Contemporary
Theories of
Schizophrenia

Contemporary Theories of Schizophrenia

Review and Synthesis

Sue A. Shapiro

McGraw-Hill Book Company

New York   St. Louis   San Francisco   Auckland   Bogota   Hamburg
Johannesburg   London   Madrid   Mexico   Montreal   New Delhi   Panama
Paris   Sao Paulo   Singapore   Sydney   Tokyo   Toronto

Library of Congress Cataloging in Publication Data
Shapiro, Sue A
  Contemporary theories of schizophrenia.
  Includes bibliographical references.
  1. Schizophrenia. I. Title. [DNLM: 1. Schizophrenia. WM203.3 S529c]
RC514.S46   616.89'82   79–27499
ISBN 0–07–056423–X

123456789 DoDo 8987654321

Acknowledgment is gratefully made for permission to reprint the following copyright material: An excerpt from *The Origin and Treatment of Schizophrenic Disorders,* by Theodore Lidz, © 1973 by Theodore Lidz, Basic Books, Inc., Publishers, New York. An excerpt from "The 'double-bind' hypothesis of schizophrenia and three-party interaction," by John H. Weakland, in *The Etiology of Schizophrenia,* edited by Don D. Jackson, © 1960 by Basic Books, Inc., Publishers, New York.

The editors of this book were Lawrence B. Apple and Suzette H. Annin. The designer was Al Cetta, and the production supervisor was Paul Malchow. It was set in Garamond by Western Publishing Co., Inc.

It was printed and bound by R. R. Donnelley & Sons.

For Maria Fried (1900–1978)

and

Dora Golding (1877–1973)

Women ahead of their time—inspirations

Contents

My aim in this book is to review the major current theories of schizophrenia and then provide a general organizing principle to integrate the data. This book is not about the treatment of schizophrenia, although a brief chapter on that subject is included, as well as some references to major work in that area. Rather, this book is an attempt to summarize current theory and research on the etiology and phenomenology, or experience, of schizophrenia. In my opinion, knowledge and understanding of these data are critical to developing and selecting treatment strategies.

This book grew out of my doctoral dissertation, which was to be an experimental study of well siblings of schizophrenics. When I began to review the literature on schizophrenia in preparation for my own work, however, I found that, despite the vast literature on the subject, there were very few comprehensive summaries or reviews that could serve as starting points. Earlier, during my internship at McLean Hospital in Boston and when starting an inpatient unit at Brooklyn State Hospital, I had been struck by the same lack. About a year after beginning my own review of the literature on the etiology of schizophrenia, I felt a need to pull together current findings; to that end I developed an organizing principle aimed at bridging the gap between the "hard data" of the laboratory and the "soft data" of clinical experience. Since developing this principle, I have found that Zubin and Spring (1977) have offered something similar in their work on vulnerability.

I hope that this book will serve as an introduction to the field for people working with schizophrenics as well as for the general student of human behavior.

This book has been many years in the making—critical years in my professional and personal development. During that period many people have helped shape the course of this book, both through specific discussions of its contents and through the support and encouragement they gave me. My interest in schizophrenia was sparked by my undergraduate work with Brendan Maher and by my experiences at Boston State Hospital. Later, at the Bronx VA Hospital, I had the opportunity to work intensively with a real pro—a patient of twenty-two years' standing, who was one of the best teachers I have had. My teachers and supervisors during my internship at McLean made that year the most exciting and intense learning experience I have had. Specifically, my work with Alfred Stanton and his belief in me spurred my desire to write a "serious" dissertation. My work with Benjamin Wolstein helped me to actualize that dream. Carl Auerbach, my dissertation sponsor, showed enormous patience over the years as we learned to work together, and many of the ideas expressed in this book grew out of our discussions. It was he who suggested a cybernetic principle for my developmental model. Chapter 11 is an abbreviated version of our collaborative efforts. Drs. Lucille Erlenmeyer-Kimling, Arnold Friedhoff, and Bonnie Spring gave helpful criticisms and suggestions for the chapters on genetics, biochemistry, neurology, and psychology. Less formal discussions with Christopher Morse and Daniel Jones were valuable in shaping the section on psychoanalytic theory. I want to thank Tony Bell, Peggy Kinder, Asya and Ted Berger, Phyllis Meshover, and Merri Weingarten for their encouragement and support during the writing of my dissertation. And I thank Don Stern, Allison Stern, Morris Eagle, David Wolitzky, Robert Stolorow, Leo Goldberger, and my editor, Larry Apple, for their helpful criticisms and encouragement to rewrite my dissertation for publication. I also want to thank Suzette Annin for her patience in working with me, teaching me just how much care goes into making a book. Nora Lapin gets very special thanks for her painstaking editing of an early draft of the manuscript. Finally, my special thanks to my husband, Clark Sugg, who was so supportive and helpful in the last months of work on this book—for living through it with me.

Grateful acknowledgment is made for permission to reprint copyright material from the following sources:

F. G. Alexander and S. T. Selesnick, *The History of Psychiatry,* New York: Harper & Row, Publishers, Inc.

M. P. Altschule, "Disease entity, syndrome, state of mind or figment?" In R. Cancro (Ed.), *The Schizophrenic Reactions: A Critique of the Concept, Hospital Treatment, and Current Research,* New York, Brunner/Mazel, 1970. © 1970 The Menninger Foundation.

American Psychiatric Association, *DSM-II: Diagnostic and Statistical Manual* (2nd edition), Washington, D.C., 1968.

American Psychiatric Association, *DSM-III: Diagnostic and Statistical Manual* (Draft), Washington, D.C., 1978.

E. J. Anthony, "The syndrome of the psychologically invulnerable child." In E. J. Anthony and C. Koupernick (Eds.), *The Child in His Family: Children at Psychiatric Risk,* Vol. 3, New York: John Wiley & Sons, Inc., 1974.

E. Bleuler, *Dementia Praecox, or the Group of Schizophrenias,* New York: International Universities Press, Inc., 1950.

E. Callaway, "Schizophrenia and interference," *Archives of General Psychiatry,* 22:193–208, 1970. Copyright 1970, American Medical Association.

L. Corbett, "Perceptual dyscontrol: A possible organizing principle for schizophrenia research," *Schizophrenia Bulletin,* 2:249–265, 1976.

R. L. Cromwell, "Attention and information processing: A foundation for understanding schizophrenia?" In L. C. Wynne, R. L. Cromwell, and S. Matthysse (Eds.), *The Nature of Schizophrenia,* New York: John Wiley & Sons, Inc., 1978.

B. Freedman, "The subjective experience of perceptual and cognitive disturbance in schizophrenia," *Archives of General Psychiatry,* 30:333–340, 1974; reprinted in R. Cancro (Ed.), *Annual Review of the Schizophrenic Syndrome 1974/75,* Vol. 4, New York: Brunner/Mazel, 1976. Copyright 1974, American Medical Association.

J. Gunderson and L. Mosher (Eds.), *Psychotherapy of Schizophrenia,* New York: Jason Aronson, 1975.

C. F. Hoover and J. Franz, "Siblings in the families of schizophrenics," *Archives of General Psychiatry,* 26:334–342, 1972. Copyright 1972, American Medical Association.

A. R. Kaplan (Ed.), *Genetic Factors in Schizophrenia,* 1972. Courtesy of Charles C Thomas, Publisher, Springfield, Illinois.

T. Lidz, S. Fleck, and A. R. Cornelison, et al., *Schizophrenia and the Family,* New York: International Universities Press, Inc., 1965.

A. McGhie and J. Chapman, "Disorders of attention and perception in early schizophrenia," *British Journal of Medical Psychology,* 34:103–117, 1961. Reprinted by permission of The British Psychological Society.

E. P. McNeil, *The Psychoses,* Englewood Cliffs, N. J.: Prentice-Hall, 1970.

H. Y. Meltzer and S. M. Stahl, "The dopamine hypothesis of schizophrenia," *Schizophrenia Bulletin,* 2:19–77, 1976.

L. Mosher, "Etiological implications of studies of identical twins discordant for schizophrenia," *Journal of Orthomolecular Psychiatry,* 42:60–67, 1972.

J. Neale and R. L. Cromwell, "Attention and schizophrenia." In B. Maher (Ed.), *Progress in Experimental Personality Research,* Vol. 5, New York: Academic Press, 1970; reprinted in R. Cancro (Ed.), *Annual Review of the Schizophrenic Syndrome 1972,* Vol. 2, New York: Brunner/Mazel, 1973. Reprinted by permission of Academic Press, Inc.

P.-N. Pao, "Notes on Freud's theory of schizophrenia," *International Journal of Psycho-Analysis,* 54:469–476, 1973.

W. Pollin, J. Stabenau, and J. Tupin, "Family studies with identical twins discordant for schizophrenia," *Psychiatry,* 28:60–78, 1965. Reprinted by permission of the William Alanson White Psychiatric Foundation, Washington, D.C.

D. Rapaport (Ed.), *Organization and Pathology of Thought,* New York: Columbia University Press, 1951. Reprinted by permission of E. R. Strasser.

H. A. Rosenfeld, *Psychotic States,* New York: International Universities Press, Inc., 1965.

M. Singer and L. Wynne, "Thought disorder and family relations of schizophrenics: III. Methodology using projective techniques. IV. Results and interpretations," *Archives of General Psychiatry,* 12:184–212, 1965. Copyright 1965, American Medical Association.

J. Stevens, "An anatomy of schizophrenia?," *Archives of General Psychiatry,* 29:177–189, 1973. Copyright 1973, American Medical Association.

H. S. Sullivan, *Clinical Studies in Psychiatry,* New York: W. W. Norton, 1956.

H. S. Sullivan, *Schizophrenia as a Human Process,* New York: W. W. Norton, 1962.

N. Wiener, *Cybernetics,* Cambridge, Mass.: M.I.T. Press, 1965.

L. Wynne, I. M. Ryckoff, J. Day, and S. I. Hirsch, "Pseudomutuality in the family relations of schizophrenics," *Psychiatry,* 21:205–220, 1958. Reprinted by permission of the William Alanson White Psychiatric Foundation, Washington, D.C.

L. Wynne and M. Singer, "Thought disorder and family relations of schizophrenics: I. A research strategy. II. A classification of forms," *Archives of General Psychiatry,* 9:191–206, 1963. Copyright 1963, American Medical Association.

J. Zubin, "Problems of attention in schizophrenia." In M. Kietzman, S. Sutton, and J. Zubin (Eds.), *Experimental Approaches to Psychopathology,* New York: Academic Press, 1975.

Introduction

Schizophrenia is an enormous, expensive public health problem. Estimates vary but, according to the U.S. Commerce Department's *Statistical Abstract of the United States* for 1974, a total of 444,777 people were admitted to state mental hospitals and approximately 92,000 entered private hospitals in that year. The total population of state hospitals was 1.7 million, a figure that included acute and chronic patients. Another 4 million people were treated in outpatient clinics. These figures do not include those in private outpatient treatment or those who are able to disguise the reasons for their hospitalization through, for example, admission to a general hospital because of "exhaustion." The vast majority of people hospitalized and many of those seen in state outpatient clinics are diagnosed schizophrenic. The money spent on their treatment, the loss of income, the money needed to support their families and eventually care for the psychological victims of parental hospitalization amounts to billions of dollars (Friedrich, 1977; Gunderson & Mosher, 1975).

The huge, ever-expanding mass of data from studies of schizophrenia can be overwhelming. Corbett (1976) remarked on this problem:

> There is an overwhelming amount of information in the schizophrenic literature; generations of effort have led to much confusion and disappointment. Such a situation is characteristic of the early stages of development of any complex field of knowledge. Accordingly, the need for a strategy of synthesis is perhaps even more pressing than the need for further analysis or description [p. 249].

Schizophrenia has been approached by many disciplines: genetics, bio-chemistry, neurophysiology, psychology, psychoanalysis, and social psy-chology (including family and group). Their common interest in and contributions to understanding schizophrenia are undermined by the fact that each discipline, and even differing theories within a discipline, has its own language and terminology. Without a common language and efforts at inte-gration, we are doomed to repeat the fable of the three blind men and the elephant, missing the whole for the particulars. Norbert Wiener commented on this problem in the introduction to his book *Cybernetics:*

> For many years Dr. Rosenblueth and I had shared the conviction that the most fruitful areas for the growth of the sciences were those which had been neglected as a no-man's land between the various established fields . . . science has been increasingly the task of specialists in fields which show a tendency to grow progressively narrower. . . . The specialist will be filled with the jargon of his field and will know all its literature and all its ramifications, but, more frequently than not, he will regard the next subject as something be-longing to his colleague. . . . There are fields of scientific work . . . which have been explored from the different sides of pure mathematics, statistics, electri-cal engineering, and neurophysiology; in which every single notion receives a separate name from each group, and in which important work has been triplicated or quadruplicated, while still other important work is delayed by the unavailability in one field of results that may have already become classical in the next field.
>
> It is these boundary regions of science which offer the richest opportunities to the qualified investigator. They are at the same time the most refractory to the accepted techniques of mass attack and the divison of labor [1965, p. 2].

For practical reasons as well as scientific ones, we should seek an integra-tion. Research costs are soaring; longitudinal research is especially costly and is available only to a few, even though it is often the research strategy of choice. Thus combined interdisciplinary research is the most efficient way to proceed.

An integrative principle has heuristic value as well. It is important that psychotherapists comprehend and be able to integrate psychological, physio-logical, and biochemical findings with their dynamic understanding of the schizophrenic's experience, if they so wish. We are, after all, talking about the same phenomenon, whether from a neurological or an experiential van-tage point, and that fact might become clearer with the aid of an integrative principle—an Esperanto of theories of schizophrenia. Such a principle will be presented in Chapter 11.

In an ideal world, the theorists of schizophrenia would start out with a general agreement about who is schizophrenic and what is known about such people. This ideal is compromised in several respects:

1. There is no general agreement on definition, nor is it clear how to arrive at one. It is also not clear whether schizophrenia represents a single "disease" entity or a syndrome with many etiologies.
2. The validity of findings is in dispute. Some findings have not been replicated; others have not been adequately tested, or have been tested on very different populations.
3. Even if true, not all findings are of equal value. Some are merely descriptive; others do point to underlying causes.
4. The field is stratified into partial theories. Schizophrenia has been approached by many different disciplines, each offering a partial explanation. Only an interdisciplinary analysis can approach the total phenomenon.

The issues listed above dictate the organization of this book. In Chapter 1, I shall discuss the problem of definition and arrive at some practical solution for the remainder of the book. In Chapter 2, I shall give a historical overview of the field. The eight subsequent chapters review major theoretical works and are attempts to validate them experimentally. Chapter 11 describes an organizing principle for these theories; Chapter 12 applies this principle; and Chapter 13 offers some concluding remarks about treatment and future trends.

The Problem of Definition and the History of the Concept

The Problem of Definition and Diagnosis	Chapter One

Despite almost a century of research on the nature of schizophrenia, we lack a commonly accepted definition. I first became clinically aware of the ambiguities of the term when I found many people in state or veterans hospitals hastily diagnosed SCUT (schizophrenia, chronic undifferentiated type), even on first admission to a hospital, which is almost a contradiction in terms. Even in training institutions, where considerable time is spent on diagnosis, there are no consistent criteria, and practices differ from school to school, region to region.

There is also confusion in the research community. This can be seen in comments made at a panel discussion on schizophrenia at the Menninger Clinic in 1969 (Cancro, 1970). Altschule (1970) stated: "Psychiatrists differ today about what the word schizophrenia means. . . . The word, I'm sorry to say, will probably last forever for two reasons. One is that it is meaningless and the other is that it's euphonious" (p. 89). Not everyone at that conference was as cynical as he, and several definitions of the concept were offered, each bearing the mark of its creator's theoretical bias. No consensus was reached regarding the definition of schizophrenia.

One of the difficulties in defining schizophrenia is that it is both a diagnostic category and a theoretical entity. The early descriptive and the later factor-analytic schools devote considerable time and care to determining the diagnostic criteria of schizophrenia. The descriptive features of schizophrenia can be gathered from these reports, but we cannot infer the essence of schizophrenia from this collection of symptoms. Theoretical works, on the other hand, seek to clarify the nature of schizophrenia but offer little to the person who wants to know a schizophrenic when he or she sees one.

We will look at several current working definitions of schizophrenia in terms of this distinction. *Diagnostic and Statistical Manual,* second edition (DSM-II), the diagnostic bible of American (but not British or European) psychiatry, defines schizophrenia as follows:

> This large category includes a group of disorders manifested by characteristic disturbances of thinking, mood and behavior. Disturbances in thinking are marked by alteration of concept formation which may lead to misinterpretation of reality and sometimes to delusions and hallucinations, which frequently appear psychologically self-protective. Corollary mood changes include ambivalent, constricted and inappropriate emotional responsiveness and loss of empathy with others. Behavior may be withdrawn, regressive and bizarre. The schizophrenias, in which the mental status is attributed primarily to a thought disorder, are to be distinguished from the major affective illnesses which are dominated by a mood disorder [American Psychiatric Association, 1968, p. 33].

DSM-II then goes on to describe the various Kraepelinian subtypes of schizophrenia. As can be seen by the continued quest for a commonly acceptable definition (W. Carpenter, Strauss, & Bartko, 1976; Gunderson, Autry, & Mosher, 1974), the DSM-II definition has proved to be inadequate because its descriptions are vague. For example, "alteration of concept formation," a key element of the definition, is not defined. And although the schizophrenic's mental status is attributed "primarily to a thought disorder," neither the meaning nor the origin of this thought disorder is explained. Nor does the manual elaborate on the essence of schizophrenia. DSM-II's vagueness about these matters has caused wide disagreement among the diagnosticians who need to apply its criteria.

A recent example of a core definition of schizophrenia can be found in Gunderson's introduction to *Psychotherapy of Schizophrenia* (Gunderson & Mosher, 1975). He offers a composite definition of schizophrenia based on the responses of the participants in a National Institute of Mental Health study on schizophrenia to the question, "What is schizophrenia?"

> Schizophrenia is a disorder of ego functioning caused by developmental, parent-child experience (which may include biological-constitutional elements) which results in an inability to separate out and maintain accurate internal representations of the outside real world. This inability, in turn, causes the production of restitutional symptoms (delusions, hallucinations) which are most prominent when the individual is confronted with the stresses of developing independent, mature, trusting adult relationships [p. xx].

This definition seeks the essence of the disorder at the expense of diagnosis.

A schizophrenic cannot be reliably identified on the basis of this description alone.

The vagueness of DSM-II and the increased breadth of research strategies (e.g., the WHO International Pilot Study on Schizophrenia), which require a universally accepted definition of schizophrenia, have led to increased operationalizing of the concept, as can be seen in the current draft of DSM-III. I quote here from the section on schizophrenia. (See Appendix 1 for the complete version.)

SCHIZOPHRENIC DISORDERS

The essential features of this group of disorders* are: disorganization of a previous level of functioning; characteristic symptoms involving multiple psychological processes; the presence of certain psychotic features during the active phase of the illness; the absence of a full affective syndrome concurrent with or developing prior to the active phase of the illness; a tendency towards chronicity; and the disturbance is not explainable by any of the Organic Mental Disorders.

As defined here, at some time during the illness a Schizophrenic Disorder always involves at least one of the following: delusions, hallucinations, or certain characteristic types of thought disorder. No single clinical feature is unique to this condition or evident in every case or at every phase of the illness, except that by definition, the diagnosis is not made unless the period of illness has persisted for at least six months.

The limits of the concept of Schizophrenia are still unclear. Some approaches to defining the concept have emphasized the tendency towards a deteriorating course (Kraepelin), the presence of specific underlying disturbances in psychological processes (Bleuler), or pathognomonic symptoms, or symptom complexes (Schneider). The approach taken here does not limit the concept to illnesses with a deteriorating course, although a minimal duration of illness is required because of the accumulated evidence that suggests that illnesses of briefer duration (here called Schizophreniform) are likely to have different correlates. The approach taken here also excludes illnesses without overt psychotic features, that have been referred to as latent, borderline, or simple schizophrenia. Such cases are likely to be diagnosed in this manual as having a Personality Disorder. Furthermore, individuals who develop either a depressive or manic syndrome before, or concurrent with psychotic symptoms, are not classified as having a Schizophrenic Disorder, but rather as having either an Affective or Schizoaffective Disorder. Thus, this manual utilizes clinical criteria that include both a minimal degree of chronicity and a characteristic symptom picture, in an effort to identify a group of conditions

* Although this classification acknowledges that Schizophrenia is a group of disorders, common usage refers to Schizophrenia. Therefore, throughout this manual whenever the term Schizophrenia appears it should be understood that conceptually the more accurate terminology would be Schizophrenic Disorders.

that has validity in terms of differential response to somatic therapy, presence of a familial pattern, a tendency towards onset in early adult life, recurrence, and severe functional impairment.

Disorganization of a previous level of functioning. Schizophrenia always involves a disorganization of a previous level of functioning. Significant impairment always occurs in areas of routine daily functioning, such as work, social relations, and self-care. Family and friends often observe that the person is "no longer himself."

Characteristic symptoms involving multiple psychological processes. Invariably there are characteristic disturbances in several of the following areas: language and communication, content of thought, perception, affect, sense of self, volition, relationship to the external world, and motor behavior. It should be noted that no one of these features is invariably present or seen only in Schizophrenia.

Diagnostic criteria for a Schizophrenic Disorder.

A. *Characteristic schizophrenic symptoms.* At least one symptom from any of the following 10 symptoms was present during an active phase of the illness (because a single symptom is given such diagnostic significance, its presence should be clearly established):

Characteristic delusions

(1) Delusions of being controlled: Experiences his thoughts, actions, or feelings as imposed on him by some external force.
(2) Thought broadcasting: Experiences his thoughts, as they occur, as being broadcast from his head into the external world so that others can hear them.
(3) Thought Insertion: Experiences thoughts, which are not his own, being inserted into his mind (other than by God).
(4) Thought withdrawal: Belief that thoughts have been removed from his head, resulting in a diminished number of thoughts remaining.
(5) Other bizarre delusions (patently absurd, fantastic or implausible).
(6) Somatic, grandiose, religious, nihilistic or other delusions without persecutory or jealous content.
(7) Delusions of any type if accompanied by hallucinations of any type.

Characteristic hallucinations

(8) Auditory hallucinations in which either a voice keeps up a running commentary on the individual's behaviors or thoughts as they occur, or two or more voices converse with each other.
(9) Auditory hallucinations on several occasions with content having no apparent relation to depression or elation, and not limited to one or two words.

Other characteristic symptoms

(10) Either incoherence, derailment (loosening of associations), marked illogicality, or marked poverty of content of speech—if accompanied by
either blunted, flat or inappropriate affect, delusions or hallucinations,
or behavior that is grossly disorganized or catatonic.

B. During the active phase of the illness, the symptoms in A have been associated
with significant impairment in two or more areas of routine daily functioning,
e.g., work, social relations, self-care.

C. *Chronicity:* Signs of the illness have lasted continuously for at least six months
at some time during the person's life and the individual now has some signs
of the illness. The six month period must include an active phase during which
there were symptoms from A with or without a prodromal or residual phase,
as defined below.

Prodromal phase: A clear deterioration in functioning not due to a primary
disturbance in mood or to substance abuse, and involving at least *two*
of the symptoms noted below.

Residual phase: Following the active phase of the illness, at least *two* of the
symptoms noted below, not due to a primary disturbance in mood or to
substance abuse.

Prodromal or Residual Symptoms

(a) social isolation or withdrawal
(b) marked impairment in role functioning as wage-earner, student, home-
maker
(c) markedly eccentric, odd, or peculiar behavior (e.g., collecting garbage,
talking to self in corn field or subway, hoarding food)
(d) impairment in personal hygiene and grooming
(e) blunted, flat, or inappropriate affect
(f) speech that is tangential, digressive, vague, overelaborate, circumstantial, or metaphorical
(g) odd or bizarre ideation, or magical thinking, e.g., superstitiousness,
clairvoyance, telepathy, "sixth sense," "others can feel my feelings,"
overvalued ideas, ideas of reference, or suspected delusions
(h) unusual perceptual experiences, e.g., recurrent illusions, sensing the
presence of a force or person not actually present, suspected hallucinations

Examples: Six months or prodromal symptoms with 1 week of symptoms from
A; no prodromal symptoms with six months of symptoms from A; no prodromal symptoms with two weeks of symptoms from A and six months of residual
symptoms; six months of symptoms from A, apparently followed by several
years of complete remission, with 1 week of symptoms in A in current episode.

D. The full depressive or manic syndrome (criteria A and B of Depressive or
Manic Episode) is either not present, or if present, developed after any
psychotic symptoms.

E. Not due to any Organic Mental Disorder [American Psychiatric Association, 1978].

The DSM-III definition is clearly descriptive and offers no statements or judgments about the "essence" of schizophrenia.

As I have illustrated, there is indeed a lack of agreement about the definition and diagnosis of schizophrenia. For further discussion of this problem, the reader is referred to *Schizophrenia Bulletin,* No. 11 (1974), especially the article prepared by the United States–United Kingdom Cross-National Project, which describes how the same patients were diagnosed differently by doctors in different facilities.

The task of defining schizophrenia, as long as there is no independent test of it and no known etiology, presents a major dilemma. This dilemma has two main features. The first is historical and has been frequently cited. It is impossible to compare results and assess data from past studies, because the criteria for diagnosing schizophrenia are often not spelled out, and even when specified, they differ from study to study. For example, there is even disagreement about whether schizophrenics are by definition psychotic (out of touch with reality). They are certainly psychotic by DSM-III criteria and probably so by DSM-II criteria, although not necessarily by Gunderson's core definition. He describes a chronic characterological state that can blossom into a full-blown psychosis. Some reports on psychoanalytic treatment of schizophrenics seem to use a characterological definition that includes a population vastly different from the one described by researchers who work in back wards of state mental institutions. These inconsistencies in definition and diagnostic criteria are gradually being rectified by increasing standardization of procedures.

The second feature of the diagnostic dilemma is that if we use operational definitions, we may be including patients suffering from disorders with different etiologies under the same diagnostic label. If this arbitrary categorization is not kept in mind, the identification of etiologies will be greatly impeded. Diagnosis by symptom cluster has traditionally posed problems in medicine. A famous example is the case of childbed fever, a form of blood poisoning arising from septic conditions in hospitals. Diagnosis by specific symptom cluster linked the disease with childbirth, obscuring investigation of its true etiology.

Closer to our own subject matter is the example of general paresis. Until the discovery of the spirochete in 1906 and the subsequent understanding of the course of syphilis, people suffering from general paresis were often grouped with people suffering from functional (nonorganic) psychoses and were considered schizophrenic. For that matter, we still frequently misdiagnose toxic pyschoses as schizophrenias because we do not know the history of ingestion of a specific toxin, e.g., amphetamines, cortisone. Undoubtedly there are unidentified toxins, viruses, and vitamin deficiencies whose symptom pictures match the requirements of the DSM-III definition of schizophrenia. If we seek a specific toxin in a random sample of "schizophrenics," our results may be statistically nonsignificant. However, this toxin may be a significant feature of a subgroup of the sample currently being called schizophrenic. This argument has been made in regard to the need to distinguish paranoid from nonparanoid, and process from reactive, lest the differences between subgroups cancel each other out.

The above remarks represent some of the difficulties presented by operational definitions of schizophrenia. On the other hand, core definitions lead to circular reasoning and thus are useless in defining a research population. Because all current core definitions are sets of hypotheses, they can generate research but cannot be used for collecting subjects.

Recently new tactics have been employed, namely, operationally defining a subgroup of schizophrenics with a specific biological or neurophysiological marker (e.g., low platelet levels of MAO as discussed in Chapter 4, or augmenting patterns in studies of averaged evoked potentials as discussed in Chapter 5). At present these tactics are used only in specific research designs and have not become part of clinical practice.

In summary, the problem of definition is that a diagnostic category with no known etiology can contain many different "diseases" with different etiologies but with the same presenting symptoms. Core definitions are only hypothetical; they must be operationalized before they can be used to separate hypothetical populations for further testing. In the following nine chapters, the term schizophrenia is used loosely, in accordance with usage in the literature under discussion.

History of the Concept	Chapter Two

Although not called schizophrenia until Eugen Bleuler coined the term in 1911, "madness" has been around as long as recorded history. Although the precise nature of the manifest symptoms may change from age to age and culture to culture, there have always been people whose logic has not conformed to the logic of their peers, whose behavior has seemed decidedly odd and out of synchrony with that of their sociocultural, temporal brothers and sisters. Lidz, commenting on the universality of schizophrenia, wrote: "Indeed, this path [schizophrenia] is so clearly open to man that if we did not know of a syndrome such as schizophrenia we would have to search for it as an anticipated anomaly of the developmental process" (1973, p. 10). Descriptions of madness that resemble what we now call schizophrenia are found in the art, literature, and philosophy of all periods. The explanations for these behaviors and the methods of treatment have changed over the years, however, reflecting the beliefs and prejudices of the times.

Although I shall not offer a thorough historical review of the concept, I believe a brief presentation will provide an important perspective on the current spate of writings and theories about schizophrenia. The reader is referred to Alexander and Selesnick's *History of Psychiatry* (1966) from which much of this discussion is drawn. As Redlich and Freedman have noted, "It is never surprising but always sobering to discover that much of what we cherish as contemporary achievement existed before, and much of what we decide was obsolete and shameful still plagues us" (quoted in McNeil, 1970, p. 4).

Thousands of years before the Greeks, some basic psychological truths had been recognized by the Babylonians, Egyptians, and Hebrews. The Babylonians knew the power of confession and suggestion in healing physical illnesses. The Egyptians, like the Greeks after them, recognized the brain as the seat of mental functions and practiced forms of milieu and sleep therapy. However, they attributed cures to the gods. In their religious writings, the Hebrews described the psychological mechanisms of projection and scapegoating; they also recognized the function of dreams as expressions of forbidden impulses. Talking freely was recommended as a cure for mental illness.

Under the direction of Aesculapius, the early Greeks erected temples to serve as beautiful, soothing retreats in which patients could rest while seeking council and ritual treatments from priests. The Greeks initiated the controversies about our true nature that have persisted to this day: the mind-body problem and voluntarism versus mechanism.

In the fifth century B.C. the early mysticism of Aesculapius gave way to the more rational explanations of Hippocrates, who attempted to explain all diseases in terms of natural causes. He was also the first to recognize the importance of the brain: "Men ought to know that from the brain, and from the brain only, arrive our pleasures, joys, laughter, and jests, as well as our sorrows, pains, griefs, tears . . . wherefore, I assert that the brain is the interpreter of consciousness" (quoted in Alexander & Selesnick, 1966, p. 54). Hippocrates believed that the functioning of the brain was affected by the balance of the humors, which in turn were affected by diet. He described organic delirium, depression, and postpartum psychoses, and even sensed the sexual origins of hysteria, recommending marriage and frequent intercourse as treatment. His most important contribution was to demystify illness. He always sought a natural cause and recognized the importance of taking an accurate case history. Hippocrates also emphasized the nature of the doctor-patient relationship and the effect it could have on the course of treatment.

Other classical philosophers addressed psychological issues. Plato (427–347 B.C.) recognized a basic tenet of psychosomatic medicine, namely, that bodily states reflect psychological states. Aristotle considered reason divine, but claimed that thinking aims to increase pleasure and decrease pain.

Aretaeus (50–130 A.D.), a Greek follower of Hippocrates who lived in Rome, described manic-depression and realized that not all mental illness leads to deterioration. Earlier, Asclepiades had distinguished hallucinations from delusions, and acute from chronic illnesses. Paranoia and delusions of persecution had also been recognized. Cicero, following Plato, believed that bodily ailments are often the result of emotional factors. He introduced the idea that melancholy has psychological origins. Galen (131–200 A.D.) integrated Hippocratic observational medicine with a firm belief in a spiritual force linking mind and body. He made significant observations on the nature of cranial nerves, the transmission of nerve impulses, and the possibility that brain lesions cause emotional disturbance.

In summary, the Greeks and Romans, expanding on more ancient ideas, described the major emotional "illnesses" (paranoia, dementia, melancholia, manic-depression, postpartum psychoses, and hysteria), understood that mental states influence physical states (psychosomatics), considered the brain as the origin of consciousness, and recognized major treatment modalities. They also recognized or initiated major philosophical debates that at times inhibited the furtherance of knowledge: namely, the mystical or divine nature of reason, the split between mind and body, and the subsequent division between the world of the senses and the world of ideas, which placed reasoning above observation. Interestingly, they abandoned observation in favor of reasoning because they saw the subjective nature of perception, failing to recognize that reasoning too can be subject to individual psychology.

The reliance on "divinely inspired" reasoning that is not subject to scientific inquiry, along with the development of Christianity and its moral injunctions, laid the foundation for the intellectual stagnation of the Dark Ages.

In the Middle Ages, the prevailing belief was that madness was an expression of the will of God; its cure was a religious ritual that often made the psychotic the target of persecution. Madness was interpreted as a sign that cultural religious taboos had been violated; openly sexual women were "possessed by the Devil." This view has persisted into the twentieth century in the belief that excessive masturbation leads to madness. The frequency with which masturbation appears as a central concern in patients' delusions can be considered evidence of the impact of such cultural myths.

For over a thousand years the mad were subjected to scapegoating and punishment—exorcism, witch-hunts, and exile to "ships of fools." The last witch was executed in 1782 (Foucault, 1965).

During the Dark Ages, there were some notable exceptions to the spirit of the time. St. Augustine (354–430 A.D.) valued introspection despite its revelation of asocial impulses, but his views were buried beneath the forces of Scholasticism. In Persia, Rhazes (865–925) kept alive the spirit of empirical observation in his attempt to correlate mental and bodily states. He took patients' pulses, while talking with them, to determine which topics caused excitement.

During the Renaissance, society's attitude toward mental patients lagged behind developments in the arts. The revival of humanism rekindled an interest in observation, as seen in Johann Weyer's notes on the verbalizations of mental patients. (Weyer was also one of the first to condemn witch-hunts.) Concurrently, there was a growing belief that intellect (or reason) was subservient to emotions, as well as a conviction that a distinction must be made between the psychology of human behavior and morality.

Seventeenth-century rationalism replaced the divine order with a world of reason and observation governed by man. Psychological issues were now back in the province of philosophers, who were again separate from the church. The major philosophical issue was the mind-body problem (which is still in dispute today). Descartes was the major proponent of a dualistic theory, and Spinoza and Stahl paved the way for an identity theory with their views on psychophysical parallelism.

Spinoza, although not concerned with madness, did introduce psychological ideas of self-preservation, homeostasis, repression, and ambivalence. Robert Burton, in *The Anatomy of Melancholy,* published in 1621, described the psychodynamics of melancholia.

The eighteenth-century scientific community, whose primary concern was the symptomatic classification of bodily illnesses, attempted to classify mental illness as well. They stressed experimental method and detailed observation. Attempts were made to localize brain pathology, as in the studies by Haslam at Bethlehem Hospital. During this period, early forms of shock treatment were in use.

The political reforms of the eighteenth century led to humanitarian reform in the care of mental patients and the cessation of witch hunts. Pinel, a major advocate of hospital reform, was also one of the first in recent history to view mental illness as the result of emotional problems. His contemporaries, Müller and Reil, distinguished between organic and functional disturbances and were the first doctors to specialize in psychiatry.

The nineteenth century was characterized by a Romantic rebellion against reason and a resurrection of the primacy of emotions—of passion and instinct. Once again, introspection replaced empiricism. During the first half of the century, much of the groundwork for Freudian dynamic psychology was laid. Reil stressed the role of emotional factors, especially that of sexual excitation, in mental illness. Esquirol undertook the first study of precipitating events that led to mental hospitalization. He differentiated hallucinations from illusions and stressed the subservience of human intellect and reason to emotional needs.

Moreau stressed self-knowledge as a prerequisite for an understanding of others and showed the similarity between dreams and hallucinations. He also theorized a relationship between schizophrenia and genius—an idea that was not taken seriously by Alexander and Selesnick in 1966, but that has now regained respectability.

Heinroth (1773–1843) was moralistic and religious in his assumption that mental illness was caused by sin, but he recognized the importance of conflict and guilt and also described three levels of psychic functioning that closely resemble Freud's id, ego, and superego. His contemporary Falret developed a sociological theory of schizophrenia that stressed social alienation as a causative factor.

In 1859 Pasteur discovered bacteria and Darwin published *The Origin of the Species.* Both events profoundly affected man's view of himself and swung the pendulum back to careful, controlled observation and systematic recording of those observations. Once again a reaction occurred against the looser, more speculative thinking typical of the Romantic period in favor of a more objective empiricism. Pasteur's work also sparked a return to an organic approach to mental illness and a conviction that if the history, symptoms, and course of the illness were accurately described, eventually the germ that caused it would be found. This is an example of a phenomenon we shall see repeatedly: the discovery of a causal agent in one area of science leads to the expectation that a similar agent is at work in all unexplained syndromes, including schizophrenia.

The increased interest in the history and course of illnesses led to the work of Kraepelin and Bleuler, the masters of descriptive psychiatry. Although Kraepelin is easily criticized for his "callous" questioning of patients on display in the great amphitheaters of medical schools (see Laing, 1960/1965a), his descriptions and classifications of dementia praecox remain instructive. It should be recalled that he was not trying to be therapeutic in these demonstrations. His intention was to point out general characteristics of the disorder and he did so in the style of medical training then current.

In the hundred years before Kraepelin, a number of terms were used to describe what were thought to be different mental illnesses. Vogel used the term "paranoia" in 1764, Kahlbaum described catatonia in 1868, and Hecker coined the term "hebephrenia" in 1870 (Freedman, Kaplan, & Sadock, 1972, p. 218). Kraepelin (1896) was the first to bring these clinical entities together under the general term "dementia praecox." The fundamental characteristic of this group of psychoses was its morbid prognosis— the patient's condition would deteriorate. The syndrome received its name because of its resemblance to dementia; however, its onset was considerably earlier.

In keeping with the spirit of the times, Kraepelin stressed specific symptoms: hallucinations (especially auditory ones), delusions, thought broadcasting and influencing, poor judgment, disturbances of emotional expression, bizarre and stereotyped behavior, and negativism. In his descriptions of patients' premorbid functioning he was sometimes amusingly overinclusive, failing to distinguish between cause, effect, and mere coincidence. Like the witch-hunters of the Middle Ages, Kraepelin was struck by the heightened sexuality of his patients.

Kraepelin distinguished dementia praecox from the organic psychoses by the absence of delirium or gross deficits of intelligence. Orientation, memory, and comprehension remained intact (Bemporad & Pinsker, 1974). He subdivided dementia praecox into three types: catatonia, hebephrenia, and paranoid, eventually adding a fourth type—simple. Kraepelin believed that an organic, probably metabolic, disease process was at the root of dementia praecox. A major criticism of his work is that he used the outcome of the illness as a main criterion for diagnosis—a procedure incompatible with the practical need for knowing the diagnosis in order to determine the treatment.

For the contemporary reader, Kraepelin's vivid descriptions of symptoms are flawed by his judgmental, moralistic tone, as illustrated in this typical statement: "The patients have lost every independent inclination for work and action; they sit about idle, trouble themselves about nothing" (Kraepelin, 1919/1971, p. 37). This statement follows a thorough description of frightening hallucinations and delusions. In later editions of his work, Kraepelin hypothesized that a disorder of will is central to one form of dementia praecox. The other type is marked by what Stransky called the "loss of the inner unity of the activities of intellect, emotion and volition in themselves and among one another" (cited in Kraepelin, 1919/1971, p. 72). Stransky's description corresponds to Bleuler's "split personality."

The main body of Kraepelin's work is descriptive; he made no distinction between primary and secondary symptoms (a distinction that preoccupied later researchers). The first edition of his book stressed the morbid outcome of dementia praecox to differentiate it from manic-depression. It is for this that Kraepelin is remembered. By 1919, however, in the eighth edition, he had acknowledged that 9 to 14 percent of dementia praecox patients eventually improved. Kraepelin believed that dementia praecox had an organic base, citing as evidence autopsy reports of nerve cell damage in the temporal and frontal lobes and in the higher layers of the cortex. From his description we may infer that some of his patients were probably suffering from syphilis, alcoholism, epilepsy, or physical trauma. But he did not report the cause of death, so his organic findings are highly questionable. He did, however, identify a hereditary predisposition toward dementia praecox and thus paved the way for later studies.

Toward the end of his life, Kraepelin was convinced that dementia praecox had a metabolic basis. He hypothesized that the body becomes autointoxicated, although he did not specify how the process occurred. In this he anticipated some current biochemical research that has investigated possible endogenous hallucinogens (see Chapter 4).

Bleuler and Freud were also committed to an organic or constitutional explanation of schizophrenia, but they added a new dimension: concern with the meaning and organization of symptoms. Freud's discovery of the psychogenic nature and meaning of hysterical symptoms caused a revolution in psychiatric thinking (see Chapter 7, section on Freud), and his influence can be seen in Bleuler's work.

Bleuler (1911/1950) preferred to call dementia praecox "schizophrenia" to reflect his theory that there is an underlying personality split in the patient, a loss of harmony between various groups of mental functions (Cancro, 1970, p. 7). He rejected Kraepelin's idea of necessary, progressive deterioration and stated:

By the term "dementia praecox" or schizophrenia we designate a group of psychoses whose course is at times chronic, at times marked by intermittent attacks, and which can stop or retrograde at any stage, but does not permit a full *restitutio a integruo* [1911/1950, p. 9].

Bleuler sought to understand the symptoms of schizophrenia in terms of their basic components. He stated:

The fundamental symptoms consist of disturbances of association and affectivity, the predilection for fantasy as against reality, and the inclination to divorce oneself from reality. Furthermore, we can add the absence of those very symptoms which play such a great role in certain other diseases, such as primary disturbances of perception, orientation and memory [p. 14].

These fundamental symptoms have been called "the four A's": affect, autism, associations, and ambivalence. Disturbances of affect refer to the peculiar ways in which the schizophrenic's emotional tone seems strikingly at odds with the content of speech, either through general flatness or excessive lability. Typically, the schizophrenic can tell gruesome tales of torture while laughing or appearing to be indifferent.

Autism refers to the predominance of internal life or fantasy over reality. Thus external events take on highly personal meanings—the world becomes a stage for the realization of highly personal fears and desires, with a loss of the ability to test reality. For example, a young woman admitted to the hospital described how she had been walking along when a red street light came on, which meant that she had to turn right. Then she came upon a green light, which meant that she was getting close to her destination . . . and so on, until she wound up at the docks where she was later found, having been raped and beaten.

Loosening of associations is a key aspect of what has become known as a "formal thought disorder," the primary feature of schizophrenia. Loosening of associations occurs when the person abandons the normal linguistic constraints on the potential number of words that can be used at a specific point in a sentence and allows personal, nonconsensual meanings into the flow of speech. Thus, for example, the sound qualities of a word will be responded to independently of its meaning, and the schizophrenic may start rhyming. The train of thought is no longer governed by a sense of purpose.

Psychotic ambivalence refers to a juxtaposition of opposite feelings and desires so extreme as to interfere with volition and action. An example can be seen in the behavior of a hospitalized teenage girl who first told me to "fuck off," then kissed me, and finally attacked me with a sliver of glass.

Bleuler believed that delusions and hallucinations were secondary to and derived from these four fundamental symptoms. He introduced the notion of ambulatory and latent schizophrenia, believing that people so diagnosed showed the fundamental signs, whereas delusions and hallucinations were more frequently encountered in hospitalized schizophrenics. These latter phenomena are the flashier, more obvious manifestations of the underlying loosening of associations and split in the personality.

Bleuler did not explain the origin of these fundamental disturbances, nor did he adequately explain the derivation of hallucinations from the fundamental symptoms. He did, however, begin to integrate the work of Freud in his assumption that delusions and hallucinations are meaningful expressions of wishes. His major contribution lies in the thoroughness of his descriptions and in his effort to construct a hierarchy of symptoms.

While Kraepelin actively searched for, and others awaited, evidence of somatic damage in brain autopsies of patients, Jung (1907/1944, 1939) believed that the toxin which produced schizophrenia was caused by psychological conflicts and their associated intense affects. According to Jung, the complexes in hysteria and the other neuroses did not generate a toxin, whereas the complexes in the psychoses did. The toxin was psychogenic and caused psychotic symptoms, but it could be inhibited through psychoanalytic work. Jung, the first to formulate a fully psychological theory of schizophrenia, was more optimistic about treating psychotics than was Freud.

Freud and his followers excited the intellectual community, totally altering the way people view themselves. A great many people now believe that somatic symptoms, memory failures, and so forth, are psychological or psychogenic until proved otherwise. The positive effect of this view has been an increased effort to understand, know, and help schizophrenics, but the negative result has been the reinforcement of the mind-body split that has characterized humanity's view of itself throughout history and a consequent inattention to biochemical and genetic findings.

While the psychoanalytic movement was gaining momentum, the rest of the scientific community was entering a golden age of discovery and specialization. In 1906, the spirochete was discovered to be the cause of syphilis, and the course of the illness thus became understood. The similarity in appearance and symptoms of general paresis and schizophrenia led to speculation about the origin of schizophrenia. In 1934, phenylketonuria (PKU), a form of mental retardation, was found to be the result of a single autosomal recessive gene. This gene caused faulty metabolism of an amino acid, which then led to faulty brain development. The discovery of the cause of PKU spurred the search for a genetic basis for schizophrenia. Four years later, Kallmann (1938) published the first of his studies on concordance rates in families of schizophrenics.

The work of Sullivan and Fromm-Reichmann at Chestnut Lodge in the 1930s and 1940s sparked a renewed psychoanalytic interest in schizophrenia. Freud's conviction that schizophrenia was an untreatable narcissistic disorder had led to a relative paucity of interest in this syndrome during the first three decades of the twentieth century. Sullivan's (1953, 1956, 1962d) "interpersonal theory of psychiatry," and increased work with hospitalized schizophrenics, initiated an interest in the family's role in the genesis of schizophrenia. Fromm-Reichmann (1948/1959a) coined the term "schizophrenogenic." Simultaneously, English psychoanalysts (Fairbairn, 1952a; Winnicott, 1958, 1965a, 1965b) were becoming more interested in understanding early child development and the psychological experience of infants. Melanie Klein's theory, derived from child analysis, provided a metapsychology for exploring psychotic states. At this same time, Freudian analysts were continuing their efforts to understand the function of the ego. Since Freud never completed a revised view of psychosis from the vantage point of his structural model, that task devolved upon the ego psychologists.

Concurrently, academic and experimental psychologists in the first half of the twentieth century carried on the empirical tradition, seeking to know specifically how schizophrenics were different from normal people. Their studies began to fall into broad categories concerning such functions as attention, perception, and memory, which are similar to the categories that Bellak identified as critical ego functions (Bellak, Hurvich, & Gediman, 1973).

The increased specialization characteristic of this period eventually led to an identification of basic organismic functions such as attention and perception. Since these are more easily reduced to physiological and biochemical mechanisms than are intrapsychic functions, a beginning interdisciplinary bridge was found. Various familial studies were undertaken, some examining communication patterns, others focusing on concordance rates and the effects of adoption on the children of schizophrenics. In the 1960s, biochemical research aimed at finding a body-made hallucinogen; transmethylation and several other key biochemical theories owe their birth to the discovery of lysergic acid diethylamide (LSD). At the same time, LSD had a profound effect on the way an entire generation viewed "madness." Laing's brilliant early work (1960/1965a, 1965b) was obscured by a cult worship that oversimplified his insights into the belief that sanity was madness, that madness was the only true sanity, and that one could learn from psychotic experiences. Social and political conditions in the United States and other countries led to a politicization of Laing's view, exemplified in some sociological theories of madness—for example, Szasz's (1961) *The Myth of Mental Illness.*

Work proliferated, and the number of journal articles on schizophrenia grew at an enormous pace. In the last five years, several publications devoted solely to this topic have been established, among them the *Schizophrenia Bulletin* (a publication of the National Institute of Mental Health) and Cancro's *Annual Review of the Schizophrenic Syndrome.*

During the late 1960s and 1970s, the pendulum swung once again. A variety of social, economic, and scientific factors contributed to a trend away from theoretical speculation and back to a more cautious empiricism. Several longitudinal projects are currently attempting to identify factors that define vulnerability in people at high risk for schizophrenia. These studies are interdisciplinary and often international in scope. Technological advances in computer design have made broader data collection feasible. And, increasingly, the need for standardized diagnostic criteria and definitions of terms becomes more acute.

Review of the Major Theories of Schizophrenia

PART

2

<table>
<tr><td>Genetic and
Constitutional Theories</td><td>Chapter
Three</td></tr>
</table>

GENETIC THEORIES

For may years the argument has raged over whether schizophrenia is an inherited disease. The continuing debate reflects the larger, nature-nurture controversy.

During the last thirty years, the debate over the origin of schizophrenia has grown in part out of the nonscientist's naïve view of genetics. Social scientists often regard genes as absolute determinants of traits. Perhaps they fear that, if schizophrenia is genetically caused, the social sciences are irrelevant to its treatment. Geneticists are not nearly as opposed to psychological-environmental explanations of schizophrenia. According to A.R. Kaplan (1972), contemporary geneticists have demonstrated that:

> An individual's genotype only determines his norm or range of reactions. In other words a gene or group of genes determines an indefinite, but limited, assortment of phenotypes, the different phenotypes being associated with differences in environment and/or with differences in other aspects of the total genotype [p. 561].

One's genetic inheritance may be influenced by the pre- and postnatal environments, which include psychological and physical stress, drugs, etc. Genes differ in their penetrance, in the degree to which the presence of the gene alone leads to the phenotype. Even the sexual morphology of the neonate has been shown to be dependent on the prenatal environment (Money & Ehrhardt, 1972).

Thus environmental influences are not alien to geneticists, whereas those who prefer to see the infant as a tabula rasa, on which parents, family, and society inscribe, find the "genetic" quite threatening. But in fact, as will be demonstrated below, the major current genetic theory, the diathesis-stress model, is easily integrated with many psychoanalytic concepts.

The major early investigators—Kraepelin, Freud, and Sullivan—assumed a constitutional, hereditary factor in schizophrenia. Because of the nature-nurture controversy, however, most early genetic research was directed toward establishing firm proof of this assumption. This research was epidemiological, studying the prevalence of schizophrenia among family members of index cases compared to the prevalence in the population at large. The risk of developing schizophrenia within one's lifetime is about 1 percent if one lives in an industrialized nation. Geneticists have studied and compared morbidity or risk rates in first-degree relatives (parents, siblings, and children) who have 50 percent genetic overlap, second-degree relatives (grandparents, half siblings, uncles, nephews, and grandchildren) who have 25 percent genetic overlap, third-degree relatives (cousins) who have 12.5 percent overlap, and monozygotic twins who have identical genes or 100 percent overlap. The risk rates for genetically determined conditions increase proportionately with the increase in genetic overlap. Gottesman (1979), in his excellent introduction and review of genetic factors in schizophrenia, provides two very useful tables that I reproduce here. Table 1 illustrates the difference in risk rates for a "simple" genetic disorder, such as Huntington's chorea, and a complex disorder, such as schizophrenia. Table 2 shows the lifetime risks for developing schizophrenia among various relatives of schizophrenic probands. As this table clearly shows, the risk for developing schizophrenia increases with the degree of blood relationship to the proband.

Having established this general trend, researchers began to focus on concordance rates (agreement re presence or absence of a trait) for schizophrenia among monozygotic (MZ) and dizygotic (DZ) twins. Gottesman reports that the risk rate for schizophrenia among both MZ and DZ twins in the general population is no greater than the risk within the population at large. As Table 3 shows, the reported concordance rates in studies of MZ and DZ twins with one schizophrenic proband vary considerably. However, even the most conservative studies support a genetic factor.

This variance can be explained by differences in:

1. The definition of schizophrenia—schizophrenia spectrum or "true" schizophrenia.
2. The selection of index cases. Studies that select schizophrenics from hospital populations, and tend to include the more seriously ill, chronic patients, show

TABLE 1: Comparative Risks in Siblings for Developing Schizophrenia in Comparison to Mendelian Disorders, Congenital Malformations, and Common Diseases

Condition	Population Risk (a)	Proband's Sibling Risk (b)	Comparative Risk (b/a)
Huntington's chorea	0.00005	0.5	10,000
Phenylketonuria	0.00004	0.25	6,250
Clubfoot	0.001	0.025	25
Diabetes mellitus	0.003	0.028	9
Schizophrenia	0.0085	0.087	10

SOURCE: Table 1 from "Toward Understanding Uncertainty," by Irving I. Gottesman, in *Psychiatric Annals,* Volume 9, 1979.

a higher concordance rate than do studies that draw schizophrenics from a nonhospitalized population. An example of the latter is the study by Tienari (1968), who screened 70 percent of the adult monozygotic twins in Finland

TABLE 2: Lifetime Risks for Developing Schizophrenia among Various Relatives of Schizophrenic Probands

Relationship	Total Relatives	Schizophrenic Number (a)	Schizophrenic Number (b)	Schizophrenic % (a)	Schizophrenic % (b)
Parents	7,675	336	423	4.4	5.5
Sibs (all)	8,505	724	865	8.5	10.2
Sibs (neither parent schizophrenic)	7,535	621	731	8.2	9.7
Sibs (one parent schizophrenic	675	93	116	13.8	17.2
Children	1,227	151	170	12.3	13.9
Children of mating schiz. × schiz.	134	49	62	36.6	46.3
Half sibs	311	10	11	3.2	3.5
Uncles and aunts	3,376	68	123	2.0	3.6
Nephews and nieces	2,315	52	61	2.2	2.6
Grandchildren	713	20	25	2.8	3.5
First cousins	2,438	71	85	2.9	3.5

(a) Diagnostically certain cases only; (b) also including probable schizophrenics. Both columns of risk figures are age-corrected.

SOURCE: Table 2 from "Toward Understanding Uncertainty," by Irving I. Gottesman, in *Psychiatric Annals,* Volume 9, 1979.

TABLE 3: Approximate Concordance Rates for Schizophrenia in Monozygotic and Dizygotic Twins

	Estimated Concordance Rate in Percent	
Study	MZ Twins	DZ Twins
Luxenburger, 1928–1934	55	2.1
Rosanoff et al., 1934–35	61	10.0
Essen-Möller, 1941	42	13.0
Kallmann, 1946	73	12.2
Slater, 1953	70	12.3
Inouye, 1961	48	9.0
Tienari, 1963, 1968	6	4.8
Gottesman and Shields, 1966	50	9.1
Kringlen, 1967	31	9.0
Fischer et al., 1969	37	9.5
Pollin et al., 1969	15.5	4.4

Note: These are not necessarily the rates reported by the investigators. They indicate this author's estimate of the rate that might best represent the data in each study, but the reader should know that a simply expressed concordance can be misleading, that it masks or disregards much information necessary to understand the basic data on which the rates are based.

SOURCE: Table 25–2 from "The Genetics of Schizophrenia," by David Rosenthal, in the *American Handbook of Psychiatry,* Second Edition, edited by Silvano Arieti, Volume 3, © 1974 by Basic Books, Inc., Publishers, New York.

for schizophrenia. He then determined the concordance rate among pairs and found it to be comparatively low.

3. Criteria for establishing zygosity. Tests for zygosity have become more stringent over the years (W. Carpenter, Strauss, & Bartko, 1976; Kety, 1969).

4. Length of follow-up and ages of twins at the time of the study.

For a further discussion of these issues, see Kety (1969) and Rosenthal (1974).

Kallmann's early studies, done in 1938 and 1946, reported the highest concordance rates (73 percent for MZ twins) yet found. They are among the most frequently cited results, although they are also the most frequently criticized (Kety, 1969; Shields, 1968; Slater, 1968) because his figures seem to be inflated. Recent Scandinavian studies (Kringlen, 1968; Tienari, 1968) had a much broader sampling base. This kind of broadly based study is possible only in countries with good birth registries and low migration rates. Tienari found only a 6 percent concordance rate in MZ twins when he used a strict definition of schizophrenia. However, further follow-up brought the rate up to 35 percent (see Gottesman & Shields, 1976).

Shields (1968) cites as evidence of genetic transmission the relatively constant rate of schizophrenia in the world. He also cites the fact that 70 percent of the nonpsychotic children of schizophrenic parents are "normal." He argues that if schizophrenia were strictly environmentally determined, one would expect these children to be more influenced by conditions at home. One possible criticism of this argument is that a clearly schizophrenic parent does not necessarily constitute a schizophrenogenic environment. Rather, it might be the parent who "passes" that is the more troubling to the child (see Anthony, 1971a, 1971b).

Shields also cites evidence of an environmental factor—namely, that a slightly higher (although not statistically significant) concordance rate exists in DZ twins than in other siblings, and a higher incidence in same-sex siblings than in those of opposite sex. He considers the latter observation to be significant because schizophrenia is clearly not caused by a sex-linked gene, and thus the difference in concordance rates might well be a function of the way in which the siblings were reared.

Another leading behavioral geneticist, Rosenthal (1974), points out that the use of risk and concordance rates to support a genetic theory of schizophrenia is questionable because these rates can also be explained by family theories of schizophrenia. Thus the schizophrenogenic family is likely to affect all the siblings; the more similar the siblings are (e.g., same sex, or twins), the greater the similarity of parental treatment. In addition, MZ twins tend to be very strongly identified with each other, often contracting the same physical illnesses (with no known genetic basis) within weeks of each other.

In view of this criticism, Rosenthal (1974) cites five critical studies that separated genetic and family factors. Heston (1966) compared children of schizophrenic parents adopted away at birth with other adopted children and looked at the rate of schizophrenia. His findings were in the predicted direction: 16.6 percent of the forty-seven adopted-away children of schizophrenics were later hospitalized for schizophrenia, compared to none of the controls. Karlsson (1966) found a greater incidence of schizophrenia among biological siblings of adopted schizophrenics than among their foster siblings. Wender, Rosenthal, and Kety (1968) studied the rate and form of pathology in biological and adoptive parents of schizophrenics and normals and found that the biological parents of schizophrenics showed more pathology than the adoptive parents of schizophrenics. However, the adoptive parents of schizophrenics showed significantly more pathology than the adoptive parents of normals. This finding is used by critics of family theories of schizophrenia, who argue that much of the odd behavior noted in families of schizophrenics is a function of having to cope with a schizophrenic; that it is caused by, rather than causative of, schizophrenia.

In a later study, Wender, Rosenthal, and Kety (1974) found that normal children adopted by families in which one parent later became schizophrenic did not have a statistically significant higher-than-base-rate risk for developing schizophrenia.

Kety et al. (1968) studied adopted schizophrenics and a control group of adopted nonschizophrenics, comparing the incidence of schizophrenia spec trum disorders in the adoptive and biological parents and siblings of both groups. Among the biological relatives there was a significant difference between relatives of schizophrenics, who more often had spectrum disturbances, and relatives of controls, who did not. There were no differences between adoptive relatives of the two groups.

Rosenthal (1974) studied the rate of schizophrenia in adult adoptees whose biological parents were schizophrenic. Using a pyschiatric mental status examination, done blind, he found an insignifcant rate of schizophrenia when a strict definition of schizophrenia was used and a significant rate when a broad spectrum definition was used. Rosenthal suggests that "rearing in an adoptive home may indeed protect children of a schizophrenic parent from developing the disorder themselves" (p. 593).

Although there is considerable evidence of a genetic component in at least some forms of schizophrenia, there is much disagreement and confusion regarding the means of genetic transmission. As early as 1916 Rüdin, in the first genetic studies on schizophrenia, noted that it does not follow a simple Mendelian law of genetic transmission. In other words, the morbidity rates for schizophrenia do not fit a simple model of recessive or dominant gene transmission. Any theory of genetic transmission of schizophrenia must account for the atypical prevalence rates.

The ambiguity and inconclusiveness of schizophrenia as a diagnostic category constitute a critical problem for establishing that it is indeed genetically transmitted in a certain percentage of cases. At present there is a tendency to include two sets of statistics, one for clear cases of schizophrenia and the other for schizophrenia spectrum disorders. Rosenthal (1974) concludes that the classical subtypes of schizophrenia, as well as the less disturbed schizoid and borderline personalities, are genetically related. However, he believes that true reactive schizophrenics, those with good premorbid histories and good outcomes, probably do not share the same genetic background.

Theories of genetic transmission of schizophrenia posit either single-gene or polygenic models. In general, diathesis models, which suggest that what is inherited is the diathesis or liability for schizophrenia, tend to be polygenic, whereas most bioamine theories are monogenic. Monogenic theories postulate that schizophrenia is caused by a single recessive or dominant gene. Single-gene theories have the advantage of being easier to investigate experimentally and easier to prove or disprove. They hold out the hope that a single twisted molecule causes the twisted mind (Rosenthal, 1971, p. 104).

Polygenic theories are more difficult to research because they do not follow simple Mendelian laws. Traits that are polygenically determined tend to be continuous and normally distributed; they have only recently been studied statistically. On a more positive note, diathesis-stress theories are more easily integrated with psychodynamic and environmentalist views.

Genetic heterogeneity theories state that several different monogenic and/ or polygenic conditions exist, each of which may underlie schizophrenia. Although most of the literature (e.g., morbidity and concordance rates) supports the view of genetic homogeneity, some investigators find evidence for a genetic distinction between chronic, deteriorating schizophrenia and a periodic form.

Monogenic Bioamine Theories

Historically, the first theories of genetic transmission of schizophrenia were monogenic, and their simplicity is appealing. Kallmann (1946) proposed that schizophrenia is caused by a single recessive gene in conjunction with polygenic constitutional modifiers. That is, schizophrenia appears only in the presence of *both* this recessive gene and other constitutional factors that are themselves inherited. The *genetic context* (constitution) is critical. According to Kallmann, all schizophrenics possess this recessive gene, but not all people who possess it become schizophrenic. This assumption was an effort to account for the atypical prevalence rates mentioned earlier. However, as Rosenthal (1977) points out, Kallmann failed to explain why at least 50 percent of MZ twins are discordant for schizophrenia. Both twins have the same genetic material—the same polygenically determined constitution—but only one becomes schizophrenic.

Böök (1953) and Slater (1958) proposed that a single dominant gene causes schizophrenia. Slater argued that all homozygotes become schizophrenic, while only some heterozygotes manifest the disease. He studied the incidence rates found by other investigators and, on the basis of these figures, hypothesized the gene frequencies, the proportion of homozygotes in the schizophrenic population, and the proportion of heterozygotes who develop schizophrenia. He did not explain the nature of the modifying factors in heterozygotes that determine whether they will become schizophrenic.

Karlsson's (1968) genealogical studies of schizophrenics led to his polygenic bioamine theory of schizophrenia. He hypothesized that schizophrenia is caused by one dominant and one recessive gene; other combinations of these genes (the other genotypes) lead to three other personality types (Karlsson, 1972), including a creative one. Although this theory, and particularly the hypothesized link between genius and madness, is of interest, no independent studies of it have yet been conducted.

Diathesis-Stress Theories

The critical feature of these theories is the claim that what is inherited is a liability or a diathesis for schizophrenia rather than the disease itself. An early example of a monogenic diathesis-stress model is Meehl's (1962) hypothesis of an inherited neural integrative deficit based on a single gene which caused a prenatal structural aberration. Meehl suggests that persons with this genotype, schizotypy, can become schizophrenic through social learning. The core traits of schizophrenia—cognitive slippage, anhedonia, and interpersonal aversiveness—all develop over time. Thus he proposes a two-stage theory of schizophrenia: the first stage is an inherited central nervous system deficit, the diathesis, the second stage is learned. Although this model is appealing in its bridge of hereditary and environmental arguments, it cannot be easily investigated. A later example of a diathesis-stress model was proposed by Mednick (1958, 1970; Mednick & Schulsinger, 1968) who argued that the preschizophrenic has inherited a high anxiety responsiveness which is habituated slowly.

Most recently, researchers have formulated theories of genetic transmission based on the application of statistical genetics, developed by Falconer (1965), to a polygenic model of schizophrenia. Gottesman and Shields (1967, 1973) are key figures in this work. The basic premise of the polygenic models is that the action of genes at different loci produces similar, cumulative effects. One becomes schizophrenic when one inherits too many culpable genes. These genes for liability are normally distributed.

Monogenic bioamine theories have led to biochemical studies searching for specific metabolic changes in schizophrenics. In contrast, the diathesis-stress model asserts that it is futile to search for consistent metabolic changes in adult schizophrenics. This latter theory can be integrated with the neurophysiological, cognitive, and attentional deficit studies of schizophrenics. It can also be related to the psychoanalytic postulate of a weak stimulus barrier and its role in early ego development.

Some recent studies (A. R. Kaplan, 1972; Vartanyan & Gindilis, 1971; see Rosenthal, 1974) point to nonspecific chromosomal abnormalities in schizophrenics that may increase psychological and physiological stress and vulnerability. This and the diathesis-stress theory describe a threshold phenomenon: the genetically determined disposition lies on a continuum and becomes phenotypically different once a certain threshold is reached.

CONSTITUTION AND TEMPERAMENT

I am defining constitution and temperament as those factors that are present in the infant at birth. They are products of the infant's genetic makeup and intrauterine experience, and are probably related to genetically based neurophysiological differences. They are described here from a behavioral and phenomenological point of view.

An early theoretical work by Bergman and Escalona (1949) on children with unusual sensitivities presaged the diathesis-stress theory and the studies of Thomas, Chess and Birch (1969) and Karlsson (1968). Bergman and Escalona state that a number of schizophrenics had unusual sensitivities in one or more sensory modalities from birth onward. For example, while many neonates can sleep regardless of sounds in the environment, some of these schizophrenics had been, as infants, hypersensitive to sound. Others had been easily disturbed by smells or by certain colors.

Bergman and Escalona hypothesize that hypersensitive children make unusual demands on their parents. For the mother to provide an adequate stimulus barrier (protection from overstimulation) for an infant with unusual sensitivities, she must know what constitutes an impingement. She is at a distinct disadvantage if she doesn't share the infant's sensitivities. For example, a color-blind mother would have trouble discriminating the colors that disturb her child.

Bergman and Escalona hypothesize that if the parents *are* able to adjust themselves to the heightened sensitivity and unique needs of their infant, their child may be able to use this heightened sensitivity in an adaptive, often creative, way (note how compatible this is with Karlsson's [1968] hypothesis).

However, all too often parents are either unable to adjust or fail to set limits, so that the child becomes a tyrant, as Wilson (1968) so aptly describes in *This Stranger, My Son.*

Thomas, Chess, and Birch have published a series of articles and books reporting early temperamental differences in infants. They define temperament as the "behavioral style of an individual child, the how or manner of his behavior" (1969, p. 4). Level of energy expenditure and sensory thresholds are major dimensions of temperament. Some attributes and patterns are more likely than others to make a child vulnerable to damaging interaction with the enviornment. The fit between the child's temperament and that of the parents is critical and may help explain some later behavioral differences among siblings. For example, a parent who is indifferent to noise will have trouble adjusting to a baby who is very sensitive to noise. On a noise dimension, this pair is much more at risk than any other combination. If the child doesn't mind noise and the parent does, conflicts will arise, but not until much later.

The parent who easily adjusts to a first child, and finds effective ways to discipline and introduce new stimuli, may have trouble recognizing the different needs of a second child. Thus a second child, who is afraid of new situations and has a sibling with an easy temperament, may be at a greater disadvantage than a firstborn with a similar problem. Parental expectations and subsequent disappointments lead to heightened anxieties with the second child, which then increase the child's anxiety, creating a vicious circle.

Many of the attributes Thomas et al. subsume under temperament (activity level, rhythmicity, approach-withdrawal, adaptability, quality of mood, intensity of reaction, threshold of responsiveness, distractibility, attention span, and persistence) are likely to have polygenic bases. Thomas et al. divide their infants on the basis of temperament into easy, difficult, and slow to warm up. Longitudinal follow-up found that difficult children were at highest risk for personality problems.

Biochemical Theories	*Chapter Four*

Biochemical explanations of schizophrenia lie midway between theories of genetic etiology and descriptions of behavioral, neurophysiological, and psychological functioning. If there is a genetic basis for schizophrenia, it will probably show up biochemically (See Chapter 3, the monogenic bioamine model). If a specific biochemical change can be isolated, we may be better able to predict and treat schizophrenia as well as gain a better understanding of normal neurochemistry and neurophysiology.

Many reports of a biochemical agent in schizophrenia have been made (e.g., Friedhoff & Van Winkle, 1962; Heath, 1954; Heath et al., 1957; Hoffer, Osmond, & Smythies, 1954), only to be refuted when findings could not be replicated. This history of dramatic, often conflicting, claims can be explained by the methodological complexities of research in schizophrenia. Diagnostic criteria, age of onset, duration of episode, length of hospitalization, diet, exercise, history of physical illnesses, current and past medication, and shock treatments may all affect current biochemistry and thus should all be controlled. In addition, many biochemical anomalies initially attributed to schizophrenia were later found to be related to stress. Researchers have rarely used adequate controls, e.g., a group of nonschizophrenic psychotics, a group of normals under stress, as well as the more readily available "normals" (see Kety, 1969; Matthysse, 1976a).

Probably more than any other kind of investigation of schizophrenia, biochemical studies are dated almost as soon as they are published. Many of the hypotheses that were considered worthy of serious attention in 1971 (see Cancro, 1972) were dismissed four years later. The following review of major biochemical theories is based primarily on critical reviews of the literature in the 1974/1975 *Annual Review of the Schizophrenic Syndrome* (Cancro, 1976a), the *Schizophrenia Bulletin,* Volume 2, No. 1, 1976 (Durell & Archer, 1976; Meltzer, 1976; Meltzer & Stahl, 1976; Rosengarten & Friedhoff, 1976; Wyatt & Murphy, 1976), Frohman and Gottlieb (1974), and *The Nature of Schizophrenia* (Wynne, Cromwell, & Matthysse, 1978).

Biochemical investigations of schizophrenia have often been spurred by what is in vogue. After a specific enzyme deficiency, caused by a single gene, was found to be the basis of phenylketonuria in 1934, the search was on for a similar cause of schizophrenia (the mental deficiency model). While in the 1960s LSD influenced Laing's language and theories, leading to what has been called the psychedelic theory of madness, it also gave rise to the transmethylation theory of schizophrenia, which states that the body produces its own psychotomimetic drugs or endogenous hallucinogens. Currently, advances in virology have led to speculation that a slow-acting virus (perhaps originating in utero) causes schizophrenia (Torrey & Peterson, 1976). Another cause of rapid change in biochemical theories is that the level of sophistication of biochemical research, more than research in other areas, is a function of the current, rapidly changing technology.

At present, most biochemical researchers see schizophrenia as a syndrome, the end product of many possible disturbances—genetic, biochemical, environmental. A biochemical disturbance may be the end product of faulty genetic coding, the observable result of an endogenous or exogenous toxin, or a biochemical reaction to environmental stress.

During the last twenty-five years, many unusual substances and/or abnormal amounts of normal substances have been "discovered" in schizophrenics. I shall discuss several of the major findings and their current status.

Kraepelin believed that schizophrenia was a metabolic disorder. For a time, he and others studied the general body metabolism of schizophrenics, but their findings were later attributed to poor diet and lack of exercise (Kety, 1969, p. 167). The focus of biochemical research has since largely shifted to the metabolism of amino acids and bioamines. This shift was related both to the elegant simplicity of the discovery of phenylketonuria (PKU) and the subsequent hope for a similar solution in schizophrenia, and to the increased interest in LSD and the hypothesis that the schizophrenic produces an abnormal, toxic protein that acts like LSD. More recently researchers have argued that the biochemical abnormality is more subtle still. For if there were a gross alteration in biochemistry, leading to either a structural anomaly or a specific enzyme deficiency, it would be more readily observable in autopsy (if structural) or in body by-products in consistent and significant amounts. This is not the case in schizophrenia, leading researchers to anticipate a regulatory rather than a structural deficit (A.J. Friedhoff, personal communication, 1978).

In 1954, Heath reported that a substance extracted from schizophrenics' blood caused some schizophrenialike symptoms when injected into nonschizophrenic volunteers. It also caused monkeys, spiders, and other laboratory animals to act bizarrely. He found a relationship between the presence of this chemical and unusual septal spiking in EEG recordings. Heath hypothesized a relationship between this substance and an increased permeability of cell membranes. He found this substance only in the acute stages when there were flamboyant symptoms. The report of induction of schizophrenialike symptoms in humans has not been supported by most investigators, although Bergen et al. (1962) did report abnormal septal spiking in monkeys who had been given taraxein (the name given to Heath's substance). Durell and Archer (1976) report that taraxein and other substances previously thought to be specific to schizophrenia are in fact products of "acute phase reaction" or stress.

More recently, a number of laboratories, in their search for the schizophrenogenic toxin that produces bizarre behavior in animals, isolated the protein alpha-2-globulin, since referred to as "the S protein." As the nature of this protein was pursued, the picture became increasingly complex. A summary of the course of these investigations will illustrate the complexity of biochemical evidence. Presence of the S protein was found to increase the lactate/pyruvate (L/P) ratio when plasma containing it was incubated with red cells. This increase in L/P ratio had been considered a significant, possibly causal, feature in schizophrenics' biochemistry; it affected the uptake of tryptophane (an amino acid); when injected into cows, they produced dimethyltryptamine (DMT), a known hallucinogen. Lozovsky et al. (reported in Frohman & Gottlieb, 1974) found that the activity of this protein varied during the course of the illness.

At first it was believed that there was simply more S protein in schizophrenics than in controls. With more exacting methodology the levels were found to be the same in both groups, but the shape of the protein was different. Frohman et al. (1971) isolated an anti-S protein and found that levels of this protein were four times higher in the nonschizophrenic patients. This disparity could be responsible for the difference in the shape of the S proteins, which appears to affect tryptophane uptake. One of the by-products of tryptophane metabolism is the hallucinogen DMT. This work, however, has not been replicated.

Durell and Archer (1976), in their review of the research on plasma proteins and schizophrenia, raise the serious criticism that these studies lacked appropriate controls. When hospitalization, medication, and stress are accounted for, the changes appear to be due to stress. A significant shortcoming of much plasma protein research is that the controls were not nonschizophrenic psychiatric patients. An exception is the work of Boch, Weeke, and Rafaelson (1971), who studied the blood sera of sixteen acute schizophrenics, eleven manics, five borderlines, and thirty-two "healthy controls." The patients had been off neuroleptic drugs for at least one month before testing. In eleven of the patients Boch et al. found a pattern of change in serum protein that was similar to an acute phase reaction. Whatever differences existed were thought to be related to stress rather than to schizophrenia per se. However, we encounter another methological problem here: hospital wards that maintain schizophrenic patients off medication frequently have strict admission criteria and thus an atypical sample of schizophrenics.

Currently there are two main biochemical theories of schizophrenia: transmethylation and dopamine. The transmethylation theory began with the work of Hoffer, Osmond, and Smythies in 1954. They were among the first to note the structural similarity between the catecholamine dopamine and mescaline. They hypothesized that abnormal methylation of dopamine would produce a mescalinelike substance, an endogenous hallucinogen that they called DMPEA. There is in fact an N-methylating enzyme that is involved in the normal synthesis of epinephrine, and this or a similar enzyme might create DMPEA. In 1962, Friedhoff and Van Winkle reported on an abnormal amine found in the urine of fifteen of nineteen schizophrenics but in none of the normal controls, and this was identified as DMPEA. Research by other investigators, however, has yielded contradictory findings. DMPEA has been found in the urine of normals as well as schizophrenics. Nevertheless, a recent study by Friedhoff et al. (1977), using more sophisticated technology, found significantly higher levels of DMPEA in the urine of acute, nonmedicated schizophrenics than in the urine of normals. Patients on phenothiazines showed lower levels of DMPEA. The significance of this finding is unclear and is especially curious since DMPEA is a by-product of dopamine metabolism and thus of interest in the dopamine hypothesis of schizophrenia as well as the transmethylation hypothesis.

Since Hoffer, Osmond, and Smythies's first reports (1954), scientists have been able to isolate and recognize several indoleamines that show structural similarities with known hallucinogens. The original 1952 methylation hypothesis was expanded and renamed "transmethylation" by Kety (1969). This expanded theory postulates that schizophrenia arises from an abnormal accumulation of N- or O-methylated biogenic amine derivatives, which are psychotogens. The expanded theory, although not disproved, has failed to yield conclusive findings. Methylated derivatives have been found in normals as well as in schizophrenics.

In addition to studying amine levels in body by-products (e.g., plasma and urine), researchers have tested the transmethylation theory by attempting to control production of the psychotogen by loading the system with a specific amino acid. Thus, some studies loaded subjects with methionine, a methyl donor. Psychotic symptoms increased and mental status deteriorated in these subjects. However, this could result from a toxic psychosis, rather than through exacerbation of the schizophrenia. Nicotinamide has been used by megavitamin therapists and by some researchers in an effort to block bio-amine methylation and thereby reduce psychotic symptoms. Careful studies of this approach do not support its utility as a primary therapeutic measure (Lehmann, 1975; May, 1975a, 1975b).

Although no conclusive evidence supports transmethylation, it has not been disproved, so the search for a specific methylated bioamine continues.

In a recent review article, Rosengarten and Friedhoff (1976) conclude that, although a higher concentration of hallucinogens is found in schizophrenics that in controls, we do not know what role these substances play. They suggest that such substances are related to symptom formation and thus are secondary, rather than central, to the etiology of schizophrenia. This idea is a biochemical analogue to the belief of Bleuler and others that hallucinations are secondary phenomena. In other words, an unidentified event or substance sets up an unusual biochemical state in which the body begins to manufacture endogenous hallucinogens.

Recently, many researchers have rejected the emphasis on an endogenous hallucinogen with its implicit basis in an LSD model of madness. This shift occurred following more careful observation and comparison of LSD-in-duced alterations of consciousness and those found in schizophrenia. These states were found to differ in the presence/absence of hallucinations, delu-sions, and thought disorder. It was therefore suggested by many that LSD states are not an adequate model for schizophrenia. This conclusion is disput-ed by some, including Friedhoff (personal communication, 1978), who points out that most people on LSD know that they have taken a drug and are, moreover, experiencing an acute reaction. Schizophrenics, on the other hand, if they are showing the effects of an endogenous hallucinogen, do not know of its existence and have been subject to its effects for a longer period of time. Friedhoff states (personal communcation, 1978) that people who have unwittingly taken LSD show a very different presenting picture, one that more closely resembles schizophrenia.

Some researchers have shifted from an LSD model to trying to understand the action of neuroleptic drugs. They reason as follows: given that neurolep-tic drugs, e.g., Thorazine, alleviate schizophrenic symptoms, understanding their chemical structure and their pharmacological activity in the brain might help us understand the biochemistry of schizophrenia. Initially the phenothia-zines were used simply for their sedating powers, but it soon became appar-ent, both clinically and experimentally, that these drugs were more effective than the barbiturates and minor tranquilizers. Tranquilization alone was not the answer. The question then arose: What do neuroleptics do biochemically that is critical for their antipsychotic activity? Investigators of this question were aided by the fact that there are several phenothiazines which have no effect on psychotic symptoms (although chemically they are quite similar to those that do), as well as a group of effective antipsychotic drugs, the butyrophenones, that are chemically quite different from the phenothiazines.

Research focused on the numerous biochemical effects of phenothiazines and other antipsychotic agents. For the most part the clinically ineffective phenothiazines are chemically similar to the effective ones. The one effect that correlates closely with therapeutic efficacy is the influence of the drug on dopamine transmission: the clinically effective phenothiazines all act to block dopamine receptors.

Since the original dopamine hypothesis offered by Carlsson and Lindgvist in 1963, numerous studies have confirmed that the clinical effectiveness of a neuroleptic is correlated with its potency as a dopamine blocker (Sachar et al., 1978; Snyder, 1978).

The other route to the dopamine hypothesis was through the observation that while LSD experiences are not prototypical of schizophrenia, amphetamine psychoses are. Long-term use of amphetamines can produce a state clinically indistinguishable from paranoid schizophrenia. Both amphetamines, which cause the release of catecholamines (dopamine and norepinephrine), and L-dopa, a precursor of dopamine, exacerbate preexisting schizophrenic symptoms. These two lines of evidence led Snyder to conclude that "one can titrate symptoms by manipulating brain dopamine" (p. 87).

There is a third, somewhat weaker, line of evidence for the dopamine hypothesis, based on findings of lowered plasma levels of monoamine oxidase (MAO). MAO is an enzyme which breaks down neurotransmitters, including dopamine. It has been suggested that depression may be related to high levels of MAO, which result in excessive breakdown of norepinephrine. Thus depression is frequently treated with MAO inhibitors. Wyatt and Murphy (1976) found that identical twins discordant for schizophrenia both had low levels of MAO, which suggested an inherited vulnerability or a genetic marker. Low MAO activity would mean less breakdown of dopamine and norepinephrine. In addition, Davis (1978) points out that schizophrenia, a disease of young adulthood, occurs at a time in the life cycle when MAO levels are at their lowest. The clinical finding that some borderline patients can become schizophrenic if they are given MAO inhibitors may also be related to the fact that the balance between the neurotransmitter dopamine and the enzyme MAO is critical for mental life. But the question must be asked why most people given MAO inhibitors do not become schizophrenic. One possible explanation is that borderlines have a subclinical chemical abnormality, namely, low MAO, that is not sufficient to cause schizophrenic symptoms unless further decreased by MAO inhibitors.

Meltzer and Stahl (1976) summarize the dopamine theory as follows:

> In its simplest form, this hypothesis states that schizophrenia may be related to a relative excess of dopamine dependent neuronal activity. It is derived

from pharmacological evidence that drugs that decrease dopamine activity (e.g., phenothiazines) may be anti-psychotic, and drugs that promote dopamine activity (e.g., amphetamines) may be psychotomimetic. The particular means by which "too much dopamine" is produced in schizophrenia is not yet known [p. 19].

While there is incontrovertible evidence that antipsychotic drugs block dopamine, and it is likely that their clinical efficacy and beneficial effects are related to dopamine blockade, we cannot yet conclude that dopamine level plays a central, causal role in schizophrenia (see Davis, 1978; Snyder, 1978). I shall return to this question later; first I shall summarize what is known about dopamine.

Dopamine is one of two principal catecholamines in the brain; the other is norepinephrine. These are major neurotransmitters. Usually dopamine is converted into norepinephrine, a transformation catalyzed by the enzyme dopamine-B-hydroxylase. However, this enzyme is lacking in some parts of the brain, and there dopamine is the principal neurotransmitter. One of these dopamine pathways, the nigrostriatal pathway, is the locus of the trouble in parkinsonism. We do not yet know the dopamine pathway that is critical to schizophrenia. Researchers have investigated several possibilities, e.g., the limbic system and the septal region (see below, Chapter 5). There are some data to suggest that disturbances in central dopamine pathways lead to schizophrenialike symptoms.

Our understanding of neuroleptics is still somewhat crude. They seem to lower the overall availability of dopamine within the brain, not only in the critical or therapeutic pathways but in others as well, frequently causing parkinsonian side effects. The general lowering of dopamine availability can be achieved in several ways: (1) blocking dopamine receptors; (2) lowering the stores of dopamine (as in the case of reserpine); and (3) blocking the synthesis of dopamine. This last action is achieved by alpha methyl paratyrosine (AMPT), which by itself does not have antipsychotic properties but which may potentiate the activities of neuroleptics.

Davis (1978) and others have suggested that the usual methods of monitoring dopamine levels do not adequately record the activity in the dopamine pathway critical to schizophrenia. These methods might not be sensitive enough to detect the critical metabolites, or the metabolites might not reach the cerebrospinal fluid directly. For example, while prolactin level is sufficiently affected by dopamine to monitor whether patients are taking medication (Sachar et al., 1978), the level reaches a plateau before clinical improvement occurs. It reaches maximum levels with low doses of medication and after only a few hours. Dopamine receptors in at least some pathways are blocked by phenothiazines long before psychotic symptoms disappear.

These data led Davis (1978) to suggest a two-factor theory of schizophrenia. He hypothesized a nondopaminergic first factor that may initiate a schizophrenic episode, and a second factor, dopamine stimulation, in a related neural system. This increase in dopamine may aggravate the first factor and increase the severity of the episode. Antipsychotic medication, which blocks dopaminergic activity, may interrupt this cycle and allow normal healing. Davis suggests that this theory could explain the slow time course of the medication. In addition, the first factor in the theory could be mediated by psychological and/or physiological factors.

Friedhoff and Alpert (1978) argue that the relatively long time (six weeks) before symptoms subside suggests that the therapeutic action of neuroleptics may result not from the blockade of dopamine receptors but, paradoxically, from the compensatory increase in the sensitivity of postsynaptic receptors to the available dopamine.

Matthysse (1976b) speculates on the way schizophrenic behavior might arise from too much dopamine. Analogizing from the known effect of dopamine level on motor behavior (it "acts by disinhibition to permit the emergence of movements from subthreshold state" [p. 191]), he proposes a corresponding dopamine effect on subcortical mental functioning, namely, a disinhibition that permits the myriad associations to events to come to consciousness, causing loosening of associations. He then somewhat less convincingly describes how the increase in dopamine may lead to the disorder of affect described by Bleuler; that is, incapacity to modulate affect, and rigid, exaggerated, and theatrical affect. He sees again the analogy to motoric symptoms of increased dopamine, namely, hyperkinesis. He also addresses himself to the problem of identical twins discordant for schizophrenia. Matthysse suggests that, although a biochemical predisposition to increased dopamine may be genetically determined, environment greatly affects the other critical aspects of schizophrenia, especially interpersonal relations. He describes a possible neuronal mechanism at work in interpersonal relations which may be affected by dopamine, but which is also very much influenced by the environment, and reminds us that phenothiazines are least effective in combating the interpersonal variable. These ideas are compatible with Meltzer's (1976a) hypothesis of a biochemical predisposition that, in conjunction with stress-related chemical events, leads to schizophrenia. Meltzer goes on to describe the limits of a theory of biological defect: "All aspects of the multifaceted behavior we comprehend by the term schizophrenia are unlikely to be tightly linked to a specific biochemical defect" (p. 14). As supportive evidence, Meltzer cites Woolf's (1967) study of identical twins, both with PKU, one with an IQ of 55, the other with an IQ of 100. This difference in IQ scores is used to illustrate that the outcome of even a relatively clear-cut genetic disorder involving a specific enzyme is not yet understood.

Bowers (1974) proposed that "clinical schizophrenia consists both of certain maladaptive characterological traits and a biologically based propensity to psychedelic states" (quoted in Meltzer, 1976a, p. 14). Thus an understanding of vulnerability to schizophrenia must include an evaluation of the varying capacities of individuals to compensate for inherent chemical deficits such as unusual levels of dopamine. This is similar to Anthony's (1974b) theory of the psychologically invulnerable child, which will be discussed further in Chapter 8.

Recent advances in virology have led to a viral hypothesis of schizophrenia: that a slow-acting virus may cause schizophrenia. The existence of similar syndromes caused by known viruses, e.g., encephalitis, is cited as evidence. Also noted are the peculiar fingerprints and seasonal variation in birth rate of schizophrenics. Since viruses are known to be more prevalent at different times of the year, the seasonal variation in schizophrenics' birthdays could be explained within this theoretical framework (Torrey & Peterson, 1976). The emergence of schizophrenic behavior may be related to genetic factors, a slow-acting virus, pubertal changes, recent unrelated infections that affect immune systems, and/or environmental stresses that can also affect these systems.

Biochemical abnormalities may be a function of genetic factors, viruses, nutrition, or stress. They may be simply the physical expression of certain mental phenomena, correlates that are in no way causal. Most biochemical theorists do not address themselves to the psychological import of their findings. One study, by Sachar et al. (1972), stands out as an attempt to integrate these different levels of observation. They studied fluctuation in the adrenocortical stress response as measured by increase in corticosteroids and epinephrine excretions during periods of ego disintegration and reintegration in their subjects. They found that the level of these hormones increased when a person was in an acute panic at the start of a psychotic episode. When delusions were formed (the "psychotic insight" of Sullivan), and anxiety theoretically diminished, the level of these substances decreased. When in the course of therapy the patients's delusions began to crumble, the level of these hormones increased. Sachar et al.'s study had clear diagnostic criteria and indicated the interconnectedness of biochemical and psychological aspects of schizophrenia. The implication of this study is that affective and cognitive developments influenced, or were influenced by, chemical levels. In either case, the changes occurred simultaneously.

Some clinical observations have yet to be explained. Not all diagnosed schizophrenics respond to phenothiazines with a reduction of symptoms. Some people have a toxic reaction to these drugs and exhibit flamboyantly psychotic behavior; others remain unchanged. These findings may suggest faulty diagnosis or the existence of several unclassified subtypes of schizophrenia. Mark Vonnegut (1977) concluded from his own experience that there are many subtypes, each with a different medication responsiveness, each with a different underlying biochemical disturbance. While his contention that schizophrenia is caused solely by biochemical disturbances is extreme, his assertion of the existence of subtypes that may be approachable via their differing responses to medication is worth considering.

My experience with schizophrenics leads me to concur with those who argue that the flamboyant characteristics of schizophrenia (especially hallucinations) are related to a biochemical imbalance. These characteristics, however, seems to occur abruptly after years of marginal functioning that may have an entirely different psychological or biochemical explanation. For example, one might be a temperamentally difficult person and have had profoundly impoverished experiences in living, but be free from clear schizophrenic symptoms until stress, physical illness, or some unknown mechanism causes the chemistry to shift, creating an altered state of sensory experience.

<table>
<tr><td>Neurophysiological
Theories and Findings</td><td>Chapter
Five</td></tr>
</table>

This chapter focuses on those theories and experiments that deal directly with the study of brain functioning through electrical stimulation, EEG recordings, and average evoked potentials (AEP). It also discusses studies of involuntary behaviors regulated by the central nervous system (CNS), such as nystagmus and eye-tracking movements. Buchsbaum (1976) states that such measures of brain functioning are more direct and immediate, and thus closer to clinical behavior, than biochemical approaches, which investigate substances assayed in blood and urine produced over a period of time ranging from hours to days. For this reason such studies are becoming increasingly popular. In addition, these measures are relatively unaffected by volition and motivation—problems common in behavioral research. Many neurophysiological findings are expressions or correlates of biochemical and/or psychological events. To some extent, therefore, this chapter overlaps Chapters 4 and 6.

Spring and Zubin (1977) note that researchers have not yet determined whether specific attributes found in schizophrenics are state-dependent characteristics (occurring only in the midst of schizophrenic episode) or enduring traits that are part of an ongoing vulnerability. This distinction has implications for early identification of those at risk for schizophrenia and for the possible objective identification of the start of acute episodes. It is thus an important consideration in biochemical, physiological, and psychological research.

It seems reasonable to assume that schizophrenic disturbances are reflected in brain functioning. Many researchers have attempted to isolate the portion of the brain responsible for schizophrenia. Heath (1954) described abnormal spiking in the septal region of schizophrenics' brains. Sem-Jacobsen (reported in Shagass, 1969) found that stimulating the parietal lobe could produce psychosislike symptoms and that LSD produced parietal spiking on EEGs, both of which were eliminated by Thorazine. Mednick (1970), in his work on high-risk children, found more perinatal complications and anoxia in children who became schizophrenic. He hypothesized that the locus of damage from perinatal complications was the hippocampus. He subsequently discovered that rats with hippocampal damage showed some of the same learning difficulties as did preschizophrenic children. Hippocampal damage may permit oversecretion of adrenocorticotropic hormone (ACTH) during periods of stress and could explain schizophrenics' excessive arousal. Another possible explanation of schizophrenics' chronic overarousal may be the hippocampus's defective capacity to inhibit the recticular formation, leading to a constant state of alertness.

Another strategy for identifying portions of the brain implicated in schizophrenia has been to monitor cerebral blood flow. Cerebral blood flow has been found to vary with mental tasks and is also related to the amplitude of EEG recordings (Buchsbaum, 1980; Ingvar, Sjolound, & Arno, 1976). Although schizophrenics and normals do not differ in total cerebral blood flow, chronic schizophrenics were found to have lower flow in frontal lobes and higher postural flows (Kety et al., 1948). This finding has caused Franzen and Ingvar (1975a, 1975b) to speculate that these flows are associated with a syndrome of unusual elaboration of sensory messages and perceptual disturbances. The finding that variations in blood flow correlate with EEG amplitude strengthens the use of EEG recordings as a noninvasive way of assessing localized brain functioning.

It may be too simple to assume that schizophrenia could be caused by a defect in any single part of the brain. Corbett (1976) states: "The intimate association between perception, affect, and thought observed clinically is reflected in the inextricable interrelations of the neuronal circuitry subserving these functions. There is a diffuse sharing of common neurotransmitter systems" (p. 259). He goes on to describe the critical interplay between the reticular activating system and the limbic system.

Other researchers have attempted to link the dopamine theory of schizophrenia with an understanding of neuroanatomy in order to better locate the site of schizophrenic disturbance (Meltzer & Stahl, 1976; see also Chapter 4, this book). Perhaps the most elaborate work in this area has been done by Stevens (1973). She reasons that if "excess production or oversensitivity to locally released dopamine is crucial to the development of schizophrenia, recent advances . . . [enable us] to provide a framework into which symptoms and signs of schizophrenia may also find an anatomical reference" (p. 177). She goes on to review evidence that dysfunctions of the corpus striatum, particularly the limbic striatum, are basic to the schizophrenic process. Her hypothesis is that a "neostriatal gate" exists. The function of the "gate" is to prevent inundation of consciousness both by general sensory and motor afferents (via caudate putamen neurons) and by primitive memories (from limbic system storage). Interference with control of limbic system function could lead to precursors of schizophrenic symptoms including hypervigilance, hyperaggressiveness, and automatisms of fear and sexual activity. Such symptoms are actually found with lesions of the amygdala, a limbic system structure. Behaviorally this might be manifested in poorly focused attention, overinclusiveness, and motor stereotypy (especially in regard to food). As evidence for a "neostriatal gate" she cites: (1) the strategic placement of the limbic striatum between the cerebral mantle and pathways leading to the thalamus, brain stem, and hypothalamus; and (2) the presence of dopaminergic pathways analogous to those in the corpus striatum, which is involved in motor information processing and central to parkinsonian diseases.

Most researchers have been less concerned with locating the site of brain dysfunction than with establishing the involvement of the central nervous system (CNS) in a general way. Hertzig and Birch (1966) and Gittelman and Birch (1967) found a high incidence of mild neurological impairment indicated by intellectual assessment, adventitious motor overflow, auditory-visual intersensory integration, and clinical neurological exams in children and adolescents diagnosed schizophrenic. Gittelman and Birch concluded that 80 percent of these children had some CNS pathology and suggested a connection with the high incidence of perinatal complications in these children's histories. Hertzig and Birch found that the degree of CNS disturbance in adolescents correlated with the severity of their psychotic illness. Ornitz (1971) has found similarities between autistic children and schizophrenics and hypothesizes that both syndromes are due to faulty homeostatic regulation of input, a finding consistent with Stevens's (1973) theory. Ornitz suggests that there is a fluctuation between excessive and insufficient sensory stimulation which leads to secondary symptoms. He cites as evidence the variability of evoked response patterns in schizophrenics (see below). Support for this idea also comes from sensory deprivation studies.

Although studies of childhood and adolescent schizophrenia may offer clues to the etiology of adult schizophrenia, their relevance must be evaluated with caution. It seems probable that the earlier a disorder manifests itself, the more likely it is to be caused by organic factors. In addition, it is not clear that "childhood schizophrenia" is related to any form of adult schizophrenia.

EEG PATTERNS

Schizophrenics' EEGs have been studied in an effort to isolate specific patterns. In a 1969 review article, Shagass reports various differences in schizophrenics' EEG patterns but states that no consistent findings have yet emerged. Itil, Saletu, and Davis (1972) state that there appears to be no EEG pattern pathognomonic for schizophrenia. Most recently, Fink (1978) describes great methodological advances in both recording and data analysis techniques. He suggests that these changes call for renewed attention to schizophrenics' EEGs, especially since EEG patterns have proved useful in providing objective diagnostic indicators in other disorders. He concludes his review of the literature on EEG patterns with two cautionary notes: (1) most findings reveal group differences and are not reliably informative for the individual case; and (2) the failure to find a correlation between diagnosis and physiological indices may reflect the poor validity of clinical diagnosis. He argues that EEG criteria may provide an independent means of identifying homogeneous populations whose behavior and prognosis may then be observed.

Fink reports that some investigators (Goldstein & Sugarman, 1969) have found low correlations between EEG recordings taken from various areas of the scalp in schizophrenics. Other investigators (Itil, 1975) have tried to describe specific differences in schizophrenics' EEG patterns, for example, greater variability in amplitude, greater amounts of fast activity, and great amounts of theta activity. In addition, Itil et al. (1975) have correlated changes in EEG recordings with treatment and clinical improvement. Dasberg and Robinson (1969) have shown that those schizophrenics with "hyperstable" EEG patterns are the least responsive to treatment.

All of the above are group EEG differences. Although schizophrenics as a group differ from controls, not all schizophrenics display any given EEG pattern, and some normal subjects may even show the EEG anomaly. Recent investigations (discussed in Fink, 1978; e.g., Stevens, 1973) have examined EEG changes in persons progressing through different clinical states. Studies in which EEG patterns are monitered during sleep or in drug-induced states (Halasz & Nagy, 1965; Struve & Becka, 1968) have suggested an association between the presence in a given individual of B-mitten patterns and psychotic decompensation—suggestive of a state-dependent finding.

AVERAGE EVOKED POTENTIALS (AEP) STUDIES

EEG recordings have also been used to monitor schizophrenics' reactions to stimuli. In this procedure, reactions to stimuli are monitored by EEG, and average evoked potentials (AEP), also known as average evoked responses

(AER), are produced. Because this technique is relatively unaffected by volition and motivation, it avoids one of the major confounding factors in research on information processing. As Sutton and Tueting (1978) note, evoked potentials (EPs) are a way of looking at brain activity associated with specific conscious processes. EPs have proved to be sensitive to changes in sensory characteristics of stimuli (e.g., intensity, color), perceptual changes (geometric form), and cognitive changes (e.g., uncertainty). EPs even measure response to the absence of an expected stimulus. Different components of EP recordings are differentiated according to length of time since the presentation of a stimulus. At 100 msec, EPs reflect processing of the sensory characteristics of the input; at 200 msec, EPs reflect attentional and perceptual elements; and at 300 msec, EPs mirror cognitive dimensions. These measures are exceedingly sensitive and thus might be affected by all the symptoms associated with schizophrenia (delusions, hallucinations, distractibility, etc.).

In general, schizophrenics' AEPs are more variable than are those of normals (Callaway, 1972; Ornitz, 1971). However, Shagass (cited in Sutton & Tueting, 1978) found that chronic schizophrenics were less variable than normals or other patient groups in the early portion (P100 msec) of the AEP. It is the later, primarily P300 msec, portion that is more variable in schizophrenics. In normals, variability of AEP tends to diminish with age, which could suggest a developmental arrest or regression in schizophrenics. In addition, researchers have found that variability of AEP is positively correlated with the degree of thought disorder. The AEP becomes less variable as the patient improves clinically—again suggesting a state-related pattern. Variability is also negatively related to IQ: the more variable the AEP, the lower the IQ (Inderbitzin, Buchsbaum, & Silverman, 1973).

Studies showing greater variability of AEP in schizophrenics may have been contaminated by other characteristics of the schizophrenic population used. Interbitzen et al. (1973) found that variable AEPs correlated with lower Wechsler Adult Intelligence Scale (WAIS) scores and lower performance on other cognitive tasks. They also found that schizophrenics showed little increase in AEP amplitude with increased intensity of stimuli and that those with stabler AEP patterns had stabler performances on other measures.

Levit, Sutton, and Zubin (1973) looked at EPs for stimuli of varying complexity in both schizophrenics and normals. They found that the normals' EPs showed higher mean amplitudes than the schizophrenics' and more increase in amplitude as the stimulus became more complex. Levit et al.'s finding is consistent with the common hypothesis that schizophrenics do not attend properly to new information. A question has been raised: Are the EP findings a function of medication level rather than schizophrenia? Levit et al.'s observation of two schizophrenics who were tested while receiving no medication supplies an answer. The EP pattern of a clinically improved, unmedicated schizophrenic was similar to that found in normals. In contrast, the EP of a drug-free schizophrenic who was not clinically improved was abnormal. Levit et al. conclude that drugs alone do not account for the changes in EP. They relate their findings to studies in which both the reaction time (Grice & Hunter, 1964; Mowrer, 1941; Zahn, 1970) and the amplitude of normals' EPs (Sutton et al., 1965, 1967; Tueting, Sutton, & Zubin, 1971) increase under conditions of greater uncertainty. In schizophrenics under such conditions, the corresponding changes in both measures are much smaller. Levit et al.'s findings suggest that some of the observed differences in reaction-time studies (see Chapter 6) are not due merely to motivational factors but, rather, reflect an altered physiological state of readiness to respond in schizophrenics.

Sutton and Tueting (1978) point out another important difficulty in this research, namely, controlling confounding influences on AEP amplitude. Distraction, body movements, and attention to internal cues can all affect the AEP. They cite two current research strategies aimed at avoiding this difficulty: (1) "Full demand" situations, in which the experimenter aims at eliminating distractibility by making the task engaging, difficult, and potentially quite rewarding. (Even given these controls, Sutton and Tueting found a difference between schizophrenics and normals in the P300 msec range, where schizophrenics have lower amplitude.) (2) A "no instructions" procedure, in which the goal is to eliminate the differential effects of instructions and personal differences in responding to instructions. (However, Sutton and Tueting criticize this strategy, stating that we cannot be sure the schizophrenic is not self-instructing.)

In reviewing neurophysiological studies of schizophrenia, Buchsbaum (1977b, 1980) stresses the potential of a psychophysical approach to identifying objective internal states. Vaughan (1978) even more optimistically suggests that we can "contemplate the development of an objective neurophysiology of mental processes utilizing approaches from psychophysical methodology" (p. 207).

Evoked potentials represent some aspect of sensory information processing, and it is assumed (but not, according to Vaughan, tested) that evoked potential amplitude reflects the magnitude of neural processes related to subjective intensity. Vaughan is conservative in his evaluation of EP findings and their interpretation. He stresses the need to link EPs with simple concrete tasks like reaction time, focusing on such questions as what the source of delay is in the slow RTs of schizophrenics.

Buchsbaum (1977a) appears to be more convinced by current EP findings. He reports that EPs are very similar in indentical twins, much more so than in fraternal twins, and concludes from the available literature that aspects of EPs are inherited. He is most interested in the middle evoked response components, which involve P100, P140, and P200. P140 is a correlate of selective attention; P200 is associated with habituation and novelty effects. These middle components are most sensitive to attention and arousal— critical problem areas for schizophrenics—and very reactive to medication; in general, phenothiazines reduce the amplitude and increase the latency of these components, a pattern different from that caused by minor tranquiliz- ers. Patients who showed the greatest clinical improvement on phenothia- zines showed the most changes in EPs. Buchsbaum suggests that the study of EPs might help to identify the subgroup of schizophrenics for whom the dopamine hypothesis is valid and phenothiazines are most effective.

Buchsbaum (1977a, 1977b, 1980) reports that a number of investigators, using different techniques, have found a relationship between MAO metabo- lism and EP patterns. Low platelet MAO—a genetic trait—was used to screen a group at risk for schizophrenia (Wyatt & Murphy, 1973). This group performed less well on a test of attention than did subjects with high levels of MAO. Schizophrenics' low reactivity to novelty or uncertainty as mea- sured by EP amplitude can be seen either as support for the view that the schizophrenic's basic defect is in the low threshold for disorganization with increased stimulus input (consistent with the views of Mednick, Venables, Broen, and Storms, as discussed elsewhere) or as indicating a compensatory neurophysiological control.

Haier et al. (1980) conducted several studies of a "biologically high-risk group" of college students. They used two biological measures as indepen- dent variables: (1) platelet level of MAO; (2) AEPs in the P100 range. Both these measures are relatively stable and are under genetic control. A person whose AEP *increases* (the P100 range) when stimulus intensity increases is called an "augmentor"; such a person lacks sensory protection. A person whose AEP *decreases* (the P100 range) when stimulus intensity increases is called a "reducer"; such a person *has* sensory protection. The dependent variable in these studies is the psychopathology level as measured on the MMPI. Earlier studies found that when AEP and MAO are both used to predict pathology, they contribute unique variances. However, there ap- peared to be a strong inverse relationship between MAO level, AEP reduc- ing/augmenting, and psychopathology. Indeed, this inverse relationship was confirmed in Haier et al.'s study. Serious psychopathology was significantly more likely to occur in group members with low MAO levels and augment- ing AEPs and/or high MAO levels and reducing AEPs. They explain their findings as follows: low MAO level is associated with stimulus seeking (both sensory and social), high MAO with stimulus avoidance. The low MAO augmentor seeks stimulation and has no sensory protection; such a person may tend to be hyperactive as a child and tend to be overaroused. The high MAO reducer avoids stimulation and reduces that which comes in, tending to be underaroused and withdrawn. Environmental variables (e.g., parental behavior, discipline) would differentially affect the sensation-seeking behavior of the low MAO augmentor and the withdrawn behavior of the high MAO reducer. Patients with chronic schizophrenia tend to have low MAO and to be augmentors.

These findings suggest an exciting area of research—that of combined factors, both of which may be inherited, and which are benign when they occur singly but in combination lead to a vulnerability to severe pathology—a biologically at-risk group.

Buchsbaum has been interested in the possibility of identifying state and trait dimensions of AEPs. He has found some leads in the intensive study of a manic patient in whom, at P200 msec, EP components changed at the same time that manic symptoms emerged, whereas at P100 msec, EP components changed eight to ten days before behavior changed. The former change appears to be more state-dependent.

Since the early 1900s (Diefendorf & Dodge, 1908), researchers have noted deviant eye-tracking movements, which may be a genetic marker for schizophrenia. Recently Holzman (Holzman et al., 1974, 1978; Holzman & Levy, 1977) and others (Shagass, Amadeo, & Overton, 1974; Shagass, Roemer, & Amadeo, 1976) have returned to this phenomenon. Eye-tracking movements, like AEPs, are involuntary behaviors that are relatively free of motivational influence. In eye-tracking studies, subjects are asked to scan a moving object, usually a pendulum, and their eye movements are recorded. Normal subjects show smooth pursuit movements, whereas schizophrenics show deviant tracking motions, the graph of which can be spotted even by untrained observers. These deviations in tracking can be subdivided into those that result from pausing and those that result from the eyes moving more rapidly than the pendulum—what Holzman calls "positive velocity errors." It is the second kind of error that is characteristic of schizophrenics. Holzman found deviant tracking in 86 percent of chronic schizophrenics and in 44 percent of their first-degree relatives, but in only 8 percent of normals. This deviance correlated with the amount of thought disorder in psychiatric patients.

Holzman offers several possible explanations for these findings: (1) they could be another sign of disturbed attention with phasic interruptions of focus; (2) they could result from extraocular muscle pathology; or (3) the tracking deviance may represent a general defect in neuromuscular cybernetic coordination. This last hypothesis suggests a central nervous system dysfunction of interoceptive and proprioceptive feedback.

Researchers have studied schizophrenics' sleep and REM cycles partly because of the often-noted resemblance between the dream state and schizophrenic hallucinations and partly because people deprived of REM for long periods show signs of delusion formation and hallucinations. The indoleamine serotonin has been implicated in the regulation of REM periods and also in the possible formation of an endogenous hallucinogen. The lack of REM rebound noted in schizophrenics may affect the level of serotonin in the body and may also exacerbate the effects of insomnia, which often occurs before an acute episode.

Psychological Theories	Chapter Six

From studying the observable behavior of schizophrenics, experimental psychologists have drawn inferences regarding underlying processes, and these have in turn generated further research. The study of observable behavior has the virtue of bringing the schizophrenic's experience and behavior into the foreground, but it carries the burden of two major confounding variables that are not mediating factors in other areas of research: the schizophrenic's level of motivation and understanding of the task.

Sutton (1975) points out that schizophrenics usually do worse than normals on experimental tasks, regardless of the nature of the specific task. Schizophrenics have an understandable bias against reporting the presence of a stimulus since they have often been hospitalized for hearing or seeing things that "aren't there." Researchers have also found that schizophrenics are less influenced by positive reinforcers than are normals. This finding raises the issue of how context and meaning affect experimental behavior. Although this problem is a major one in all research, it seems especially relevant here. "Normal" control subjects are often concerned with achievement and social prestige, whereas schizophrenics may not be. For example, a paranoid patient may view any experimental situation as part of a conspiracy, and all hospitalized schizophrenics are likely to view any experimental procedure occurring within the hospital as related to their potential discharge.

Sutton (1975) and Spring and Zubin (1977, 1978), representing the biometric research group approach, suggest that, whenever possible, the experimenter should use tasks in which schizophrenics generally perform better than normal controls. Spring (1975) reports a technique of Collins in which schizophrenics demonstrated a visual discrimination that normals were not able to make. The problem of schizophrenic response bias has also led to increased use of physiological measures (see Chapter 5). Chapman and Chapman (1973) have noted that, given schizophrenics' response bias, generally slower reaction time, more variable performance, and greater difficulty with more complex tasks, it is easy to prove almost any statement about them via methodological inconsistencies. In order to increase the validity of test findings, tests should be matched for complexity and reliability. In addition, careful explanation of experimental procedures has improved schizophrenics' performance (Spring, 1975).

Psychological studies are also subject to the already-mentioned methodological problems that affect all research with schizophrenics. There is considerable evidence that experimental behavior is affected by the dimensions of acute/chronic, process/reactive, and paranoid/nonparanoid; these subgroups ought therefore to be tested separately. Medication can also affect test behavior. For example, a recent review and replication (Spohn, Cancro, & Thetford, 1976) of size estimation and visual scanning studies done with unmedicated schizophrenics reversed earlier findings of studies using medicated schizophrenics (Harris, 1957; Silverman & Venables, cited by Maher, 1966). Technological advances, too, have led to reversals of experimental findings, as methodology becomes more sophisticated.

Psychologists have classified behavior into general processes such as attention, motivation, and learning. The study of these processes raises yet another specific methodological problem—the definition of the intervening process (see Neale & Cromwell, 1973). In addition, these processes are interrelated. Recent advances in understanding brain function have made it clear that these classifications are arbitrary and do not reflect a real separation of loci in the brain (Corbett, 1976). Nonetheless, some separation is required to organize the massive data. The experimental literature on schizophrenia is voluminous and replete with contradictory findings and controversies. In this review I am necessarily selective, seeking to represent major research trends and findings, especially those leading to or deriving from etiological theories.

PHENOMENOLOGICAL REPORTS

Autobiographical accounts and reports by astute observers (see B. Freedman, 1976; B. Kaplan, 1964; McGhie & Chapman, 1967; Sechehaye, 1951a) provide the starting point for an understanding of schizophrenia. Patients and former patients report their psychotic experiences—it is these phenomenological events which all theories must explain.

Although Bleuler minimized sensory and perceptual alterations, schizophrenics themselves stress changes in intensity of perception, depth perception, size constancy, figure-ground distinction, and the sound of their own voices. These alterations are pronounced during acute episodes and are sometimes associated with a sense of euphoria and mystical enlightenment, at other times with dread (B. Freedman, 1976, pp. 100–105).

McGhie and Chapman (1961) and B. Freedman (1976) cite numerous examples of patients complaining of difficulty in focusing attention. For example: "My thoughts wander around in circles without getting anywhere. I try to read even a paragraph in a book, but it takes me ages, because each bit I read starts me thinking in ten different directions at once" (Freedman, 1976, p. 108).

Freedman summarizes descriptions of alterations in thinking, such as feelings of heightened or diminished efficiency, racing or slowed thoughts, increased yielding to associative connections between ideas, loss of control of thoughts, loss of meaning, memory deficits, thought blocking, confusion, trouble concentrating, and changes in perception of time. Freedman concludes: "There is no one set of phenomenological experiences that can be identified as a universal 'schizophrenic experience.' However, the multiform possible alterations in perception and cognition do lead rather reliably to the progressive loss of a sense of self and to the depersonalized feeling of loss of control over one's thoughts, feelings, and behaviors" (p. 117). As we shall see, many of these reported experiences have been experimentally confirmed and have become known as the distinguishing features of schizophrenia.

PERCEPTUAL STUDIES

Studies of size estimation (summarized by Buss & Lang, 1965; Maher, 1966; Neale & Cromwell, 1973; Spohn, Cancro, & Thetford, 1976) have found that schizophrenics do indeed have trouble with size constancy. Early studies by Harris (1957), Silverman (1964a, 1964b), and Venables (1964) found that paranoids and acute schizophrenics underestimated the size of distant objects, whereas nonparanoids and chronics overestimated the size. These researchers hypothesized that size estimation was a function of visual scanning behavior, which was in turn related to level of arousal. They reasoned that acute schizophrenics and paranoids showed hyperscanning, while nonparanoids and chronics showed hyposcanning owing to withdrawal from the enviroment. Spohn et al. (1976) cite McKinnon and Singer (1969), who obtained the opposite results with drug-free patients. They also found that measurements of size estimation did not correlate with visual scanning behavior. The latter behavior, measured by eye movements, was lower in medicated subjects than in nonmedicated subjects. Spohn et al. found that normal subjects displayed relatively consistent patterns of hyper- or hyposcanning, whereas schizophrenics showed greater variability.

Pupillary response to light, an indicator of psychological arousal, may also affect perception. Lidsky, Hakerem, and Sutton (1971) found that schizophrenics show less pupillary contraction when exposed to light than do normals. The above findings suggest that secondary symptoms of visual hallucinations could be caused by these unusual pupillary reactions and loss of size constancy. Lidsky et al. point out that the behavior of schizophrenics' pupils is consistent with Venables's (1964) theory of increased sympathetic tonus in schizophrenia (see section on arousal, this chapter).

Many studies, directly or indirectly, tap perceptual acuity. Some measure reaction time to a stimulus (signal detection); others study perceptual discriminations through a conditioned learning task. But as performance on these tasks is affected by readiness to respond and/or attention span, researchers are increasingly using physiological measures, such as AER, to study perceptual acuity. To date it appears that the difficulty is not in the reception and transmission of sensations to the cortex but, rather, in the integration of sensory impressions into a context and/or the attribution of meaning.

COGNITION AND INFORMATION PROCESSING

Historically, schizophrenic thought disorder has been a focus of interest; it is therefore not surprising that schizophrenic cognition has been much studied. I shall consider general cognitive theories before dealing with theories of schizophrenic language.

Lane and Albee (1965), Mednick (1970), and others have reported that adult schizophrenics had lower IQs as children than did their nonschizophrenic siblings. Hertzig and Birch (1966) and Gittelman and Birch (1967) also found below-average IQs in schizophrenic children. The meaning of this finding is unclear because performance on IQ tests is subject to all of the motivational problems mentioned above. In addition, if the preschizophrenic child is preoccupied, school performance will probably suffer.

Given these reports of lower IQ in preschizophrenic children, any study of cognition in adult schizophrenics should carefully control IQ and educational background. Unfortunately, Kilborg and Siegel (1976) neglected such factors in their study of schizophrenic functioning using Piagetian dimensions, leading to questionable results. They predicted that schizophrenics would do poorly on a test of formal operations and that process schizophrenics would do less well than reactive schizophrenics. In their attempt to utilize the process-reactive distinction, Kilborg and Siegel arbitrarily defined as reactive schizophrenics those with less than twelve years in the hospital. This is not what is generally referred to in the literature as reactive. In addition, their patient-subjects had had electroconvulsive therapy (ECT) and were receiving varying doses of medication. While the results were in the predicted direction, they were highly correlated with level of formal education and performance on the vocabulary subtest of the WAIS. Kilborg and Siegel's measure of formal operations was a series of sophisticated verbal and mathematical analogies which we would expect to correlate with IQ. In addition, schizophrenics generally perform poorly on complex tasks, and this fact alone could account for the findings. Similar methodological problems flaw the work of Kasanin, Hanfmann, Cameron, Goldstein, and von Domarus (Kasanin, 1944/1964). Unfortunately, there have been few studies of schizophrenics from a Piagetian orientation (see, e.g., Solod & Lapidus, 1977), and it remains a fruitful area for further research.

Shakow (1962, 1963, 1974) was one of the first to integrate research findings into a general cognitive theory of schizophrenia. He made several general observations: (1) Schizophrenics show increased variability of performance. (2) Schizophrenics usually show neophobia. (3) Schizophrenics have consistently slower reaction times than do normals, and the speed correlates with the degree of mental health. (4) Schizophrenics have more difficulty with tasks which provide or demand more autonomous behavior than with tasks the experimenter controls. Normals, in contrast, prefer to be in charge and do better when they have more autonomy.

Shakow believes that the fundamental disorder in schizophrenia is an inability to maintain a "major set" or state of readiness to respond. Instead, many other sets, other ways of responding, interfere. In other words, schizophrenics cannot filter out irrelevant stimuli and distractions because they cannot "keep their eyes on the ball," cannot keep the goal in mind.

In developing his theory, Shakow (1962) considered two critical features of adaptation: (1) *novelty,* which demands the right amount of arousal for perceptual narrowing and focusing on critical aspects of the situation; and (2) *reduced arousal* when the stimulus becomes familiar. The schizophrenic fails on both counts. This is consistent with findings that schizophrenics are slow to habituate (see Mednick, 1958, 1970) and have a chronic disorder of arousal.

Shakow (1974) describes the same phenomenon in different terms when he speaks of the "signal to noise ratio" in schizophrenics' experience. He states that there is too much "noise" in the system; that schizophrenics lack an adequate "filtering mechanism," to use Broadbent's (1958) term. This theory is related to theories of attentional deficit, which will be discussed below.

McReynolds's (1960) theory of schizophrenia is based on an information-processing concept, that the rate of information flow is critical. He stated that there is an optimum rate of perceptualization, or stimulation, for the organism. Too little stimulation (e.g., sensory deprivation) or too much stimulation is harmful and anxiety-provoking. Deriving ideas from Piaget, he explored the relation between schema and stimulus input, stating that ordinarily, stimuli are assimilated to one's schemas and schemas accommodate to novel stimuli. However, if the volume or novelty of stimuli is too great and new percepts or schemas are needed to handle the input, anxiety occurs. Anxiety, then, is seen as a consequence of too much incongruous and/or unassimilated material. New situations and life crises always result in some anxiety of this type. Persons who have previously developed an adequate system of constructs can struggle through these times, whereas those whose system of constructs is inadequate or erroneous are likely to experience extreme novelty and discrepancy a good part of the time. Similarly, persons with a small range of schemas are more likely to experience novelty.

McReynolds reasoned that the schizophrenic, who is anxious in response to the pileup of unassimilated percepts, withdraws to avoid stimuli and eventually hallucinates in response to this defensively induced state of sensory deprivation. Some limitations of McReynolds's work are that it is basically descriptive and that his explanation of the origin of hallucinations seems to account for only one group of patients, the chronic schizophrenics.

The idea of an optimum rate of perceptualization can easily be integrated with biochemical and neurophysiological findings of increased arousal and decreased chemical inhibition of neurotransmitters. It is also congruent with Kelly's (1955) personal construct theory (a cognitive view of personality development), which has been experimentally researched by Bannister (1965), Bannister and Fransella (1971), and Corbett (1976). Kelly views humans as scientists, continuously "construing" their world and revising those constructions (similar to percepts or schemas). He defines anxiety as "the recognition that the events with which one is confronted lie outside the range of convenience of one's construct system" (p. 495). One way of dealing with increased anxiety, according to Kelly's model, is through "loosening," which stretches the meaning of constructs (similar to overinclusiveness) and eventually renders them useless. This theory has been supported by Bannister and Fransella (1971), and loose construing has been attributed to serial invalidation of constructs during development. It is also consistent with family theories of double binds and mystification.

Callaway, in his 1972 article "Schizophrenia and Interference," seeks to clarify the processes at work in schizophrenia through analogy with a malfunctioning computer. To this end he utilizes concepts of Miller, Galanter, and Pribram (1960). He argues that the massive quantity of experimental and theoretical data on schizophrenia need to be organized. He reasons that since a parallel exists between thought processes and computer programs, and since thought disorder is of cardinal importance in schizophrenia, perhaps a model for schizophrenia can be found in computer technology.

Callaway observes that when schizophrenics have a clear goal and a well-practiced means of attaining it, they function appropriately (e.g., escaping a fire). But in most circumstances these same schizophrenics show classic signs of schizophrenia: "They had shifting, unstable 'segmental sets,' their associations showed 'lawful disorganization,' their language reflected 'disattention deficit,' and their behavior suggested 'perceptual inconstancy'" (1972, p. 572). Callaway suggests that these classic symptoms of schizophrenia are analogous to an interference in the running of a computer program, and describes a computer that in fact gave inappropriate, schizophrenialike responses.

Callaway notes that others before him have emphasized the role of interference in schizophrenia and quotes Buss and Lang (1965):

> When a schizophrenic is faced with a task he cannot attend properly or in a sustained fashion, maintain a set, or change the set quickly when necessary. His ongoing response tendencies suffer interference from irrelevant, external cues and from internal stimuli which consist of deviant thoughts and associations. These irrelevant, distracting, mediated stimuli prevent him from maintaining a clear focus on the task at hand and the result is psychological deficit [quoted in Callaway, 1972, p. 573].

Callaway states that, although persons show interference and/or interruption of programs after sleep deprivation and in other psychological states, schizophrenic interference is peculiar in that it not only disrupts or stops the program but may divert it or retain it after it should have been diverted (perseveration), leading to the extreme variability of schizophrenic performance.

Referring to Miller et al.'s (1960) conception of hierarchically organized plans that structure human behavior, Callaway mentions Luria's (1961) discovery that language plays a critical role in regulating behavior. Callaway infers that programs are likely to become more complex when they are stored in verbal symbols (1972, p. 576). Miller et al. call the sequences for all self-regulating machines (from thermostats to computers and human beings) TOTEs. TOTE stands for Test, Operate, Test, Exit. For example, Test is the room at the right temperature; Operate, start the air conditioning; Test, check the temperature again; and so on, until the temperature is right, and then Exit or end plan. TOTEs are organized hierarchically.

Human and computer errors occur very frequently, but most of them are in the "O" unit of the TOTE and thus not seriously disruptive, since they are recognized by the "T" and corrected. Low-level errors are not very disruptive, whereas errors occurring higher up in the structure, especially those closest to the executive TOTE, are quite serious. Significant errors usually occur in the "T" sections of the plan. In general, the more organized a system, the more redundancy is built into it and the more resistant it is to interference. When well-organized plans are interrupted, visceral arousal signals a potential emergency. Thus Callaway argues that schizophrenic over-arousal is at least partly a function of the schizophrenic process, the primary feature of which is the interruption of programs. He cites experiments indicating the inadequacy of the traditional view that overarousal precedes the cognitive disturbance, since increased arousal can improve the schizophrenic's performance. However, Venables would have a different explanation of this. Callaway stresses the existence in acute schizophrenia of a positive feedback loop, in which interference causes arousal and then arousal causes more interference.

Callaway briefly describes how this theory is consistent with a view of schizophrenia as a syndrome in which interference can arise from various sources, since plans are affected by genetics, biochemistry, neurophysiology, and learning, as well as by the current demands of a situation.

Recently, Corbett (1976) has presented a theory of perceptual dyscontrol which, he suggests, can serve as a general organizing principle for work in schizophrenia. Recognizing the need to organize existing knowledge, Corbett returns to the patient's experience to ascertain the primary disturbances reported in schizophrenia, namely, perceptual, cognitive, and attentional changes. He states that perception:

> . . . implies a complex interpretive function in which sensory data are processed, discriminated and related to other processes such as memory, affect, thinking and language so that the person can react to the original experience. The data not only come from without but also from within the body. This is a reciprocal relationship because the pre-existing state of the individual markedly affects the perception. There is a unique interaction between perception and memory, one which involves the reperceiving of organized stored data [1976, p. 251].

According to Corbett, normal perception contributes to a sense of environmental stability through perceptual constancies, attribution of meaning, integration of experience from different sensory modalities, categorization of experience, and the provision of some form of "gating" or selective inattention. These functions are all disturbed in schizophrenics. Corbett maintains that changes in perception and attention are primary and that anxiety is a consequence of the influx of new, difficult-to-assimilate data (in the form of unusual perceptions derived from the breakdown of perceptual constancies). He asserts that it is specious to try to separate perceptual from attentional processes since they have a neurophysiological interconnection. He also argues that, to the extent that perceptual-attentional deficits are inherited, the parents of schizophrenics would themselves be handicapped by a faulty perceptual apparatus. A history of stress and potential social alienation, deriving from unusual, nonconsensual perceptions, would create a distinctive defensive pattern that might disturb the preschizophrenic offspring. In psychotherapy with schizophrenics, I think it is important to be aware of experimental work on schizophrenics' cognitive impairment. If schizophrenics are indeed functioning on the level of concrete operations, what are the implications for therapeutic work? Perhaps Sechehaye's (1951b) use of symbolic realization can be seen, in light of cognitive deficits, as an equivalent of play therapy with children. In the future, it might be useful to include level and quality of cognition in evaluating a patient for treatment.

LANGUAGE

Perhaps the single most striking feature about schizophrenics is their peculiar use of language. All writers seriously concerned with understanding schizophrenia at a behavioral level have noted this peculiarity, and many have attempted to explain it. Kraepelin (1896) and Bleuler (1911/1950) gave detailed descriptions of this "language"; Bleuler (1911/1950) and Jung (1907, 1960) went further in seeking the communicative meaning of this language and some of the "laws" of its disorganization. Many other theorists, including psychoanalysts and family therapists, have tried to understand and explain schizophrenic language. Those readers with a special interest in this area are referred to Chapman and Chapman's book, *Disordered Thought in Schizophrenia* (1973), in which the authors focus on schizophrenic language and thought disorder in a review of psychological theories of schizophrenia.

Kasanin's book (1944/1964) remains the classic introduction to early work in this field. Experimental support for the theories presented is, to our modern eyes, often scanty and poorly controlled, but this is more than compensated for by the research generated by these theoretical pioneers. Early theorists debated whether language and thought are inextricably linked processes and whether schizophrenic thought disorder is due to regression, deterioration, or a unique alteration.

Bleuler believed that language difficulties in schizophrenia were caused by loosening of associative connections, loss of goal-directed behavior, and strong emotional needs. Chapman and Chapman (1973) criticize Bleuler's formulation, citing recent research which suggests that schizophrenics *do* have access to normal associative responses, but frequently give idiosyncratic responses. In other words, although the associative threads do not appear to be broken, response errors are consistent with the theory or view that they have lost goal-directed behavior.

A major explanation of schizophrenic language, one so prominent that it was incorporated into DSM-II, is the loss of "abstract attitude." The two theorists most associated with this view are Vygotsky (1962) and Goldstein

(1944/1964). Unfortunately, Goldstein's use of the term "abstract attitude" differs markedly from its common usage and thus has caused some confusion.

Vygotsky's theory of normal cognitive development was brought to this country by Hanfmann and Kasanin (1936). Using his own object-sorting test, Vygotsky studied the way normal subjects of different ages and adult schizophrenics grouped objects. From their performance he inferred their methods of concept formation. He reported that the stage of cognitive development directly preceding mature abstract thought, a stage found both in normal adolescents and in adult schizophrenics, showed the use of "pseudoconcepts." These pseudoconcepts have the same names as true abstract concepts but are used inconsistently—the person uses the right word without fully grasping its meaning. Based in Vygotsky's work, Kasanin (1944/1964) described a developmental movement from physiognomic thought (syncretistic, animistic) to concrete thought to abstract thought. He viewed the personalized language of schizophrenics as a regression to concrete and physiognomic thought.

Goldstein's (1944/1964) early work was with brain-damaged patients. Through this work he defined two distinct attitudes of thought: abstract and concrete. The abstract attitude, according to Goldstein, is *voluntary* and *reflective.* That is, the person is not tied to the immediate properties of the stimulus but, rather, is free to reflect on its properties and choose a response. The concrete attitude is evidenced by a variety of errors, including excessive anchoring to a situational context, inability to assume a mental set to initiate an action, inappropriate shifting of sets, loss of as-if behavior (loss of playfulness and metaphoric style), loss of abstract meanings of words, inability to integrate different stimuli, and inability to abstract common qualities of form concepts. Goldstein found that schizophrenics were less consistent in their attitudes and more influenced by personal ideas and preoccupations than were persons with organic disorders. Chapman and Chapman (1973) criticize the breadth of Goldstein's concepts, the difficulty in testing his theory that all schizophrenic errors are due to the concrete attitude, and his failure to explain why manifestations of concreteness vary from patient to patient.

Von Domarus's (1944/1964) work, especially as modified by Arieti (1955), has been very influential in the field. Chapman and Chapman (1973) note its lack of experimental support and attribute its tenacious hold on our imaginations to the fact that it is clinically compelling. According to von Domarus, schizophrenic language and thought are a regression to "paralogical" thinking. Normal adults use the "mode of barbara," in which identity is based on identity of *subjects.* For example:

All *A*'s are *B*		All men are mortal
C is an *A*	or	John is a man
∴ *C* is a *B*		∴ John is mortal

Schizophrenics, however, reason as if identity were based on identity of *predicates* as well as subjects. For example:

A is a *B*	Jesus Christ suffered
C is a *B* or	I suffer
∴ *C* is an *A*	∴ I am Jesus Christ.

The Virgin Mary was a virgin
I am a virgin
∴ I am the Virgin Mary.

Arieti's (1955, 1974a) conception of "paleologic" thought is based on von Domarus's work, with the additional idea that schizophrenics use regressed thought in the service of emotional needs. The Chapmans (1973) point out, however, that Arieti and von Domarus were mistaken in their belief that normal adults reason "logically" and not "paleologically." Quite the contrary, they report that logical errors based on identity of predicates are statistically "normal" among college students and are adaptive in everyday life, in which probabilistic reasoning is the best way to determine appropriate action. Gottesman and Chapman (reported in Chapman & Chapman, 1973) found that, although schizophrenics were less accurate than normals on a test of syllogistic reasoning, the percentage of errors based on the von Domarus principle was no greater for schizophrenics than for normals. Nor was there a difference on affective or neutral syllogisms. The greater inaccuracy of the schizophrenic subjects seemed to be due to increased randomness of responses, which is typical of schizophrenics on multiple-choice tests.

Other psychoanalytic theorists too have argued that schizophrenic language and thought are disrupted by the conflictual or affect-laden nature of the material being discussed. Researchers have attempted to differentiate schizophrenics' responses to affective and nonaffective communications. A difficulty in this research is determining what constitutes an affective stimulus for a specific patient. For example, Blumenthal (1964) used questions about patients' parents as affective stimuli, and questions about their life in the hospital as neutral, nonaffective stimuli. In my opinion, this distinction is a questionable one. Chapman and Chapman (1973) state that two-thirds of the literature they reviewed supports the hypothesis of increased deficit in response to emotionally charged items. However, the emotionally charged and neutral items differed in many other ways (such as complexity) known to affect schizophrenics' performance.

Cameron (1944/1964) and Sullivan (1944/1964) both reject a regression model of schizophrenia. Cameron, who views language as a function of social environment, believes that a schizophrenic's basic difficulty is "disarticulation," or the inability to take the "other's" role. In normal circumstances, a person can assume the role of the other during misunderstandings and failures of communication, and can alter his or her language accordingly. The schizophrenic is too alienated or "disarticulated" to do this. According to Cameron, a schizophrenic's difficulty in understanding causality is due to his or her inability to limit attention to relevant aspects. Schizophrenic thinking is overinclusive, and personal themes and idioms interpenetrate. He considers schizophrenic language to be distinct from both organic language and the language of normal children, and thus he rejects the notion of regression. The Chapmans (1973) believe that Cameron's various tests for overinclusion have little relationship to each other because of his excessively broad, loose formulation of overinclusion, which fails to yield unifying principles.

Like Cameron, Sullivan (1944/1964) believes that language is heavily influenced by social factors. But he clearly distinguishes between thought—which he describes as the refinement of reverie—and language—a social communicative device. He states that, in childhood, language is autistic and magical, replete with personal associations and meanings. Gradually, it becomes socialized and is used primarily to satisfy needs and gain security. In other words, language plays a critical role in defensive interpersonal operations, or "security operations." Sullivan describes two factors that contribute to schizophrenic language development: (1) The schizophrenic has lost hope of achieving satisfaction and uses language primarily to gain security. (2) We all use an "auditor" to make certain that our language is ready for social consumption, but the schizophrenic's "auditor" is inadequate and immature and therefore does not properly censure bad, nonconsensual language. Although Sullivan's ideas are consistent with a regression model, he deliberately avoids such a conclusion.

Chapman and Chapman (1973) believe that schizophrenic language disturbance is caused by an excessive yielding to normal response biases. That is, the associations which intrude in schizophrenic speech are not completely idiosyncratic; they reflect the normal associations to words in a sentence if those words are taken out of context. This explanation fits with clinical experience, in that one can almost predict the points in a sentence where a schizophrenic will get "derailed." These points tend to be words with several meanings and/or several associations, where the most common meaning is not used. For example, there is a strong tendency for normal subjects to associate the word son to the word father. However, this tendency is easily held in check when they are talking about "father time." Response biases also change over time—there are developmental differences in normal associative links. Rattan and Chapman (1973) showed that schizophrenic errors were not due simply to chance. They designed a multiple-choice test in which subjects were asked to pick the correct definition of a stimulus word from among several alternatives. One of the choices was irrelevant, one was correct, and in some cases, one was an associate. For example:

Shoot means the same as
rifle (associate)
rug (irrelevant)
sprout (correct)
none of the above [quoted in Chapman & Chapman, 1973, p. 123].

Normal subjects tended to pick an associate when they did not know the definition. They made the same number of errors whether or not associates were present. Schizophrenics made more errors when associates were included in the list. Dull normal subjects made equal numbers of errors under the two conditions.

The Chapmans (1973) argue that their theory is of greater value than Bleuler's in predicting where associative threads will be broken. Many of the errors predicted by Chapman and Chapman could also be accounted for by theories of narrowed attention (with the subsequent loss of contextual cues), regression to earlier modes of thought (since preferred meanings are often those earliest learned), and/or loss of abstract attitude (since associations tend to be more concrete). The Chapmans present research supporting their conviction that normal response bias is the most predictive and inclusive theory of schizophrenic language and thought.

Maher (1972), on the other hand, considers attentional deficit to be the most promising explanation of schizophrenic language peculiarities. As we shall see in the next sections, there is considerable overlap in predictions based on the work of Chapman and Chapman, Cameron, and Shakow and the attention/arousal work of Broen and Storms and others.

ATTENTION AND AROUSAL

As noted above (see phenomenological reports), schizophrenics frequently report difficulty in attending. Theorists starting with Kraepelin have remarked on this attentional deficit, and researchers have investigated it through a variety of means. I have chosen to group attention and arousal theories together at the end of this chapter for several reasons: (1) Although many investigators report cognitive and perceptual changes in schizophrenics, these changes are often considered to be sequelae to alterations in attention or arousal, rather than fundamental symptoms. (2) Anxiety level, arousal level, and ability to attend selectively are often discussed by the same author.

Attention is a psychological concept concerned with why some events reach consciousness and others do not. Arousal, on the other hand, is a physiological concept concerned with measuring autonomic nervous system responses to stress, e.g., heart rate, respiration, pupil dilation, and galvanic skin response (GSR). Both terms are often defined vaguely and used loosely; both are also frequently implicated as central processes disturbed in schizophrenia. As we shall see, research in these areas overlaps with research in cognition and perception.

Cromwell (1978) puts this problem well:

> Another question concerns the relationship of arousal to attentional deficit. Is the disorder of arousal, whether overresponding or underresponding, a necessary antecedent to the disorders of attention and information processing? Or, are the attentional and information-processing disorders the more primary features? Does the schizophrenic experiencing information-processing difficulties become aroused, or does the arousal disorder create the difficulty in processing? As other alternatives, neither or both cause-effect relationships may exist [p. 222].

Attention

Kraepelin (1896) considered attention disturbances to be fundamental in schizophrenia. Bleuler, noting the difficulty that schizophrenics have in attending, stated: "The selection which attention exercises over normal sensory impressions may be reduced to zero [in schizophrenia] so that almost everything that meets the senses is registered" (quoted in McGhie, 1973, p. 102). Many other researchers have also considered attentional deficits as central to schizophrenia. However, hypotheses of attentional deficit in schizophrenia suffer both from inadequate definition of attention (Neale & Cromwell, 1973, p. 73) and from its multiform nature—its impact on and interference with a broad spectrum of behavior. On the one hand, attention is difficult to isolate and measure in a pure form; that is, without tapping physiological measures of arousal, motivational components, cognitive capacities, sensory thresholds, and emotional meanings. And on the other hand, attention is involved in (even when not viewed as a central feature of) many areas of research into schizophrenics' performance: For example:

> *Perception research:* deviant perceptions, disruption of size constancy, perceptual scanning. . . .
>
> *Cognition research:* poor conceptual performance, incidental learning, field articulation studies, overinclusion research, information processing, memory deficit, word association disturbances, language deficits . . . stimulus overload in distraction studies.
>
> *Attentional tasks:* span of apprehension, simple discrimination, cross-modal reaction time, perceptual vigilance, disattention studies.
>
> *Psychophysiology and neurophysiology:* states of high drive and autonomic arousal as indexed by GSR, heart rate . . . EEG and evoked potentials, correlates of orienting behavior . . . [see previous chapter].
>
> *Psychopharmacology:* behavioral response to phenothiazines.

Studies of children at risk for schizophrenia.
Attitudinal, motivational components in schizophrenic performance, studies of set and expectations [Garmezy, 1977, p. 365].

In addition to the above-mentioned difficulties, Kopfstein and Neale (cited in Nuechterlein, 1977) have found that low intercorrelations characterize the performances of chronic and acute schizophrenics on five laboratory tasks considered to be measures of attention. Until we are better able to define and isolate what we mean by attention, our claim that schizophrenics have an attentional deficit may be equivalent to saying that they don't function well— an obvious and uninformative statement. Given the scope of work on attention, this review will be selective, aimed at describing major theoretical formulations and the most widely used experimental procedures.

Bleuler (1911/1950) and others distinguished between passive and active attention. Garmezy (1977) reports several elaborate lists of types of attention, the simplest and, in my opinion, most useful of which is Zubin's threefold classification: (1) *selection* of a portion of the environment for focusing attention; (2) *maintenance* of that focus; and (3) *shift* of that focus when required to some other part of the environment.

> Since our receptors are bombarded continuously by a wide spectrum of both internal and external stimuli, we must have some way of separating the relevant stimuli and those that we cannot ignore, those on which our adaptive adjustment depends in a given situation, from the irrelevant, those which we can ignore with safety and survive and continue undisturbed with the ongoing activity. This is selective attention. Once the sector of the environment has been selected, attention is directed toward it until we attain our goals or become satiated or bored with it. This is maintenance attention. Since we can not remain glued to the same sector forever, a switching mechanism is provided which switches our attention to some other sector. This is switching attention [Zubin, 1975, p. 141].

McGhie and Chapman were among the first to view attentional deficit as the core of schizophrenic pathology. At the outset of their research (McGhie & Chapman, 1961), they were in agreement with Federn's belief that schizophrenic symptoms are defensive activities. Their view changed, however, when they interviewed acute schizophrenics and found that the patients reported difficulty in attending as one of their first symptoms. McGhie and Chapman cite numerous descriptions by schizophrenics of their inability to attend selectively, loss of spontaneous action, increase in self-consciousness, difficulty with speech perception, etc. As one patient said: "Everything seems to grip my attention although I am not particularly interested in anything. I'm speaking to you just now but I can hear noises going on next door and in the corridor" (1961, p. 105).

McGhie and Chapman (1961) summarize their theory as follows:

> By the process of attention we thus break down and effectively categorize both the information reaching us from the enviroment and that which is internally available in the form of stored past experience. By such processes we reduce, organize, and interpret the otherwise chaotic flow of information reaching consciousness to a limited number of differentiated, stable, and meaningful percepts from which reality is constructed. Now let us suppose that there is a breakdown in this selective-inhibitory function of attention. Consciousness would be flooded with an undifferentiated mass of incoming sensory data, transmitted from the environment via the sense organs. To this involuntary tide of impressions there would be added the diverse internal images, and their associations, which would no longer be coordinated with incoming information. Perception would revert to the passive and involuntary assimilative process of early childhood, and, if the incoming flood were to carry on unchecked, it would gradually sweep away the stable constructs of a former reality [p. 105].

Schizophrenia, then, is characterized by an inability to attend selectively; this leads to a flood of stimuli, difficulty in concentrating, increased attention to irrelevant details, and attention to previously ignored aspects of experience, so that one becomes self-conscious. Schizophrenic symptoms, such as catatonia and delusions, can be understood as attempts to reduce or reorganize the sensory overload.

McGhie and Chapman's theory easily accounts for many cognitive and social symptoms, but a longitudinal study is required to check the sequence of events: which comes first—difficulty with selective attention or cognitive slippage? Or, in Shakow's (1962, 1963) terminology, does the loss of major sets precede the inability to attend selectively, or does the loss of selective attention lead to overstepping the boundaries of the major set?

McGhie and Chapman's hypothesis, based on clinical interviews, gained support from subsequent experimental studies, including Payne's (1966) study of the relationship between overinclusive thinking and difficulties in attention. He found that overinclusiveness, a quality of schizophrenic thinking originally discerned by Cameron (1944/1964), can be considered secondary to broadening of attention. McGhie and Chapman describe the normal development of mature perception and cognition as one of increasing differentiation and organization of incoming sensory data (see Chapter 8, this book, section on Wynne and Singer). In schizophrenia there is a regression to more global perception. McGhie and Chapman point out the significance of the reticular formation in signaling the cortex to attend selectively and to call up related memories and associations. If the "spotlight of attention" is too narrow, not enough information is recalled; if it is too broad, there is overinclusiveness. The latter is the case in acute schizophrenics. They

(McGhie & Chapman, 1961; McGhie, 1973) report studies correlating difficulties in abstract thinking (overinclusiveness) and size constancy. Thus, schizophrenics' difficulties in perception and cognition seem to be related and are probably caused by an underlying physiological process. McGhie (1969) uses a concept of filtering developed by Broadbent (1958), who views the development of an effective filter mechanism as essential to the categorization of incoming data. Broadbent describes how the mind structures reality to lessen the absolute number of items to which it must respond. When there is no selective attention or filtering, the person is passively assaulted by disconnected bits of information.

Efforts to conceptualize the central attentional deficit in schizophrenia have become more sophisticated over the last twenty years, often utilizing biochemical and/or physiological data. For example, Matthysse (1978) proposes that involuntary shifts in attention are under the control of a neural system that uses dopamine as a neurotransmitter. An imbalance in this system might cause an inability both to *withdraw attention* from stimuli and to *deny attention* to stimuli normally kept out of awareness.

The 1976 Rochester Conference on Schizophrenia (reported in Wynne, Cromwell, & Matthysse, 1978; summarized in Spring et al., 1977) reflected the increased sophistication of work on attention in schizophrenia. It also upheld the utility as well as popularity of some time-honored experimental techniques aimed at assessing attentional deficits: reaction time (RT) and continuous performance tasks (CPT).

Spring et al. (1977) note that RTs have been studied since 1868; Cancro et al. (1971) consider research on RT to be the closest thing to a North Star in schizophrenia research, and Nuechterlein (1977) notes that numerous hypotheses have been offered to explain both normal and pathological behavior on reaction time tasks—most of which involve attention.

Shakow's work (summarized in Nuechterlein, 1977) examined the relationship between length and regularity of preparatory interval (the time between the signal for a stimulus and the actual stimulus) and the reaction time of normals and schizophrenics. He (and others) found that normals benefit more than schizophrenics from regular preparatory intervals. Schizophrenics do especially poorly when there is a long preparatory interval. Shakow's primary hypothesis is that schizophrenics do poorly because of their difficulty in establishing and maintaining a major set to respond to the stimulus (see this chapter, section on cognition). The inability to maintain a major set and the interference of minor sets is consistent with the work of Broen and Storms (1966) on lawful disorganization, reviewed below.

In an effort to discriminate schizophrenics from normals, Shakow devised a "set index" that he hoped would be less affected by motivation, and would better indicate a person's ability to prepare and maintain a mental set, than simple RT. This index distinguishes chronic schizophrenics from other patient and nonpatient groups. It is not simply a measure of intelligence, as it discriminates low-IQ schizophrenics from mentally retarded patients. However, Nuechterlein (1977) reports that the set index fails to discriminate acute schizophrenics from psychotically depressed patients.

Shakow investigated the readiness to respond to a stimulus (an issue of attention maintenance) and invoked a cognitive attribute as an intervening variable. Zubin et al. (summarized in Spring & Zubin, 1977) investigated shifting attention in reaction-time studies, using cross-modal and ipsimodal stimuli and maintaining a constant preparatory interval. They (and others) found that schizophrenics' reaction times are significantly more retarded by changes in modality than are those of normals. They offer two main explanatory hypotheses: (1) the neuronal trace model and (2) the expectancy model.

According to the neuronal trace model, "facilitating and inhibitory neural traces have greater duration in schizophrenics than in normals" (Nuechterlein, 1977, p. 387). Zubin (1975) hypothesizes that an RT stimulus leaves a facilitating trace for similar stimuli and an inhibitory trace for dissimilar stimuli. He cites evidence that neural substrates for attention and suppression may be interconnected, supporting his theory of inhibitory traces for attention to nonpresent but potentially competing stimuli. For a series of ipsimodal and cross-modal stimuli, the facilitating or inhibiting trace from previous stimuli is assumed to center on the modality variable; for an irregular preparatory interval series, the focus is on preparatory interval duration (Nuechterlein, 1977, p. 387). Consistent with this is Zubin's finding that RTs are fastest for identical stimuli, slowest for cross-modal (e.g., auditory and visual) stimuli, and in between for ipsimodal, nonindentical stimuli. Zubin (1975) argues that the neuronal trace exists in all people, but in schizophrenics the "immediate effects of stimulations are presumed to last longer" (Nuechterlein, 1977, p. 387).

A sophisticated investigation and elaboration of this model has been provided by Allan (1978), who applies the methodology of quantitative psychophysics. Her model of attention is based on "the premise that attention can be switched from one sensory channel to another only at certain equally spaced time points" (Spring et al., 1977, p. 473). This would explain the delay in schizophrenics' reaction times under cross-modal conditions. Schizophrenics either may have difficulty in taking advantage of the earliest switching point or may require more time before switching is possible.

Reaction time is also significantly retarded by the schizophrenic's inability to attend selectively, which leads to flooding by distracting and irrelevant stimuli. McGhie and Chapman conducted a series of experiments (Chapman & McGhie, 1962; McGhie, 1973; McGhie & Chapman, 1961; McGhie, Chapman, & Lawson, 1965a, 1965b) to clarify the nature of schizophrenic distractibility. The McGhie, Chapman, and Lawson theory leans heavily on Broadbent's (1958) model of normal information processing, which stressed the limited channel capacity for incoming information (Broen, 1968; McGhie, 1969, 1973; Payne, 1966). In this model the organism normally selects from the many impinging stimuli which ones should be further processed so that its limited capacity will not be overloaded. The selection should be consistent with adaptation to the environment and is achieved through a hypothetical filtering device. McGhie (1969) locates the schizophrenic's deficit in the breakdown of this normal filtering device, as a result of which the schizophrenic is less able to attend selectively and process only relevant information. Broen (1968) believes that the deficit is due to a disorder in the use of conditional probabilities to influence selection. Thus the fundamental deficit "could be in the long-term store, the filter, or transmission to the filter" (p. 181). This deficit is greatly affected by the level of arousal and may be reversible.

Broen and Storms (1966) look at schizophrenic behavior in Hullian learning theory terms, which involve changes in response hierarchies and emphasize the level of arousal (arising from stress) as the *drive* in the schizophrenic. They view schizophrenics as suffering from "collapsed response hierarchies" that increase competition between dominant and subordinate responses to a given situation. They propose that schizophrenics have basically "normal" response hierarchies; however, the relative probability of appropriate or dominant responses is lessened, while the probability of inappropriate responses is increased. The reason why is a hypothesized lower response ceiling in schizophrenics, so that the probability of the dominant response levels off earlier than in normals, especially under conditions of arousal. This calls for some further explanation.

According to this view, drive (in this case arousal) increases the strength of the dominant response up to a certain level, beyond which it remains constant, while the strength of subordinate responses continues to increase. This is consistent with the inverted U curve that illustrates the effects of arousal on performance. For any given task there is an optimum range of arousal level; when arousal level is outside that range, performance is impaired. We know this intuitively from our experiences in studying for exams, performing for a group, engaging in competitive sports. We need to be "up" for the game or test. If we are too lackadaisical, we don't study enough, concentrate hard, or play hard. If, on the other hand, we really get the jitters, we have trouble concentrating well. The optimum level of arousal for a task is related to its complexity.

Broen and Storms distinguish two aspects of performance on selective attention tasks: (1) scanning or search habits, followed by (2) attentional responses directed at stimuli that have been important in the past. Schizophrenics show increased response competition both at the scanning level (in which nondominant scanning modes intrude) and in their disorganized attentional priorities. "The end result will be increased attention to extraneous stimuli and an apparent broadening of cue utilization due to greater randomization among competing attentional tendencies" (Nuechterlein, 1977, p. 410).

Kornetsky and Orzack (1978) have used performance, as measured by the continuous performance task (CPT), as an independent variable in studying schizophrenia. They found that compared to good performers, poor performers had significantly slower RTs, more interference from the preceding preparatory interval, less slow wave sleep, and more frequent history of mental illness in relatives. This supports their hypothesis that impaired sustained attention in schizophrenia is related to a state of central hyperarousal that interferes with the complete registration of target stimuli (Spring et al., 1977, p. 477). Their work exemplifies a recent trend toward using previously dependent variables as independent variables to identify different schizophrenic subtypes.

The CPT has also been used by Erlenmeyer-Kimling and Cornblatt (1978) in studies of children at risk for schizophrenia. They hypothesized that, if attentional disturbance is causal rather than symptomatic of schizophrenia, then children at risk should show evidence of this disturbance. They found that children at risk indeed made more errors than normal children under both distracting and nondistracting conditions. Long-term follow-up is needed to determine whether these high-risk children are the 10 percent who later develop symptoms (See Chapter 9, this book).

Some theorists have argued that the schizophrenic's poor performance is caused by lack of motivation, what some researchers have called "active attention." The question of motivation to perform on experimental tasks and/or to communicate responses has been raised by researchers with differing concerns and biases, e.g., psychoanalytic and family theorists, behaviorists, and researchers primarily interested in getting schizophrenics to perform an experimental task.

Nuechterlein (1977) reports that data do not support a solely motivational explanation of schizophrenics' performance. While schizophrenics do not benefit from social rewards and punishments in the same way normals do, they do respond to primary aversive stimulation (p. 403). Chapman and Chapman (1973) report that schizophrenics also perform better under conditions of primary positive reinforcement. The biometrics research group (Zubin, 1969, 1975; Zubin & Spring, 1977) stresses the importance of maintaining an adequate level of motivation during the experimental procedures through positive reinforcements (e.g., money). The finding that schizophrenics perform better on some tasks than do normals is a further indication that motivation is not the sole factor influencing performance. Collins's work (cited by Spring et al., 1977), in which schizophrenics made a discrimination that normal subjects cannot make, indicates that schizophrenics are sufficiently motivated to perform experimental tasks. Cancro

(1976b), however, presents some potentially opposing evidence. In a study of the eye-blinking response, he found more frequent blinking during mental that during visual tasks and a significantly higher blink proportion and frequency in schizophrenics than in normals. His findings suggest that schizophrenics are less attentive than normals to the external world.

A related issue is the question: Are schizophrenics motivated to maintain interpersonal distance, or do they lack motivation to communicate as Sullivan (1944/1964) and Cameron (1944/1964) suggest? If so, the experimental situation acquires an entirely different coloring. Shimkunas (reported in Chapman & Chapman, 1973) investigated the effects of personal disclosure —a sign of decreased interpersonal distance—on schizophrenic thought disorder. He found that the schizophrenic's thought disorder worsened in response to personal, as opposed to nonpersonal, communications. The study can be criticized because the communicatons differed in other ways that were not controlled. However, the finding does suggest that care be taken in setting up diagnostic testing sessions or research sessions with schizophrenics.

Arousal

Spohn and Patterson (1979) make a useful distinction between psychophysical studies before and after 1965, the year Lang and Buss wrote their major review of psychological theories of schizophrenia. The years before 1965 were marked by (1) studies of broad concepts such as arousal; (2) naïve research strategies; (3) inconsistent methodologies, little replicability of results from different laboratories, and numerous conflicting reports.

Like attention, the concept of "arousal" is ill-defined. It is involved in many physiological functions and is in general considered a reflection of the relative dominance of the sympathetic and parasympathetic systems. Thus, while attention is primarily a behavioral concept with hypothesized central nervous system components, arousal is a physiological term specifically related to the autonomic nervous system.

The level of arousal is inferred from peripheral responses such as galvanic skin response (GSR), pupillography, pulse rate, and respiratory rate. Unfortunately these measures, like measures of attention, do not cohere. Lacey (1967) reports that persons have "preferred" responses to stress; for example, a person's pulse rate may quickly reflect his or her general level of stress (or sympathetic dominance) while the pupils are slow to respond. Group means and variance on any given measure are thus greatly affected by individual differences in responsiveness. Gruzelier (1978) claims, however, that schizophrenics, unlike normals, have unitary arousal states (the measures do cohere).

In general, any stimulation of the organism produces an increase in arousal. In addition, Maher (1966) reports studies, using laboratory animals, in which early exposure to stress increased responsiveness to later environmental stresses and decreased responsiveness to simple environmental changes. The effects of such an increase on behavior depend on the initial level of arousal. Thus, if a person is underaroused at the time a stimulus impinges, the increase in arousal may improve performance. If he or she is optimally aroused or overaroused, the same increase in stimulation may impair performance. This paradoxical feature of arousal (the inverted U curve of efficiency described by Malmo [Malmo & Shagass, 1949, 1951] and mentioned above) may account for the opposing theoretical formulations of Mednick and Venables.

The idea that schizophrenia is a disorder of arousal is intuitively appealing. Acute schizophrenics often experience their first breakdown after an event or series of events of a clearly stressful kind. Considering schizophrenia as a disorder of arousal placed it easily on a continuum with other forms of mental disorder. However, proving that schizophrenia is a disorder of arousal is something else, as Venables's and Mednick's early work demonstrates.

According to Venables (1964; Venables & Wing, 1962), acute schizophrenics are underaroused and have a low level of parasympathetic dominance; because they cannot selectively attend, they are at the mercy of sensory input. Chronic schizophrenics, on the other hand, are overaroused, have slight sympathetic dominance, and their attention is narrowed; thus they should benefit from drugs that lower the level of arousal. This overarousal leads to social withdrawal in an effort to limit stimulation and prevent further arousal. This theory leaves unanswered the question why most acute schizophrenics also benefit from medication that decreases the level of arousal.

Mednick (1958) applied Hullian learning theory to the study of schizophrenia and derived the following hypothesis: schizophrenics are chronically overaroused persons who eventually withdraw to such an extent that they are underaroused. Potential schizophrenics have a high level of anxiety, equivalent to a high level of drive (in Hullian terms). Such a high level interferes with rather than aids performance. It leads to overgeneralization (of conditioned responses), increased avoidance of potentially anxiety-provoking stimuli (thoughts, situations, or people), and remote, autistic thoughts, which eventually lower anxiety at the cost of removing the person from reality. In the course of an acute episode, the already highly aroused preschizophrenic experiences even more anxiety, which increases the response strength of all habit tendencies, especially subordinate ones (see Broen & Storms, 1966). Increased generalization goes hand in hand with decreased differentiation and impairment on complex tasks. Irrelevant associations intrude (see also Shakow's [1962] work on loss of major set), thoughts seem to race, and the person begins to think he or she is going crazy (which adds to the anxiety). Chronic schizophrenics continually avoid anxiety. Increased arousal can also explain overinclusiveness and loosening of associations.

Some of the discrepancies reported in the literature can no doubt be accounted for by differences in patient selection, varying definitions of terms, and variable medication levels, since all these factors affect base levels of arousal. As discussed above, discrepancies in experimental findings on the effects of increased arousal (e.g., distraction) may arise from inadequate appraisal of the preexisting state of arousal. Maher (1966) reported that schizophrenics showed decreased responsiveness to stress, as indicated by the amount of chemical body by-products. Malmo and Shagass (1949, 1951) reported that acute schizophrenics were *hyper*responsive to stress whereas chronic schizophrenics were *hypo*responsive. Venables and Wing (1962) found that their withdrawn patients were highly aroused, whereas Mednick (1958) hypothesized that such patients have withdrawn to lower their level of arousal. The decreased responsiveness to stress reported by Maher might be a consequence of an initial level of stress so high that it cannot increase any further. To reiterate, choice of criteria and conditions for testing can greatly affect findings. According to Maher, "the difference in the formulation between Venables' theory and Mednick's lies in the inferences made about anxiety—if anxiety is defined as autonomic arousal" (1966, p. 340).

In general, schizophrenic breakdowns seem to occur after highly stressful life events.

Work since 1965 reflects technological advances and biochemical and neurological findings. There is also increased sensitivity to the likelihood of a schizophrenia *spectrum,* with various subgroups bimodally distributed on various psychological measures. Previous controversies have lost their force, Mednick and Venables work together on some projects, specific data have increased, and overall theorizing has decreased. There has been less emphasis on overall arousal level in schizophrenia and more concern with measurements of brain function. There has also been a shift away from studying attention per se and toward the study of preattentive stages in information processing by the use of evoked potentials as described in Chapter 5. Although Spohn and Patterson (1979) remark that "by and large it is questionable whether the term arousal has any value as a clarifying concept in schizophrenia" (p. 584), the research on heart rate (HR) levels, skin conductance, and blood pressure continues to suggest that schizophrenics are hyperaroused.

Lang and Buss's 1965 conclusion that schizophrenics are hyperaroused was based on the elevated rate of cardiovascular activity. Subsequently it has been clearly shown that medication elevates tonic heart rate level in schizophrenics (Spohn, Thetford, & Cancro, 1971; Spohn et al., 1977). However, the tonic heart rate levels of even nonmedicated schizophrenics are higher than normal. Heart rate levels of high-risk children do not differ from those of low-risk children in a neutral setting; under conditions of stress, however, the heart rates of high-risk children are significantly higher than those of low-risk

children. The meaning of the raised tonic heart rate level is unclear. Generally it is seen as a sign of overarousal, but Lacey and Lacey (1970; summarized
in Spohn & Patterson, 1979, p. 590) postulated that "cardiac deceleration
reflects cortical activation and openness to enviromental input, while acceler-
ation is defensive and represents a shutting out of enviromental stimuli."
Perhaps elevated heart rate in schizophrenia can be seen as an effort to
defend against sensory overload.

Gruzelier and Venables, Mednick, and others have moved from earlier
work with GSR to more sophisticated efforts at relating changes in skin
conductance orienting response (SCOR) and habituation to structural alterations in the brain. Before reviewing this work it is important to described a
major change in the findings on SCOR. In 1972 Gruzelier and Venables first
reported a significant number of schizophrenics in random samples who were
"nonresponders" (i.e., do not show SCOR to a stimulus). In this and other
studies (Bernstein & Taylor, 1978; Gruzelier, 1973; Patterson, 1976a,
1976b), researchers found that 49 percent of schizophrenics were nonresponders, whereas only 7 to 10 percent of normal adults were nonresponders. These data, combined with previous findings, suggest a clear bimodal distribution of schizophrenics in SCOR tasks—"Gruzelier and Venables
showed that approximately 50 percent of the patient population studied
produced no responses (i.e., were nonresponders), and the remaining 50
percept did not habituate the orienting response" (Spohn & Patterson, 1979,
p. 584). Zahn (1976) did not find such clear bimodality, but the dichotomy
has nonetheless been integrated into the literature and research that followed. Mednick (1970; Mednick & Schulsinger, 1968) had found a fast
recovery in the SCOR of children at risk for schizophrenia. Venables (1975)
interprets this finding as indicative of exceptional openness to the environment, which might lead to sensory flooding.

Relatively little is known about the control of SCOR, although Gruzelier
and Venables (1972; Gruzelier, 1978) sought to use SCOR to demonstrate
limbic involvement in schizophrenia. They and others (e.g., Mednick &
Schulsinger, 1968; Stevens, 1973) were excited by Bagshaw's (Bagshaw &
Benzies, 1968; Bagshaw, Kimble, & Pribram, 1965) findings that monkeys
with amygdalectomies were hyporesponsive to stimuli whereas those with
hippocampectomies were hyperresponsive. Gruzelier and Venables, like
Mednick, reasoned that the hippocampus/amygdala balance reflects an in-
hibitory/excitatory balance that is defective in schizophrenics. Gruzelier and
Venables saw parallels between the amygdalectomized monkeys and nonre-
sponding schizophrenics and between hippocampectomized monkeys and
hyperresponsive schizophrenics who failed to habituate.

A third distinct electrodermal group of fast habituators has been found—
this group seems to have an active inhibitory process, and these schizophrenics perform normally on tasks of sustained attention. Spohn and Patterson

(1979) suggest that this may be controlled by the level of neurotransmitters. They offer a modified limbic system hypothesis, attempting to integrate structural and biochemical findings. The hippocampus is the most cholinergic structure in the brain. Behavioral changes associated with hippocampal lesions can be produced by anticholinergic drugs. Cholinergic activity can be investigated through pupillometry studies. These studies have found a weak parasympathetic system in schizophrenics as indicated by reduced pupillary constriction in response to light (constriction is dominated by acetylcholine). Davis (1975) postulates an acetylcholine/dopamine balance that is critical in schizophrenia.

Studies of phasic heart rate—response to an orienting stimulus—are less conclusive. Gruzelier (1975) found that heart rate accelerated in responders and that in nonresponders a brief shallow deceleration was followed by a rapid return to normal. Lacey and Lacey (1970) suggest that cardiac functions modulate cognitive functions via negative feedback loops from the brain stem to the peripheral cardiovascular system and back to the brain stem.

The last fifteen years have brought interesting refinements and hypotheses in the study of schizophrenia. It seems safe to conclude that schizophrenics are generally somewhat overaroused, showing higher tonic heart rate levels and higher than normal muscle tension. Their level of "biological noise" is higher. An increase in psychopathology is signaled by a decline in efficiency —i.e., in the ratio of focused to diffuse biological activity. Normals orient their activity in either the musculature or the autonomic nervous system. Schizophrenics, on the other hand, show an increase in random activity and a decline of task-centered activity. Their hyporeactivity to specific stimuli may be a function of high basal level activity, which would diminish the amount of response possible (the law of initial value).

Psychoanalytic Theories	Chapter Seven

Each major group of theories has its own inherent problems, and psychoanalytic theories are no exception. Here we are faced with such a morass of competing terminologies that the creator of a psychoanalytic Esperanto, or an *Object Relations to Freud to Sullivan* dictionary, would be providing a much-needed service. In addition to the semantic difficulties, few of the major psychoanalytic theorists have explicitly presented statements on the etiology of schizophrenia (Redlich, 1952). Rather, they have tended to elaborate metapsychological descriptions of the schizophrenic's internal world, dynamics, way of being in treatment, the feelings he or she evokes in the analyst, etc. Etiological statements are, with but a few notable exceptions, embedded in accounts of therapy with persons who are called schizophrenic or in metapsychological accounts of the psychological processes involved in schizophrenia.

Yet another problem, one that has plagued us throughout the entire investigation, is diagnosis. Is Rosenfeld's schizophrenic the same person we meet in Sullivan and, more important, is he or she the same person studied in the biochemical, neurophysiological, and psychological experiments discussed above? Accounts of psychoanalytic treatment of schizophrenics tend to refer to an upper-class population, which leads to a further methodological difficulty: Is the schizophrenic from an upper-class family who seeks treatment at an expensive private hospital as handicapped as the schizophrenic from a lower-class family who arrives involuntarily at the state hospital? These patients vary considerably in their pre- and postnatal care, nutritional state, educational level, medical care for childhood accidents, etc. One might also argue that their familial ego functions (to borrow a term from Wynne and Singer's work on transactional thought disorder—see Chapter 8) differ in strength. Much of the experimental literature on schizophrenia has come from state hospital populations, whereas most psychoanalytic work has been with private patients.

Another difficulty in integrating these theories with experimental findings is the lack of a clear-cut distinction between psychosis and schizophrenia in the psychoanalytic literature. Thus, detailed accounts of faulty reality testing can be of use in understanding the psychotic, but do not help us understand the specific state of the schizophrenic.

Psychoanalytic theories are not strictly observational. For the most part their terms are second- and third-order inferences. Reification of terms, growth by accretion, and concern with maintaining theoretical unity have also obstructed efforts at understanding a given theoretical school's view of schizophrenia; and comparisons of schools are even more difficult.

Whatever their failings as etiological statements, psychoanalytic theories of schizophrenia do make a unique contribution to understanding schizophrenia in their perception of the significance of the schizophrenic's verbalizations and behaviors. From the standpoint of the schizophrenic's experience, it may well be poor mothering that leaves him or her feeling vulnerable, whereas from the outsider's perspective, poor mothering may have been a consequence of the exceedingly difficult temperament the preschizophrenic was born with. Psychoanalysis was the first discipline to view schizophrenics as persons to be understood, rather than shunned, mocked, or merely controlled.

One way to compare theoretical models is to distinguish between conflict and deficit models of schizophrenia. Conflict theories postulate that schizophrenia lies on a continuum with other emotional states, all of which represent responses to conflicts. According to this view, the schizophrenic differs from the neurotic in the kinds of defenses used. Deficit theories, on the other hand, use such terms as "ego weakness" and "constitutional differences" to imply that something innate or early in maturation went awry in the schizophrenic's development such that there is a basic fault which may or may not be amenable to corrective experiences in adulthood. As we shall see below, there is often no clear distinction between conflict and deficit models; e.g., though the hypothesized break with reality is in response to a conflict, the fact of a break rather than a neurotic defense is a function of a deficit of some sort.

Psychoanalytic theories must address themselves to the specific quality of the schizophrenic experience in all its sensoriperceptual, emotional, interpersonal, cognitive, and linguistic facets. Theories differ in the priority they give to these facets, in the degree to which they explicate the various aspects of schizophrenic symptoms, and in their definitions of what is fundamental to the disorder. For example, Freud (1911/1958a) argues that the schizophrenic first withdraws from reality and then attempts to repair this break with restitutive symptoms (hallucinations and delusions). On the other hand, Federn (1952) argues that misperceptions occur first, followed by estrangement and social isolation. Theories also differ on the role assigned to regression in schizophrenia.

Several issues are consistent thorns in the side of psychoanalytic theories:

1. A general dynamic, genetic formulation is open to the criticism that not everyone with those dynamics becomes schizophrenic.
2. The cardinal sign of schizophrenia—the presence of a formal thought disorder—is difficult for psychoanalytic theories to explain. Psychoanalysis has not yet integrated theories of cognitive development with those of emotional development. Despite the efforts of Rapaport, Arieti, and Wolff, much remains unknown.
3. A developmental theory of schizophrenia must explain how the preschizophrenic survives for some eighteen years before psychotic symptoms erupt. He or she survives with many ego functions intact—the very ones that will disintegrate during the acute psychotic break.
4. Most psychoanalytic work relies heavily on the single case as the testing ground for theory. Although Mahler and Bellak attempt more general testing of hypotheses, many theoretical hypotheses remain untested and/or at odds with well-established data from cognitive and developmental studies.

In this chapter I shall summarize some of the major psychoanalytic contributions to our understanding of schizophrenia. I have divided the field into three groups: Freud and the neo-Freudians, Sullivan and the "Chestnut Lodge School," and the English object-relations school. Such a division is in many ways arbitrary and unsatisfactory since there has been much overt and covert cross-fertilization over the years. Nor are these schools separable along a temporal dimension. Table 4 charts the chronology of major theoretical works and is included to afford the reader a glimpse into the intellectual context, the "siblings," of the various theories.

In addition to original sources, several summaries and reviews have proved helpful: Boyer and Giovacchini (1967), Gunderson and Mosher (1975), and Arieti (1974b).

FREUD AND HIS FOLLOWERS

Although Freud was not primarily concerned with schizophrenia, he did offer three partial theories and initiated several conflicting trains of thought on the subject. His work on the unconscious, dreams, the meaning of neurotic

TABLE 4: Chronology of Major Psychoanalytic and Family Works on Schizophrenia

1896 Kraepelin's *Psychiatrie,* 5th ed.
1907 Jung's first work on dementia praecox
1911 Eugen Bleuler coins the term "schizophrenia"
      Freud's analysis of the case of Schreber
1913 Ferenczi publishes "Stages in the Development of the Sense of Reality"
1916 Rüdin's monograph on the genetic transmission of schizophrenia
1919 Tausk's "The Influencing Machine"
1921 Melanie Klein starts publishing her work with "The Development of a Child"
1923 Freud publishes *The Ego and the Id*
      Piaget publishes *The Language and Thought of the Child*
1924 Freud publishes "Neurosis and Psychosis"
      Sullivan publishes "Schizophrenia: Its Conservative and Malignant Features"
1925 Sullivan's "Peculiarity of Thought in Schizophrenia"
1929 Sullivan's "Research in Schizophrenia"
1930 Klein's "The Psychotherapy of the Psychoses"
1931 Sullivan writes on environmental factors in schizophrenia
1932 Klein publishes *The Psychoanalysis of Children*
1934 Federn publishes "The Analysis of Psychotics"
1936 Anna Freud publishes *The Ego and the Mechanisms of Defense*
1938 Kallmann's genetic work in schizophrenia is first published
1939 Fromm-Reichmann writes "Transference Problems in Schizophrenia"
1940 Sullivan publishes *Conceptions of Modern Psychiatry*
1941 Manfred Bleuler publishes *Course of Illness, Personality and Family History in Schizophrenics*
      Fairbairn writes "A Revised Psychopathology of the Psychoses and Psychoneuroses" and
        "Schizoid Factors in the Personality"
1942 Fromm-Reichmann publishes "A Preliminary Note on the Emotional Significance of Stereo-
        types in Schizophrenics"
1943 Bychowski writes "Physiology of Schizophrenic Thinking"
      Federn's "Psychoanalysis of Psychoses"
1944 Kasanin publishes *Language and Thought in Schizophrenia*
1945 Fenichel's *The Psychoanalytic Theory of Neurosis*
1947 Rosen writes "The Treatment of Schizophrenic Psychosis by Direct Analytic Therapy"
      Rosenfeld begins to publish his work
1948 Bellak's first work on schizophrenia appears
1949 Bergman and Escalona write on children with unusual sensitivities
      Lidz publishes his first work on families of schizophrenics
1951 Sechehaye publishes *Symbolic Realization* and *Autobiography of a Schizophrenic Girl*
1952 Brody and Redlich edit *Psychotherapy with Schizophrenics*
      Fairbairn's collected papers are published
      Mahler begins to publish her work on separation-individuation
1953 Hartmann writes "Contribution to the Metapsychology of Schizophrenia"
      Rosen publishes *Direct Analysis*
1954 Jacobson publishes "Contribution to the Metapsychology of Psychotic Identifications" and
        "On Psychotic Identifications"
      Stanton and Schwartz publish *The Mental Hospital*
1955 Arieti publishes *The Interpretation of Schizophrenia*
1956 Bateson, Jackson, Haley, and Weakland write "Toward a Theory of Schizophrenia"

1958   Jackson et al. publish "Psychiatrists' Conceptions of the Schizophrenogenic Parent"
        Winnicott's *Collected Papers* are published
        Wynne's first paper on pseudomutuality appears
1959   Jackson and Weakland, and Searles, publish major papers on schizophrenia
1960   Bateson publishes "Minimal Requirements for a Theory of Schizophrenia"
        Jackson edits *The Etiology of Schizophrenia*
        Laing publishes *The Divided Self*
1961   Burton edits *Psychotherapy of the Psychoses*
        Jackson publishes "Family Therapy in the Family of the Schizophrenic"
        Will publishes "Process, Psychotherapy, and Schizophrenia"
1963   Wynne and Singer publish work on transactional thought disorder
1966-1974   NIMH research (Mosher, Pollin, Stabenau, and Tupin) on identical twins discordant
        for schizophrenia
1968   Mednick's work on children at high risk for schizophrenia begins to be written up

Our table ends here with the beginning of the 1970s and the growth of high-risk research and the relative dearth of psychoanalytic and family theorizing on schizophrenia.

symptoms, and the structure of the mind laid the foundation for future psychoanalytic inquiries into schizophrenia.

At first Freud was not interested in differential diagnosis. In his early papers (1894/1962a, 1896/1962b) he used the terms "neurosis" and "psychosis" interchangeably, a usage which was consistent with his early view that psychoses and neuroses lay on a continuum of mental illness. Both were seen as consequences of defenses against conflicts arising from faulty repression of impulses and as differing only in the kinds of defenses used. This early work is considered a statement of the conflict model of schizophrenia. However, Freud (1894/1962a) in general believed that constitutional factors may influence the development of the ego and the defenses (see Boyer & Giovacchini, 1967).

Pao (1973) and Boyer and Giovacchini (1967) have divided Freud's work on schizophrenia into three periods. The above-mentioned work of the 1890s constitutes the first period. The second period begins with the publication in 1911 of the analysis of the case of Schreber. In this paper Freud (1911/1958b) stressed the role of libido in the development of symptoms and theorized that psychosis occurs because of extreme withdrawal of cathexis from both environment and people. Following such extreme withdrawal, the prepsychotic recathects either his body or his ego. In the former case, the result is bodily preoccupation and hypochondriasis; in the latter case, it is megalomania. Eventually withdrawal can lead to restitutive symptoms in the form of delusions and hallucinations. Extreme withdrawal from the environment is sometimes experienced as an end-of-the-world delusion. Freud distinguished between paranoia—in which there is still object cathexis and regression to the narcissistic stage—and schizophrenia, which he preferred to call "paraphrenia"—where the regression is to the autoerotic stage of development.

Freud believed that persons suffering from both paranoia and paraphrenia were unsuitable candidates for psychoanalytic treatment because the extent of regression and withdrawal of object libido made transference impossible. This belief prevailed among Freudians until relatively recently and is partly responsible for the paucity of theoretical work on schizophrenia during the first half of this century.

In the second stage of his work, Freud viewed as fundamental the paraphrenic's withdrawal from the environment, a social-interpersonal aspect of schizophrenia. He stated that the schizophrenic's thought disorder results from the ego's defending itself against reality by rejecting both the idea and the affect and then behaving as though the idea had never occurred to it—denying a piece of reality. The schizophrenic withdraws not only from the external world but from the unconscious representation of it as well. The neurotic, on the other hand, represses the idea, which then emerges in fantasy. Pao (1973) summarizes:

> In schizophrenia words and not things are subject to the primary psychic processes. That is, words (and not things) are being condensed and substituted, resulting in the characteristic disorder of schizophrenic thought process. He explained that, in schizophrenia, after withdrawal of object cathexis both the thing-presentation and word-presentation of the object become decathected. But, in the attempt at recovery, the schizophrenic "sets off on a path that leads to the object via part of it, but then finds himself obliged to be content with words instead of things" (Freud . . . [1915/1957], p. 204). Characteristic of schizophrenia is that free communication between preconscious (word cathexis) and unconscious (thing cathexis) is cut off [pp. 470–471].

The third stage began in 1923 with Freud's presentation of the structural model in "The Ego and the Id" (1923/1961a). Here he emphasized the importance of the ego in mediating between the id, the superego, and reality. Although he never developed a comprehensive theory of schizophrenia based on this model, Freud began to alter his earlier theory. He now viewed psychosis as the outgrowth of a conflict between the ego and reality, in contrast to neurosis, which is caused by a conflict between the ego and the id. In his paper on "Fetishism" (1927/1961d), Freud recognized the importance of the defense of "splitting" in the development of psychosis. In this paper he described the cases of two men who denied the deaths of their fathers—thus denying a piece of reality—although they were not psychotic. He reasoned that they were able to remain "sane" because of a split in the ego, one part of which remained cognizant of reality while the other part, governed by the instincts and wish fulfillment, ignored it. As long as the balance of power favors reality, the person remains neurotic; when the balance favors the world of the wish, the person is psychotic.

Pao (1973) notes that Freud lacked sufficient knowledge of the ego to develop further his conceptualization of schizophrenia. This task was left to Freud's followers, who have tried to integrate Freud's earlier economic view of schizophrenia with later advances, i.e., the structural model and a better understanding of the importance of the ego. Freud's followers seem to have been torn between allegiance to Freud and his economic theory, and concern with accurate observation and study of schizophrenics. Jung (1907, 1960) and Freud (1911/1958a) disagreed over the role assigned to libido in the etiology of schizophrenia. Tausk (1919/1933), Ferenczi (1914/1950a, 1922/1955), and others who became interested in schizophrenia split with Freud, coincidentally or not.

A major weakness in psychoanalytic theory at the time of Freud's death was its inadequate analysis of the development of cognition. Schizophrenia, more than any other "functional" mental disorder, is manifested in peculiarities in the cognitive realm. As such, it can be seen as posing a special problem for psychoanalytic research. In this connection, Rapaport (1951) notes that:

> Philosophical psychology, the ancestor of scientific psychology, was a subsidiary of epistemology. Its major query was: How do we acquire our knowledge of the world of reality? It studied psychic functions mainly in their relation to the acquisition of knowledge of reality. . . . Freud's point of departure was different: he was concerned with the evaluation by the psychic apparatus of *internal stimuli* (drives, needs) rather than *external stimuli* [pp. 316–317n.].

It was not until 1911, in "Formulations on the Two Principles of Mental Functioning," that Freud (1911/1958a) turned his attention to the individual's relation to the external world.

Freud's theory of thought processes is centered on his theory of drives.

> Ideation is the process by which a need causes the memory image of the need-satisfying object to appear in consciousness. . . . Ideation yields its place in the course of development to the process of thought in which all ideas related to the need-satisfying object are so organized as to enable a planful search for the need-satisfying object in reality [Rapaport, 1951, p. 325].

Freud thus echoes the classical concept that thinking is the slave of the passions, but carries it to an extreme in his view that thinking originates from the prototypic experience of the hungry infant imagining (thinking) a gratifying breast. In other words, Freud believed that cognition begins when the infant, in a state of hunger, does not get fed at the moment of desire and imagines satisfaction in the form of the hallucinated breast.

Freud's work in the area of the person's relationship to reality was not as comprehensive as his work on drives and the unconscious. Hartmann and the ego psychologists addressed themselves to this point in stressing the ego's role in adaptation. In my opinion, despite the work of Rapaport and others, psychoanalytic explanations of cognitive development remain forced. Perhaps that is because the method of investigation employed by psychoanalysis is not suited to the development of a theory of thinking.

Freud's personal contact with schizophrenics was limited, which may explain the conflicting observations of his followers who had more extensive contact. Fenichel (1945) remarked that, contrary to Freud's contention that schizophrenics withdraw cathexis from the object world, one finds that they have intense, immediate transference reactions. These reactions are exceedingly labile; therefore Fenichel regarded schizophrenics as unsuitable candidates for analysis. Nonetheless, these reactions reflect the schizophrenic's continued and/or restitutional interest in the external world. This capacity for cathecting the external world and establishing a transference reaction has subsequently been noted by many workers in the field (Boyer & Giovacchini, 1967; Fromm-Reichmann, 1959c; Sullivan, 1956, 1962d). Fenichel basically elaborated Freud's view of the libidinal changes in schizophrenia and offered a more systematic explanation of schizophrenic symptoms in terms of these changes.

In the late 1920s and 1930s, Paul Federn, Paul Schilder, and Anna Freud extended our understanding of the ego in ways that had important implications for the understanding of schizophrenia. Schilder (1931) and Federn (1934) stressed the importance of the body ego in the formation of the ego, emphasizing that it is at the core of one's differentiation from others. Federn disagreed with Freud's idea of initial withdrawal of cathexis from the external world leading to hypercathexis of the ego. Instead, Federn (1952) claimed that the primary defect in schizophrenia is the decathexis of the ego, which leads to a weakening of the ego boundary (the boundary between the self and the outside world, thoughts and reality). In this state there is regression to a period before distance perception, one in which all sensations touch the ego. In Federn's view, the schizophrenic is in much the same position as the infant in need of a stimulus barrier, unable to fend off massive stimulus impingement. This view is consistent with some psychophysical findings discussed in earlier chapters. In addition to the influx of external sensations, there is the intrusion on the ego of normally unconscious material. The loss of the self-other distinction, and the influx of sensory impressions that are experienced in an unusual way (at the periphery) and must somehow be explained, give rise to a false reality. Federn saw the false reality as primary and the withdrawal as a secondary effort to limit sensation.

Federn hypothesized an early deficit in self-object differentiation, possibly arising out of poor mothering. He suggested that a narcissistic mother incapable of truly nurturing the preschizophrenic may cause weak ego development, but he also allowed for constitutional factors. His is an example of a deficit theory of schizophrenia, and he was guarded in his expectations from treatment. Basically Federn believed that there is a permanent psychotic reaction which, it is hoped, can be encapsulated by strengthening the ego boundaries. Those who follow this view would be nonregressive and oriented to reality in their treatment, and would make ego interpretations. Although many theorists believe that faulty or weak ego boundaries are basic to the development of schizophrenia, Pollin (1974) has called this premise into question. He found that identical twins, who according to the literature have hazier boundaries than the rest of the population, do not have a higher incidence of schizophrenic disturbances.

Bychowski started writing about schizophrenia in 1924, but his major work, *Psychotherapy of Psychosis,* was not published until 1952. At that time his views on schizophrenia showed the influence of Melanie Klein, Heinz Hartmann, Edith Jacobson, and others. Bychowski believed that schizophrenia is the product of regression and that constitutional or congenital differences in ego strength make some people more prone to deep regression than others. In addition to this unidentified constitutional element, environmental factors, which affect a person's introjects, either strengthen or weaken the ego. According to this view, in the course of development the immature ego expands and strengthens itself through introjection and identification. Bychowski hypothesized that schizophrenics are deprived of sufficient material for favorable identification and introjection and are instead subject to contradictory, conflicting introjects. This pattern of introjection leads to a key feature of the weak ego: the persistence of hostility as a permanent component of all object relations, which later becomes manifest in the psychotic ambivalence of schizophrenics.[1]

If we accept the ego psychologists' theory that reality testing is actually a relating of external perceptions to memory traces and internal representations of objects (see Rapaport, 1951), then an inadequate set of internal objects or introjects leaves the schizophrenic with a faulty internal map of the world, which affects not only interpersonal affective relations but thinking as well (see the discussion of Hartmann, below).

While Bychowski accepted the work of Federn and Schilder on the body ego, he maintained Freud's view of hypercathexis of the ego. However, he stated that the hypercathexis of specific organs can further weaken the ego by attacking its foundation in the physical sense of boundedness in space and separation from the other. In other words, hypercathexis of specific body parts leads to a peculiar experience of one's self in space.

Bychowski stated that the schizophrenic's superego regresses to a more

---

[1] One could translate this idea into a more cognitive conception of the schizophrenic's inability to start life with a straight, clear-cut view of things, including emotional attachments.

primitive, punitive state. The weakened ego fails to neutralize instinctual demands, fails at repression, and fails to contain the primitive superego. Bychowski saw "blocking " and "flatness" of affect as defenses that protect the ego from the disintegrating effect of affects. Depersonalization results partly from the shifts in bodily experience and in the appearance of the external world. Estrangement is characteristic of early stages of schizophrenic decompensation.

In 1953, Hartmann stated: "The outline Freud gave us in these papers [1924/1961b, 1924/1961c] and the many hints he gave us in a series of others, have so far not yet been made the basis of a systematic theory of psychosis" (p. 177). Hartmann believed that schizophrenia is caused by a deficit in primary autonomous ego functions, which leads to a decreased capacity to neutralize aggression. He arrived at this theory after reviewing Freud's (1924/1961b, 1924/1961c) last statements on the subject, in which he claimed that schizophrenia is caused by a conflict between the ego and reality. Hartmann asked why the schizophrenic's ego comes into such conflict with reality. Freud's answer had been that either the nature of reality or increased pressure from the drives leads to conflicting demands of both the id and reality on the schizophrenic's ego. Hartmann added that the ego's role as mediator may be impaired because the defensive countercathexis or the ego functions that maintain contact with reality are incompletely developed or weakened. Since schizophrenics lack an organized, integrated system of defenses, they have lowered resistance to all kinds of stress. Their defenses are more primitive and do not rely as heavily on repression as do the more mature defenses used by normals.

Hartmann postulated a deficit in the primary autonomous precursors of defense. He suggested that the schizophrenic's ego is incapable of neutralizing aggressive energy for use in countercathexis, the energy source of the defenses. Thus the ego's defenses are weakened through lack of neutralized energy; the ego is then subject to a greater amount and/or intensity of aggressive energy, since none of it has been siphoned off for use as countercathexis. But why does faulty neutralization of energy occur? Hartmann suggests that the preschizophrenic starts off with less neutralized energy than does the normal person; this, then, is the primary deficit in autonomous ego functions. Faulty regulation of drive intensity can lead to inadequate object constancy, for, as Anna Freud (1952, p. 44) stated, the achievement of object constancy follows a decrease in drive. Developmentally, then, there is a parallel between self-object and ego-id differentiation. In addition, Hartmann pointed out that in schizophrenia symbols are identified with the objects symbolized, and thus words are treated as if they were things. This last observation grew out of Hartmann's interest in cognitive and adaptive development. In his metapsychological statements on schizophrenia, Hartmann unfortunately did not adequately integrate his ideas on autonomous ego functioning with his descriptive and explanatory statements. It is beyond the scope of this review to consider further the implications of his work on cognition for our understanding of schizophrenia. Suffice it to say that, insofar as Hartmann renewed interest in the importance of explaining our cognitive skills and our capacity to adapt to our world, to reality, his was a major contribution.

Edith Jacobson, Margaret Mahler, René Spitz, and others, inspired by the work of Hartmann and his co-workers, continued to expand psychoanalytic understanding of early ego development. Mahler and Spitz are unique in that they have begun to bridge the gap between theory and laboratory research through their use of detailed infant observations. Their work is reviewed at the end of this chapter.

Jacobson (1954a), like Hartmann, believed that constitutional differences in the amount of neutralized energy available to the ego predispose some persons to psychosis. The prepsychotic ego cannot use neurotic defenses; rather, it can cathect objects and the self only with defused libido and aggression. In psychosis proper, the self- and object representations, which normally become differentiated relatively early in development, merge again into an undifferentiated self-object, leading to serious distortions in the perception of reality. Jacobson seems to be describing two different paths to psychosis. On the one hand, there is a prepsychotic development based on constitutional deficits in neutralized energy. On the other hand, there is a less insidious course to psychosis, one based on premature disillusionment with the parents and generally premature development, creating a person vulnerable to regressive defusion of impulses and refusion of self-object. The first type, the constitutional path, corresponds to the "process" schizophrenic, who has at best a primitive defensive style based on splitting and projection. The second path corresponds to the "reactive" schizophrenic, who has developed a "false," prematurely socialized self that functions reasonably well until some critical point reveals the hidden, weak core of the personality. Jacobson's theoretical constructions sound similar to those of the Kleinians, who are discussed below.

Arlow and Brenner (1969) criticize Freud's libido model of schizophrenia and try to integrate more recent knowledge of anxiety, ego, superego, and aggression into a comprehensive theory of schizophrenia. They disagree with Freud's basic assumption that the decathexis of external reality leads to an increase in narcissistic libido that eventually results in recathexis of external reality through restitutional symptoms.

In contrast, Arlow and Brenner point out that the external world is not decathected to such an extent that transference does not occur. It is not that patients fail to perceive reality, but rather that their judgment and perception are impaired, independent of cathexis. Arlow and Brenner believe that delusions, hallucinations, and hypochondriasis result from conflict and defenses.

They stress the role of disturbed ego functions: reality testing, memory, integration, perception, and judgment. This regressive alteration of reality testing is viewed as a defense against anxiety. Fantasies appear real and defend against reality. The difference between neurosis and psychosis is one of quantity, not quality, with more severe instinctual regression in the psychoses than in the neuroses. Conflicts over aggressive impulses are more intense in schizophrenics and create a special need to protect the object; this heightened aggression often disrupts ties to the external world. Because the schizophrenic's ego cannot counteract regressive reinstinctualization of function, it resorts to extreme means of defense.

Wexler (1975) presents a deficit view of schizophrenia based on his observations of decompensation in patients during classical psychoanalysis. He hypothesizes that the loss of the object representation, combined with the loss of the analyst as object through his silent, unseen position, leads to a loss of both object constancy and the sense of personal identity in certain predisposed persons. He remarks that Freud (1915/1957), in his paper on the unconscious, stressed the loss or decathexis of unconscious representatives of the object, as a result of which the schizophrenic uses words to replace lost objects. The disintegration of higher-level, complex object representations involves a progressive loss of identity, accompanied by enormous anxiety and restitutive efforts. Building on the work of Hartmann and Rapaport, Wexler states that the maintenance of object representations is essential to many ego functions. Rapaport (1951) has stated that reality testing is feedback from memory traces of internalized objects to the real world. Thus a disturbance in the area of object representations can lead to a thought disorder and disturbances in reality testing.

Most evidence in support of these theories is drawn from psychoanalytic work and for various reasons does not qualify as objective proof. Two noteworthy exceptions are: the efforts of Mahler and Spitz to create a theory of development based on observations of many normal infant-children and their mothers; and the work of Bellak on defining ego functions operationally. These will be discussed below.

SULLIVAN AND HIS FOLLOWERS

Unlike Freud, Sullivan believed that schizophrenics could be treated, and he spent a considerable portion of his professional career working with schizophrenics himself and encouraging and training others to work with them. He spent years at St. Elizabeths Hospital, Sheppard and Enoch Pratt, where he developed and ran an all-male ward, and Chestnut Lodge, where he trained and inspired a generation of psychiatrists, including Frieda

Fromm-Reichmann, Adelaide Johnson, Don Jackson, Alfred Stanton, Harold Searles, Don Block, and Alberta Szalita.

It was at Chestnut Lodge that Fromm-Reichmann (1948/1959a) developed her idea of the "schizophrenogenic" mother; that Stanton and Schwartz (1954) first studied the impact of schizophrenics on staff and vice versa; that Hannah Green was hospitalized and successfully treated by Fromm-Reichmann (the basis of *I Never Promised You a Rose Garden* [Green, 1964]). Schizophrenic families first became a legitimate area of psychological investigation when staff at the Lodge openly acknowledged their difficulties in relating to and obtaining histories from the families of schizophrenics.

Sullivan's theory of schizophrenia evolved in a series of articles starting in 1924. The early articles (1924–1939) are gathered in *Schizophrenia as a Human Process* (1962d). His continuing interest in schizophrenia is evidenced by the inclusion of ideas on this subject in all his major writings.

Sullivan's first article on this subject, "Schizophrenia: Its Conservative and Malignant Features," was published in 1924, the same year as Freud's (1924/1961b) "Neurosis and Psychosis." In his paper, Sullivan presaged his new approach to psychiatry. He defines schizophrenia as a series:

> . . . of major mental events always attended by material changes in the personality, but in itself implying nothing of deterioration or dementia. The disorder is one in which the total experience of the individual is reorganized; there is an eruption of primitive functions . . . and there is at least temporarily profound alteration of the egoistic structures of the sentiment of self-regard. It is a disorder which is determined by the previous experience of the individual—regardless of whether it is excited by emotional experience, by toxaemia of acute disease, by cranial trauma or by alcohol intoxication. . . . *That there is hereditary predisposition to the schizophrenic dissociation is fairly certain* [1924/1962e, p. 12; my italics].

Mullahy (1970), who thoroughly analyzed Sullivan's work, erroneously states that Sullivan believed schizophrenia to be a disorder of living with no organic base. However, as the above quotation shows, that was not the case. Rather, by "disorder of living" Sullivan meant that schizophrenia is only one of many fates possible to humans and, as we shall describe below, is in large part the outcome of the person's relation to society. That does not deny a hereditary or organic predisposition.

In contrast to Freud, and in anticipation of Winnicott and Laing, Sullivan stressed the "conservative," by which he meant conserving, aspects of schizophrenia. He concluded his 1924 paper with a description of this conservative aspect as:

> . . . *attempts at regression* to genetically older thought processes—to infantile or even prenatal mental functions—*successfully to reintegrate masses of life*

experience which had failed of structuralization into a functional unity, and finally lead by that very lack of structuralization to multiple dissociations in the field of relationship of the individual not only to external reality, including the social milieu, but to his personal identity [1924/1962e, p. 20].

In the later *Clinical Studies in Psychiatry* (1956), Sullivan defined schizophrenia as: "A failure of the self system to reserve attention to the types of referential processes that enjoy good repute among the intelligent . . . to the higher referential processes which can be consensually validated" (p. 182). He also noted that: "A statement of the essential characteristics in schizophrenia is not a description of the processes which go into being schizophrenic" (p. 182).

As seen above, Sullivan emphasized the thought disorder as the basic characteristic of schizophrenia. Although his etiological statements do not clearly explain the development of the thought disorder, they do offer the first dramatic insights into the probable life history and phenomenology of the preschizophrenic, and thus presage Laing's work.

According to Sullivan, the person strives to satisfy needs and to maintain security, i.e., one's sense of self-worth and one's self-esteem. The sense of self is built on the reflected appraisals of others. Very early in life, the primary others are one's family. From infancy onward, the child can sense the mothering one's anxiety, experiencing it through contagion. The child then seeks to avoid this experience. When the mothering one is made highly anxious by the child's behavior, for example, by masturbation, the child banishes that part of the self, dissociating it into what Sullivan termed the "not-me." Through a variety of security operations (what Freud called defenses) such as "selective inattention," the child, and later the adult, seeks to contain such behaviors, feelings, and attitudes outside of awareness.

Mullahy (1970) describes the existence of a dynamic balance between the self-system and these dissociated elements. In the preschizophrenic the balance is uneasy, perhaps because of the wide variety of events that caused anxiety in the parents, or because of the specific behaviors, such as autonomous action, intimacy with outsiders, and/or heterosexual activity, that became labeled "not-me." In the preschizophrenic, then, areas that are necessary for "normal" adult functioning are part of the "not-me" constellation and thus inaccessible.

Sullivan stressed the potential of the juvenile period to correct early family experience. In our culture, it is expected that a child will develop an intimate relationship with a same-sex chum in the respite before heterosexual behavior; it is also the preschizophrenic child's last opportunity to avert disaster. It was to this relatively simple juvenile social milieu that Sullivan oriented his exclusively male ward at Sheppard and Enoch Pratt.

Sullivan anticipated the later delineation of the process-reactive continuum when he noted that anyone who had achieved some intimacy with a chum before the breakdown was less likely to undergo a severe regression than the person with no experience of intimacy.

This less severely regressive form of schizophrenia, found in persons who have already achieved some level of intimacy, begins abruptly when some external event upsets the dynamic balance, confronting the person with dissociated elements of his or her personality. This leads to the collapse of the self-system and to panic. The abrupt disorganization of the self-system, which includes all collaborative, consensually validated meanings, is exceedingly confusing and makes the whole world seem incomprehensible. One's own utterances and actions no longer make sense, and are responded to by others with fear and derision. One is not aware of the specific cause of the panic, but rather, feels that everything is terrifying and that there is an urgent need to set things straight. When this failure of dissociation exists:

> The schizophrenic admits into consciousness things which the rest of us would ordinarily exclude . . . [there] is inclusion in attention of primitive, diffuse processes dealing with essentially rather terrifying states of nature. In such a situation, for example, I as a person known to me, would no longer be fixed and relatively durable but, instead, would become much more like a toy boat in a real monsoon; and other people . . . would become embodiments of rather terrifying generality [Sullivan, 1956, p. 184].

Sullivan went on to say that the schizophrenic is especially terrified of cultural mandates, prohibitions, and prescriptions that he or she can no longer follow. The schizophrenic feels totally unworthy of respect and terribly confused. He or she is flooded by thoughts and events, and may experience a sudden narrowing of attention and what Arieti (1955) refers to as "psychotic insight." With this insight, the schizophrenic's experience is no longer baffling, but rather is explained by a plot: dissociated aspects of the self are either projected onto others or are the will of an "other" who controls the schizophrenic.

In insidious schizophrenia, a morbid withdrawal from others takes place. These schizophrenics have never had a consolidation of intimacy, and they have felt inadequate and self-conscious for a long time. All their efforts at "entering" the human race have been rebuffed. Preadolescent peers have reacted to them with ostracism and withdrawal, reinforcing the preschizophrenics' own withdrawal and isolation. Their lack of social contact and exchange make their utterances increasingly autistic, as there is no opportunity for consensual validation. They are stuck in a vicious circle and suffer extreme regression when a full-blown psychosis finally emerges.

Sullivan did not distinguish Kraepelinian subtypes of schizophrenia. Rather, he viewed schizophrenia as a process, the original form of which is catatonia. He believed that treatment during this initial episode, as well as premorbid factors, determines whether or not the person will become paranoid, hebephrenic, or improved.

Fromm-Reichmann (1959c) bridged the worlds of Freud and Sullivan. She wrote primarily about the therapy of schizophrenics and was among the first to describe how, contrary to Freud's belief, schizophrenics are indeed capable of forming intense transference relationships with their therapists. She believed that the schizophrenic is powerfully distrustful and resentful of other people because of the severe early warp and rejection by important people during infancy and childhood—especially the "schizophrenogenic" mother. These early experiences deprive the preschizophrenic of a wellspring of security, self-reliance, and assurance and leave him or her with little resistance to the frustrations of adulthood. In the face of extreme frustration, the schizophrenic regresses to earlier periods and seeks autistic, delusional security. He or she withdraws from contact, but also strongly desires it. This fear of closeness derives in part from fear of hostility toward the loved one. (This idea was further developed by Burnham, Gladstone, and Gibson [1969] as the need-fear dilemma; it is also encountered in Guntrip [1969]). Because of this basic ambivalence about closeness, improvements in the course of therapy are likely to be followed by brief regressions and withdrawals.

Searles's (1965a) foremost contribution to the understanding of schizophrenia has been his rich description of psychoanalytic work with schizophrenics and the vicissitudes of the transference-countertransference reactions encountered during such work. His thoughts on etiology are eclectic, drawing primarily on the work of Sullivan and Jackson. In his paper on "The Effort to Drive the Other Person Crazy," Searles (1959/1965b) describes the six most frequent ways in which the preschizophrenic is subjected to conflicting and/or inappropriate messages and is deprived access to other, saner forms of interaction. He stresses the following six ways of driving the other crazy:

1. Pointing out areas of the other's personality of which he or she may be unaware that are inconsistent with ideal or actual self-image
2. Stimulating the person sexually in settings where attempts at gratification would be disastrous
3. Simultaneously or rapidly alternating stimulation and frustration
4. Relating to the other simultaneously on two unrelated levels
5. Switching erratically from one emotional wavelength to another
6. Switching topics while maintaining the same emotional wavelength

However, these "techniques" are often used by families that do not produce schizophrenics. In addition, Searles does not explain why usually only one sibling becomes crazy. He later brings a new element into the discussion, namely, the drive to express oneself in a loving way. He describes the preschizophrenic's love for the mother and recognition that his or her achievement of autonomy would drive the mother crazy: the mother requires symbiotic relatedness, and therefore out of 'love' the schizophrenic opts for his own craziness. Searles hypothesizes that the schizophrenic's mother's low self-esteem and primitive rage lead her to distrust her own loving feelings and to strive to protect her child from her rage. In addition, she transfers to her child the feelings and attitudes she experienced in her symbiotic relationship with her own mother. Searles states that to move on from symbiotic relatedness one must experience not only being loved, but loving someone who can accept that love. This idea is developed somewhat differently by Fairbairn (see below). The preschizophrenic's mother has not been able to give or receive love and clings to her own child symbiotically.

Arieti has written extensively on schizophrenia. In the main, his work represents an effort to integrate cognitive and emotional theories of normal and pathological development, and to analyze the structure and possible origin of schizophrenic thought disorder. In his major work on schizophrenia (1974a), he includes physiological findings without really integrating them into his own theory. Arieti presents his material in a systematic, developmental fashion that lends an air of consistency and finality to his theory. However, many of his statements are inferences that do not seem to be supported by the data. His major contribution is his continuation and broadening of Sullivan's concern with schizophrenic language and thought and his recognition of the importance of the cognitive changes seen in schizophrenia.

Arieti views schizophrenia as the outcome of an extreme lack of security in the early years of life, the lack of a trusting relatedness to the mother, and the failure to achieve what he calls "a sense of communion." This failure leads to a faulty internalization of the world, distrust and turning away from others, and dissociation from the more social parts of the self. He postulates that internalization is a consequence of trusting relatedness. This theory is in direct opposition to Fairbairn's (1952a) view that internalization is initially a consequence of frustration (see below). Arieti's theory also leaves unexplained the subsequent development of the preschizophrenic's inner world, which obviously includes some form of internalization. Another consequence of the lack of a sense of communion is the flawed development of symbolic function: in the absence of opportunities for consensual validation, the preschizophrenic can maintain primitive, autistic forms of thought. Arieti appears to say that infantile autism, childhood schizophrenia, and adult schizophrenia all lie on a continuum—but he does not elaborate his views on the subject, nor does he explain the vastly superior capacity to conceptualize and symbolize in adult schizophrenia as compared with either of the childhood psychoses.

For the adult schizophrenic, latency was a time of relatively normal, if isolated, functioning. Arieti develops the idea that the danger for the preschizophrenic in adolescence is not the great physiological changes and the increased instinctual drive that Freud postulated, nor the sociocultural expectations of autonomy and intimacy that Sullivan and Erikson suggest, but rather the magic of concepts and ideas—the growth of what Piaget calls "formal operations." According to Arieti, the preschizophrenic adolescent, whose early cognitive development was distorted, gets lost in this new world of ideas. It is at this point that the "process" schizophrenic has his or her break. The more acute schizophrenic's break occurs in ways described by Sullivan (see above). (Note that current researchers would question whether these "acute schizophrenics" are in fact schizophrenic.)

Arieti describes schizophrenic thought disorder in terms of progressive teleological regression. He considers schizophrenic thinking to be a regression to primitive patterns of thinking that are characterized by: active concretization; paleological thought involving identity of predicates; desocialization and desymbolization; and overuse of psychological or teleological causality (see Chapter 6, the section on Language).

MELANIE KLEIN AND THE ENGLISH OBJECT-RELATIONS SCHOOL

In reviewing the work of the Kleinian group, we are faced with some of the same difficulties discussed in the review of Freud and the neo-Freudians. The theoretical work of the Kleinians grew by accretion—Melanie Klein's own work spans over forty years (1921–1963), and each of the major English theorists—Segal, Rosenfeld, Fairbairn, Winnicott, Guntrip, and Laing—though accepting some of the same basic premises (most significantly, the importance of the first months of life for subsequent personality development), offers his or her own substantial modifications in terminology and theory. The differences between Klein on the one hand and Fairbairn and Winnicott on the other are quite significant: Klein retains and emphasizes Freud's life and death instincts; Fairbairn and Winnicott do not. Klein and Fairbairn disagree on the primacy of projection versus introjection and on the contents that are projected and introjected; they hold different views on aggression—Klein sees aggression as innate, whereas Fairbairn and Winnicott consider it a product of interaction with a frustrating environment. In general, Klein places considerably less emphasis on the external world, viewing it primarily as a reinforcer of innate processes of death and life instincts, whereas Fairbairn and especially Winnicott stress the importance of the "holding environment" in determining the development of the infant who enters the world untainted by aggression.

Melanie Klein's work, which is essential to this school, developed primarily from her therapeutic treatment of children. In the course of this work, she claims to have analyzed material from much earlier periods of life (2–12 months) than had Freud in his analysis of neurotic adults with primarily Oedipal (3–6 years) conflicts. Since Freudians and Kleinians agree that schizophrenia is a product of pre-Oedipal conflict, a better understanding of this stage of development should enrich our conceptualizations of schizophrenia. Whatever criticisms have been leveled against Kleinian theory, there is no gainsaying that it is remarkably descriptive of processes encountered in borderline and psychotic patients; as such it can decrease the therapist's anxiety and may correspondingly increase his or her utility. Boyer and Giovacchini (1967) have noted that Kleinian metapsychology has greatly increased our desire and ability to work psychoanalytically with psychotics.

More contemporary members of the "English school" have focused their work on the analysis of the "schizoid" personality. The use of the term "schizoid" gives rise to another set of problems. Schizoid refers to: (1) the earliest "position" of the infant (in Kleinian terms); (2) the conflicts and defenses originating in this earliest period of development; (3) a particular constellation of personality patterns and defenses; and (4) the preschizophrenic and the schizophrenic without flamboyant symptoms.

Fairbairn, Guntrip, and Winnicott view schizoid phenomena as the core pathology in most patients and consider traditional neurotic symptoms as a defense against the emergence of these issues. Schizoid is thus a very broad classification, which leads to some difficulty in understanding the specific qualities of the "schizophrenic."

It follows from the above statements that Kleinians, like Sullivanians, view schizophrenia as lying on a continuum of personality disorders.

I shall begin with a review of Klein's description of the earliest period of infancy—what she refers to as the paranoid-schizoid position—and the pathology deriving from fixation at this stage. For this discussion, I have relied on Segal's (1973) excellent introduction to Klein's work, Klein (1945, 1957), and Grotstein's (1975) and Boyer and Giovacchini's (1967) reviews of her theory. These reviews, although helpful, clearly demonstrate the opacity of Klein's work in that they differ considerably in their reports of what she says.

Klein's complex theory of intrapsychic development has been widely criticized and has proved to be exceedingly difficult to understand. Gunderson (1975) criticizes Klein for basing her theory primarily on child observation, for stressing the role of very early infant experience to the comparative exclusion of later influences on personality, and finally, for "The concepts and language [she uses, which] defy ready correlation with clinical observation, leading even sophisticated metapsychologists to admit they aren't sure they understand the position being taken" (p. 149). With that standing as a warning, I shall explicate the part of her work that seems especially relevant to a discussion of schizophrenia.

When Freud's structural approach was in its infancy, when Anna Freud, Hartmann, and others were beginning their research on the ego, and when Sullivan was initiating the interpersonal approach, Klein, through her observations and analyses of young children, was formulating a theory of psychic development rooted in the first year of life. Utilizing Freud's postulate of life and death instincts, Klein placed the death instinct, which she considered innate, and its derivative—aggression—at the center of the infant's development. She stated that, from the moment of birth, the infant has an ego, albeit an unintegrated one, which strives toward integration and the alleviation of anxiety. At times, however, during intolerable anxiety, defensive disintegration occurs (Segal, 1973, p. 25).

The primary anxiety of the first three months is persecutory and stems from the infant's efforts to deflect the death instinct by projecting it onto the original object—the breast—which is then felt to be bad and persecutory. Some of the remaining death instinct is then converted into aggression and is directed against the "persecutor." Note that according to Klein, the initial projection occurs regardless of external reality. Secondarily, frustrating, "bad" external events cluster around this fantasized originally "bad" breast. An original "good" object is also created via projection of libido and the subsequent clustering of "good" external events.

"Splitting" has now begun. It is linked with other defenses: increased idealization of the good object and omnipotent denial of the bad object. It is the goal of the ego to reduce anxiety by acquiring, keeping inside, and identifying with the good, ideal object through introjection. The introjection of good objects serves to strengthen the ego, aiding in its integration and protecting it from the bad objects and persecutory anxieties.

During this paranoid-schizoid position, the infant ideally projects the bad objects and introjects the good objects. However, the fear of persecution remains and leads to several secondary maneuvers. At times the ego may project the ideal object in an effort to save it from persecution, and bad objects may be introjected in order to gain control. Another means of maintaining control is projective identification. When all other defenses fail, the "ego fragments and splits itself into little bits in order to avoid the anxiety" (Segal, 1973, p. 30). This is destructive to the ego and is the precursor of psychotic depersonalization and confusion.

In normal development, there is a scaffolding of good and bad fantasies, with a preponderance of the good. This serves both to strengthen the ego against disintegrative experiences and to prepare it for the difficulties attending the depressive position. It is in this next stage that the perception of whole objects, with the resolution of splits between good and bad, leads to guilt and mourning.

In pathological development there are several problems. For either external or internal reasons (a nongratifying mother or an innate increase in the death instinct), the amount of persecutory anxiety is excessive, and bad objects predominate. This makes the transition to perception of the whole object exceedingly difficult because of the fear that primitive rage will annihilate the object. The failure to introject primarily good objects weakens the ego and creates a vicious circle of increasing persecutory fantasies and increased weakening and fragmenting of the ego.

In her later work Klein (1957) recognized the importance of envy, which, unlike jealousy (with which it is often confused), is a primitive emotion. Envy is defined as the feeling one can have toward the object that possesses some desired quality, e.g., milk. One aims at being as good as the object, or, if that is impossible, at spoiling the object so that it is no longer envied. Although it can fuse with greed, envy is different from pure greed, in which the destruction of the object is secondary and coincidental. For some unexplained reason, certain infants appear to have such intense envy that the "ideal object" cannot be introjected and thus cannot nourish the ego. The ideal object cannot be introjected because pathological envy necessitates its destruction. In addition, whatever has been introjected of the ideal and envied object must also be destroyed. Thus, early envy both interferes with the basic schizoid mechanism of splitting, in that good and bad cannot be adequately distinguished and separated, and weakens the ego by depriving it of nurturance from the ideal object.

Although in adults splitting is considered pathological, it is a basic defense and the precursor of repression. According to Segal (1973), it also plays a major role in cognitive development, serving both as the prototypical discrimination and as the foundation for selective attention. She describes the effects of pathological splitting: faulty perception of reality, confusion of good and bad and of inner and outer, ego weakening, bizarre fantasies, and a distrust of and attack on the links between objects. In other words, faulty splitting during the paranoid-schizoid position lays the foundation for a schizoid personality, with the potential for a psychotic break.

Klein believed that the anxieties of infancy are the same as those characteristic of psychoses and that the defenses are correspondingly similar in the two instances. Rosenfeld (1965) asserts that the acute schizophrenic's state of confusion derives from a lessening of splitting. This can result from an increase in libidinal or aggressive impulses or from the need to deal with a whole object—through either loss or "falling in love" (see Gunderson and Mosher, 1975). According to Rosenfeld:

> Psychotic parts of the personality may be split off in very earliest infancy while other parts of the self develop apparently normally . . . under certain conditions these split off psychotic parts may break through to the surface, often producing an acute psychosis, for example schizophrenia. One has to assume a certain predisposition to the psychosis exists from birth. In such cases the

destructive instinct seems constitutionally stronger and dominates the rudimentary ego . . . [1965, p. 167].

Rosenfeld stresses the importance of the infant's constitution in determining the quality of mother-child interaction.

According to Kleinian theory, in adult schizophrenia there is regression to the state of confusion that exists when splitting is inoperative or pathological. This confusion manifests itself in the formal thought disorder. Grotstein (1975) states that the schizophrenic cannot think because he or she cannot repress. It might be more accurate to say that it is the inability to "split," thus the inability to discriminate and to attend selectively, that leads to the thought disorder.

The bizarrely sexualized behavior of the schizophrenic can also be explained by pathology during this early period of development. According to Klein, extreme oral frustration spreads to other, nonoral modes of aggression. In the course of such spreading, the infant becomes aware of the potential for genital satisfactions, which leads to jealousy of the parents' satisfactions and an increase in the infant's own frustration.

I have dealt only with Klein's work on the paranoid-schizoid position and pathological envy, since these areas seem most relevant to an understanding of her views on schizophrenia. These and other aspects of her theoretical work have influenced many in the field, most notably the English school of object-relations theorists. I shall focus on the work of Fairbairn and Winnicott, both of whom have significantly modified Kleinian theory.

In the course of analytic work with adults, Fairbairn came to believe that schizoid pathology is at the basis of all psychopathology. (See Fairbairn, 1952a, his collected papers covering the years 1940 to 1951.) All of us, he says, have more or less dissociated parts and have had moments of peculiar detachment, both of which he cites as evidence of "splits" in the ego. People differ in the depth and/or degree of these splits. Splits in the ego weaken it and interfere with its adaptive and integrative functions, including its capacity to distinguish between inner and outer reality. The more the ego is characterized by splits, the more "schizoid" the personality, and the more the person is characterized by attitudes of omnipotence, isolation, detachment, and preoccupation with internal reality. Usually schizoid people unconsciously harbor an attitude of futility, a fear of loving and/or being loved, and a belief that their love is destructive. The extreme example of this pathology is the schizophrenic who has withdrawn from external reality and object relatedness into a delusional world based on internalized objects—his or her inner world. How does the schizophrenic get that way? In order to answer this question, we must first state some of Fairbairn's basic ideas regarding the structure and development of personality.

Fairbairn (1952a) believes in the "pristine unitary wholeness" of the infantile ego. The ego of Fairbairn is a dynamic structure[2] with libido, or energy, which is primarily object-seeking. The ego is directed toward objects in reality and can thus be said to be ruled by the reality principle, albeit in immature form. Under conditions favorable for adaptation, the reality principle matures as "experience expands." Only when conditions are unfavorable is the reality principle replaced by the pleasure principle, which is aimed at the relief of tension. Thus, in contrast to Freud, Fairbairn maintains that it is the pleasure principle which is derivative and secondary.

Development can be viewed in terms of changes in the quality of the ego's relation to internal and external objects. For Fairbairn, the erogenous zones of Freud's oral, anal, phallic, and genital stages represent primary paths for object relatedness.

According to Fairbairn, objects are internalized primarily under the pressure of frustration and deprivation, an extreme form of which is separation. They are internalized in an effort to maintain the "goodness" of the external object. Thus for Fairbairn, in contrast to Klein, the first defense is introjection or incorporation. The internalization of objects and the subsequent defenses against these frustrating internalized objects cause the ego to undergo splits and restructuring (see below).

The ways in which the mother (prototypical object) frustrates or deprives the child vary during development, depending on the zone of interaction. Later deprivations compound earlier ones and can trigger regression to primitive modes of defense. The primary tasks for the parents of the growing child are the offering of spontaneous affects, regard for the child's autonomy, and acceptance of the child's love (note here the similarity to views expressed by Searles).

When parental care is adequate, the child is able to progress from immature object relations based on infantile dependence (at first real and absolute) and primary identification via incorporation, to the stage of mature dependence based on differentiation of self and other. During the transitional period of development (roughly corresponding to latency and adolescence) the child, or the neurotic adult, vacillates between the two forms of dependence and defends against regression to the earlier stage.

The earliest form of dependence is appropriate when the infant is totally biologically dependent on and identified with the mother. During this early oral stage, the dependency persists and the immature ego, the 'mouth ego,' is characterized by the following features: (1) the relation to the mother is really to a part of the mother—the breast; (2) a libidinal attitude of taking rather than giving, of incorporating and internalizing, exists; (3) feelings of

---

[2] Fairbairn notes that changes in our idea of the physical world, namely, Einstein's theory of relativity, have led to his conception of the ego as a dynamic structure, integrating energy and matter.

fullness and emptiness are significant (see Fairbairn, 1952a, p. 11). Fairbairn believes that this stage is characterized by preambivalent love for the mother. However, he postulates that, owing to the aggressive component of hunger, the infant believes its sucking empties the mother of milk and goodness.[3]

The anxiety about destroying the libidinal object can be reawakened by later experiences of the parents' nonacceptance of the child's love. This anxiety is at the base of the schizoid impasse—"loving is destroying." This fear contrasts with the depressive's fear that his or her *hate* of the ambivalently loved object will destroy the object.

In his later metapsychological paper (1952a, pp. 162–179), Fairbairn states that the preambivalently loved object is still at times experienced as frustrating and as such becomes the first internalized object. It is internalized in an effort to maintain the goodness of the external object. Once internalized, the overexciting and overfrustrating aspects of the object are split off and repressed, along with portions of the ego that are identified with the object. The exciting object and the libidinal ego correspond roughly to Freud's id; the frustrating or rejecting object and the internal saboteur correspond to Freud's superego. The remainder of the internalized object, stripped of its overexciting and rejecting parts, corresponds to the ego ideal with which the central ego is identified.

Internalization increases late in the oral period, which is characterized by biting and ambivalence. The "bad" mother is internalized in an effort to maintain the image of the "good" mother. The internalized bad mother is split into exciting and frustrating parts that are repressed along with portions of the ego (as described above). These internalized objects and substructures of the ego are in dynamic relation to each other. Aggression, which was first mobilized by external frustration, is now directed against internal objects. Good external objects are internalized to lessen the impact of the internalized bad objects on the ego's sense of itself.

Fixation at and regression to the early oral period lead to a perpetuation of attitudes characteristic of that period which are inappropriate to mature affective, cognitive, and interpersonal functioning. The failure to derive from the mother a belief in one's capacity for loving and being loved leads to depersonalization of the object with regression to part objects, and to deemotionalization of object relations. There is a reemphasis on taking as opposed to giving and a dread of expressing feelings. Intellectualization, repression of affect, and detachment are manifestations of this failure. The failure to

---

[3] This last hypothesis appears to assume the infant's misapplication of the law of conservation of matter and contradicts Piaget's evidence that it takes many years for the child to develop this concept. In this respect it is a good example of the failure of psychoanalytic theory to keep pace with experimental (cognitive) findings.

relate to external reality leads to an overinvestment of internal reality and extreme narcissism.

According to Fairbairn, projection is a later defense that becomes possible with the entrance of the father—the nonbreast person—into the infant's awareness. The second external object affords the infant the opportunity to project the bad object (the rejecting aspect of the mother) onto an other, usually the father. With this addition, the external world becomes more complex. The awareness of genital sensations and subsequent frustration of the desire for genital relatedness to the parent lead to jealousy and to further complexity in internalized object relations.

One might assume that an extremely depriving and/or rejecting mother during infancy is at the root of schizophrenic development. Such a mother affords the infant's developing central ego little in the way of emotional sustenance. This would suggest a consequent structural weakness or defect, which, when awakened by the failure to achieve mature relatedness, causes not only the reemergence of early oral ego attitudes but also a failure of integrative and adaptive capacities.

Fairbairn does not account for the "psychotic break" with reality and does not sufficiently differentiate it from the ongoing schizoid state.

Winnicott, like Melanie Klein, arrived at his theory of development through work with children. Although he later became an analyst, his work was influenced by his initial experiences as a pediatrician. The language of his work is firmly rooted in the real mother-child relationship. I shall discuss only his ideas about the etiology of psychosis.

Winnicott (1958,1965b), like many others before and since, stresses the important achievement of self-other, me–not-me differentiation. This differentiation is based on the development of a sense of self, an integration of initially separate ego states. Winnicott describes early psychological development without reference to internalization and object representation. He believes that these come after the distinction between self and other is made.

The infant, born with the capacity for a true self, requires the ministrations of the "good-enough" mother to have its needs met and not be overwhelmed by anxiety. The anxiety Winnicott describes is the threat of annihilation of the self. (This is in contrast to the anxiety postulated by Sullivan, which is derived through contagion from the mother.) This threat occurs when the infant is subject to excessive impingement (stimulation) from internal or external (these two are not yet differentiated) sensations. Such excessive impingement creates an experience of extreme helplessness.

The "good-enough" mother is able to maintain the illusion of omnipotence for the infant. She responds to early infant gestures by extending their meaning and creating the illusion that the baby is not helpless. Such an experience of omnipotence is necessary before the infant can feel enough confidence in the "goodness" of the external world and in its own strength and abilities to begin to differentiate and individuate. The true self of the infant is strengthened by the mothering person's gradual failure at adaptation, which necessitates increasingly active, real movements from the infant. Through increased motility, the infant comes in contact with the world; each contact reinforces the boundary between self and other and thus defines the real limits and powers of the infant. This is in contrast to both the infant who is overcared for and has no opportunity to "exercise" the self and the infant who is overimpinged on and resorts to extreme withdrawal because of an intense, premature sense of helplessness.

To the extent that the mother is alert to the gestures of the infant, she indicates both an awareness of the infant as separate and a willingness to respond to the infant as such. The not-so-good mother does not comprehend the infant's gestures and forces the infant to accept her gestures. The mother's inadequate comprehension of the infant's gestures and the infant's experience of inordinate amounts of impingement lead to a defensive split of the infant's self into true and false selves. The false self is an effort to protect the true self from annihilation and to buy time through compliance with external reality. Through identification, the false self may take on the personality of other family members and may pass for the real self. When the false self becomes entrenched and is seen as real, a sense of futility sets in. Originally the false self is a means of buying time, of guarding the true self against annihilation by the environment's demand for compliance. When the false self predominates, the true self has no opportunity to engage with the real world—for growth, strengthening, and relatedness.

The healthy child develops the capacity to sustain the true self through periods of false self interaction with the world—in other words, he or she maintains the capacity to stay alive, vital, and spontaneous despite the social demands for modified personal expression. The preschizophrenic does not.

In psychosis there is a breakdown of the false self system. Winnicott sees in this the potential for positive development. There is the opportunity to reintegrate in the presence of a better environment (the analyst) without recourse to a false self.

Laing (1960/1965a) gives a phenomenological description of the schizophrenic of Winnicott's theory. He describes the preschizophrenic's development of a true and a false self and its dire consequences; the preschizophrenic's fears and mode of being in the world before the breakdown; and why the crackup was inevitable. The notion of a false self conforms to the common history of the preschizophrenic as a good child and model student, with so-called "friends" (who, it is later discovered, never actually *knew* the patient).

Preschizophrenics live through pretense, never revealing their "true selves." But in the process of treating themselves like "rare orchids," they neglect the very air and water, the substance of human contact, that is essential for survival. They are so terrified of engulfment, implosion, and petrification that they keep apart from others, and in so doing they condemn themselves to eventual breakdown.

The child develops a false self in the face of parental and societal expectations and demands that the child's spontaneous self cannot fulfill. We all more or less go through this when we are socialized. Laing believes that many of us live false, disembodied lives and, in the tradition of Fairbairn, Winnicott, and Guntrip, he sees a preponderance of schizoid pathology. He does not articulate the specific development of those "society" has labeled "schizophrenic."

Laing's elaboration of a theory of familial etiology of schizophrenia will be discussed in the next chapter.

PSYCHOANALYTIC EMPIRICAL RESEARCH

Psychoanalytic theories are second- and third-order inferences, often greatly removed from observable, experimentally reproducible events. Much psychoanalytic theory is based on retrospective introspection and subsequent interpretation of process and transference phenomena. All too often, ideas about early development show gross adultomorphism. Even now, most analytic theorists ignore the findings of Piaget and persist in attributing to infants fantasies that seem inconsistent with what is known about early cognitive development.

Psychoanalytic theories are resistant to research strategies for many reasons. Before language develops, the infant is frequently a projective device for the analyst. Even after language development in the child, the adult has much room for hypothesizing the nature of the infant's experience without much chance for reality testing. The argument that analytic material supports a specific metapsychology is specious since the patient's choice of material, words, and even dream symbols is a product of interaction and identification with the analyst and the desire to please the analyst.

Empirical research based on observation is difficult but necessary; two brief examples of psychoanalytic research follow. The first, Bellak's work on ego functions, represents an effort to develop an objective, operational method for defining and evaluating the "weak" ego posited by many workers.

Bellak views schizophrenia as a syndrome, "the final common path of many different etiologies manifested in severe disturbance of various ego functions" (1970, p. 11). Thus, all schizophrenics have a generally "weak" ego, but the specifics of the weakness and the pattern of disturbances in ego functions may vary according to etiology. Bellak hypothesizes that some ego functions are likely to be affected by organic and/or hereditary factors whereas others are more influenced by interpersonal factors. Describing someone's ego functioning in specific ways may give clues to the etiology of a particular disorder as well as suggest target areas for intervention. Such an approach addresses itself to the clinically noted phenomenon, observed both in diagnostic testing and during therapeutic contacts, that schizophrenics are very different from one another. Some are highly capable of abstract thinking, others are entirely concrete; some show impaired judgment while maintaining above-average short-term memory and attention, others show just the reverse pattern. Whereas the above description stems from performance on the Wechsler Adult Intelligence Scale, which measures intellectual functioning, Bellak's work addresses itself to the broader group of ego functions, including reality testing, judgment, sense of reality, regulation and control of drives, object relations, thought processes, adaptive regression in the service of the ego, defenses, stimulus barrier, autonomous functioning, synthetic function, mastery, and competence.

Bellak's system represents an effort at more detailed diagnosis and is a forerunner of the multidimensional diagnostic system proposed by some members of the biometric research group (see Carpenter, Strauss & Bartko, 1976; Keith et al., 1976). Such sharpened diagnosis can lead both to improved treatment and to a better chance of solving the etiological puzzle.

Mahler's observations of normal infants and their parents and her work with psychotic children have led her to formulate a theory of development that stresses the vicissitudes of separation and individuation (Mahler, 1968; Mahler, Pine, & Bergman, 1975). Her assumptions regarding the earliest stages of this development, which she calls the stage of normal autism (0–3 months) and the stage of normal symbiosis (3–6 months), are of necessity based on few specific observations and therefore remain questionable. Mahler makes a commendable attempt to support these observations with available neurophysiological findings, but she does not pursue this effort to its logical conclusion. She is not sufficiently thorough in her references to and explanations of potentially valuable, supportive physiological evidence. Her examination of the later stages of the separation-individuation process are, however, more clearly tied to careful observation.

In the course of her observations, Mahler has found that the path to separation-individuation is not a simple one; at different stages it requires different behaviors from the mothering one. For example, a mother who is very good with her infant during the symbiotic period may have difficulty adjusting when the infant begins to move away from her through crawling and other autonomous exploring. She may become distant and let go too abruptly, or she may continue to hold on very tightly, denying room for autonomous action.

Mahler describes how the infant's sensory and motor development influences the growth of a sense of self: of separation and individuation. Pleasure-pain sequences, maturation of perceptual organs, and increased mobility lead the infant to shift from predominantly proprioceptive-endoceptive cathexis to "sensoriperceptive" cathexis. Each infant develops uniquely. Some have rapid motor development; others, experiencing early injuries, may be confined to a cast during the normal toddler period. Various congenital handicaps, such as blindness or deafness, can also alter the child's early experience of separateness from the mother (Meshover, 1980). Some infants are constitutionally difficult and place extreme demands on the adaptive capacity of the mother. A good mother should adapt to the specific needs of her child, sensing the child's psychological needs even when they do not conform to outer motor behavior.

In Mahler's later work (Mahler, Pine, & Bergman, 1975), she differentiates the critical steps in normal separation. Following Mahler, Adler and Buie (1976) believe that borderline conditions stem from a poorly negotiated rapprochement subphase. They support this hypothesis with findings from psychotherapy with adult borderline patients. Longitudinal research on the children Mahler has observed in her nursery may give us more reliable findings on the precursors of adult psychopathology.

While Mahler studied normal infants and their mothers, Spitz (1945) took advantage of historical and cultural anomalies to study infants deprived of normal mothering. He was the first to describe the depressive response of the infant reared in sterile conditions and deprived of maternal contact. These infants first showed marasmus and then, if still uncared for, they died. Spitz's infant observations are informed by his knowledge of biology, animal psychology, and ethology. He describes the importance of critical periods in infant development, which call for new responses from mother and infant. The mother must regulate frustrations to an optimal level, especially at these critical points, if the infant's ego is to acquire strength and structure. This idea is quite similar to Winnicott's discussion of the mother's gradual failure to adapt.

In closing this chapter, it is worth stressing the need for further efforts to integrate psychoanalytic developmental theory with recent cognitive and physiological findings. Such a task is feasible and would greatly clarify our understanding of development.

Family Theories of Schizophrenia	Chapter Eight

In this chapter I shall review the major family theories of schizophrenia and describe some supporting empirical data. Family theories of psychopathology, unlike individual theories, arose specifically from interest in schizophrenia. The observations and theories that have evolved are overtly aimed at understanding the etiology of schizophrenia. However, these theories have been criticized for being based on observations made after the appearance of illness in one member of the family. Thus what is observed and reported may be a consequence, rather than a cause, of the schizophrenia.

MAJOR THEORETICAL WORK

Until the 1950s, there were very few studies of families of schizophrenics. Interest in families grew in the 1930s and 1940s with the work of Sullivan, who stressed the interpersonal nature of schizophrenia and, along with Fromm-Reichmann, showed that schizophrenics were treatable. Fromm-Reichmann (1948/1959a) coined the term "schizophrenogenic" and described schizophrenogenic mothers as aggressive and domineering, but insecure. Her work helped focus attention on the families of schizophrenics.

The earliest work on families was descriptive and is typified by Gerard and Siegel's (1950) study employing semistructured interviews to establish the personality characteristics of the schizophrenic's mother and her relationship to the schizophrenic. Gerard and Siegel and other researchers during this period constructed long lists of adjectives describing "typical" mothers, fathers, and siblings of schizophrenics. These early studies have been criticized by Sanua (1969) for their methodological weaknesses.

Family research of the 1950s was heavily influenced by the prevailing psychoanalytic view that schizophrenics had symbiotic relationships with their mothers and defective self-object discrimination. The three main schools of family research in the 1950s and 1960s were: Lidz et al. at Yale; Wynne et al. at the National Institute of Mental Health (NIMH), and Jackson, Bateson, and Haley at Stanford. Lidz, Wynne, and Jackson had all been trained as analysts and were influenced by the work at Chestnut Lodge. Bateson was interested in communication theory and general systems theory, and the broader perspective he brought to work with schizophrenics influenced not only Jackson but the others as well. For the last fifteen years, both Lidz and Wynne have increasingly focused on the transmission of meaning and language in the families of schizophrenics.

Lidz

In Lidz's early work (Lidz & Fleck, 1960; Lidz, Fleck & Cornelison, 1965), which grew out of the psychoanalytic tradition, he considered schizophrenia a disease of adolescence and looked for factors that preclude firm identity formation and emergence from the home. He believed that the acute schizophrenic's social withdrawal is the means of handling fear of loss of control of sexual and aggressive impulses.

Lidz's group intensively studied seventeen families of schizophrenics and wrote a series of articles, collected in *Schizophrenia and the Family* (Lidz, Fleck, & Cornelison, 1965), in which they describe the characteristics of the individual family members and their patterns of interaction.

For this study, the following method was employed. The subjects were from the Yale Psychiatric Center and included early diagnosed schizophrenics between the ages of fifteen and thirty who were unmarried and had both a mother and a sibling available for interviewing. Fourteen of the seventeen families studied were upper-middle-class, and the authors acknowledge that all of them were more intact than is typical for schizophrenics. All family members were interviewed at length by a social worker and at least one or two research psychiatrists. In addition, they were given a battery of projective tests. The schizophrenic subjects were in therapy, as were many of their siblings. The social worker's initial sessions with family members were structured; later ones were open-ended, and contact often lasted for over a year. In addition, home visits were made, and conjoint family interviews were recorded. The researchers also attempted to interview nonnuclear relatives, friends, and teachers, and to examine records from the patient's childhood, e.g., photographs, letters. Lidz's group found that information changed markedly over time and concluded that histories acquired early in contacts with family members were unreliable. In order to insure greatest accuracy, all material was cross-referenced to lessen biases arising from individual family members' perspectives and from lapses of memory. The researchers summarize their data collection as follows:

> The extensive material concerning each family was condensed into comprehensive summaries of the history of the family, the life and personality of each member, the interrelationships and transactions among members, the organization and atmosphere of the family as a unit; its relationships to the parental families and to the community, etc. An effort was made to include each member's view on the interrelationship among family members [Lidz, Fleck, & Cornelison, 1965, p. 24].

The study resulted in the following conclusions:

1. All schizophrenics come from families with serious emotional strife.
2. Schizophrenics' mothers tend:
   a. to be impervious to their children's needs
   b. to be extremely intrusive
   c. to confuse their children's needs with their own
   d. to give conflicting verbal and empathic signals (similar to the double bind of Jackson)
   e. to fail to recognize ego boundaries
   f. to live their lives through their children
   g. to be either too restrictive or insufficiently firm.
3. Fathers were often:
   a. insecure in their masculinity
   b. in need of constant admiration to bolster their self-esteem
   c. mildly paranoid or paralogical.
4. Schizophrenics' families tend to have unclear sexual and generational boundaries. Parents were often seductive with their children, acted like children themselves, and at times reversed sex roles.
5. "Many of these families provided a paucity of emotional shelter requiring members to erect stronger ego defenses and be less honest and trusting within the family than elsewhere. Others provided a kind of shelter that fostered distrust of all without" (Lidz and Fleck, 1960, p. 336).
6. Parents were often more tied to and identified with their own families of origin than with their current families of generation.
7. These families fail to deeroticize the child's ties to the parents and to provide an adequate structure for developing ego integration.

Lidz and his coworkers differentiated two basic types of schizophrenogenic family according to sex. The parents of male schizophrenics tend to have "skewed" relationships; the parents of female schizophrenics were characterized by great "schism."

In the skewed family, one parent (usually the mother) is seriously disturbed, but the other parent never acknowledges the emotional problems of the disturbed spouse. The mother in the skewed family is often not capable of caring for and nurturing her infant son, and as he grows older she places contradictory demands and expectations on him. On the one hand, she wants him to fulfill all her unfulfilled dreams—nothing is beyond him and she expects great achievements—but at the same time, she is overprotective, seductive, and infantilizing. The passive father in such a family is an ineffectual role model, incapable of offsetting the mother's pathological influence.

In families with marital schism, the parents are locked in continuous covert conflict and compete for their children's loyalty. Any child who tries to save this kind of marriage may wind up as the scapegoat. The father in this family often wants constant admiration; the mother tends to be hopeless, passive, and overprotective. Because the mother is actively demeaned by her husband, who tends to be seductive with his daughter but disparaging of women in general, the daughter has no one with whom to identify.

In general, both male and female children who become schizophrenic have had poor relationships with the same-sex parent. The parent of the opposite sex has been seductive and has used the child for narcissistic gratification. Both parents have been impervious to the child's needs and have tried to fit him or her into the procrustean mold of their own defenses and needs. Potential schizophrenics, trained to be hypersensitive to the needs of others, are usually quite unaware of their own needs. They feel and often *are* magically central to the parents' well-being, and this feeling of centrality may later take on delusional dimensions.

So far we have described the dynamic importance of parental interaction with the preschizophrenic, and have seen the importance of Oedipal conflicts in the development of schizophrenics who, it will be recalled, are often flooded by incestuous wishes during their breakdowns.

Lidz considers schizophrenia to be an especially human disorder and is fond of saying that "the brain permits thinking but does not guarantee its rationality" (1973, p. 10). Language and thought permit flexibility and adaptability but contain our vulnerability. As Lidz has said:

> Meanings can alter in the service of emotional needs and when a person's acceptability to himself and others is threatened, when no way out of an irreconcilable dilemma can be found, and when all paths into the future seem blocked, there is still a way. One can simply alter his perception of his own needs and motivations and those of others; one can abandon causal logic or change the meaning of events; one can regress, retreating to a period in childhood when reality gave way before the wish, when one felt central to the parent's care or even to a time when one was not fully separated from the mother—and then regain a type of omnipotence and self-sufficiency [1973, p. 10].

From the beginning of his work, Lidz considered the thought disorder to be the crucial aspect of schizophrenia, and over the years his work has focused increasingly on this issue. In his early work, Lidz spoke of the transmission of irrationality; more and more the question is: How does this transmission occur? In answering this question, Lidz has been influenced by the work of Wynne and Jackson. In "The Transmission of Irrationality," Lidz, Cornelison, and Terry (1958/1965) asserted that schizophrenics are raised in families that routinely deny obvious interpretations of reality. As the child subjugated his or her needs and experiences to the needs of the parent, he or she lost sight of what was real. In addition, the lack of sexual and generational boundaries led to diffuse identity formation, a weakened ego, and—I would add—a disturbed basis for discriminating and categorizing experiences.

Over the course of the next decade, Lidz, influenced by the work of other family theorists and by Piaget, refined his view of the origin of schizophrenic thought disorder. His theory evolved from:

> . . . the recognition that the serious disturbances of the family settings derived from the profound egocentricity of one or both parents; that the disturbance of language and thought that form the critical attributes of schizophrenic disorder are largely types of egocentric cognitive regressions to developmental stages described by Piaget and Vygotsky; and that the parents' disturbed styles of communication, which are manifestations of their egocentricities, are essential precursors of the patient's cognitive regression that occurs when he cannot surmount the essential developmental tasks of adolescence [to the idea that] the nature of the schizophrenic disorder can only be grasped if the critical role of language in ego functioning is appreciated; and how on the one hand, distortions of language and reasoning lead to gross disturbances in behavior, and on the other hand, how the human condition permits escape from insoluble dilemmas by breaking through the confines imposed by the culture's system of meanings and reasoning and by regression to early childhood types of magical thinking [Lidz, 1973, p. x].

Lidz developed the idea that overinclusiveness, often regarded as a major feature of schizophrenic thought disorder, is a form of egocentrism related to the egocentrism of the schizophrenic's parents and their capacity to alter meanings in the service of their own needs. They do not adequately convey the cultural system of meanings to their children.

Lidz believes that the primary deficiency in schizophrenia is the inability to categorize phenomena linguistically. This leads to the inability to sustain focal attention and maintain a major set, to being flooded with stimuli, and to loosening of associations. Thus, in a theory reminiscent of McReynolds's (1960) theory of perceptualization processes, Lidz views language as a filter (see 1973, p. 61), maintaining that when words are used properly, they serve to group incoming data.

In summary, Lidz believes that the schizophrenic's family fails panphasically in its nurturant role because it does not meet the child's needs throughout the various phases of development. The child's socialization is impaired because:

1. Parents provided faulty models for identification.
2. They did not believe the child could care for itself.
3. Their example led the child to believe that interdependency, for example, in marriage, is unattractive and/or dangerous.
4. Parental egocentricities and/or their distrust of outsiders made their child reluctant to bring friends home.
5. One or both parents verged on psychosis in the tendency to distort reality; in order to maintain their own shaky balance, they insisted that other family members also distort reality.

Lidz, more than other theorists, tends to stress Oedipal issues in the genesis of schizophrenia. One of the few testable hypotheses derived from his work is the expectation that same-sex siblings ought to be more disturbed than opposite-sex siblings. Research has yielded contradictory findings (Alanen, 1972; Prout & White, 1956).

The Palo Alto Group

Bateson and Jackson initially worked deductively in an attempt to determine the conditions that lead schizophrenics to strip their messages of meaning and result in a thought disorder. They hypothesized that schizophrenics' parents frequently gave "double-bind" communications (Bateson et al., 1956, 1963). This term has been popularized and misused. According to their original definition:

The general characteristics of this [double-bind] situation are the following:

1. When the individual is involved in an intense relationship; that is, a relationship in which he feels it is vitally important that he discriminate accurately what sort of message is being communicated so that he may respond appropriately.
2. And, the individual is caught in a situation in which the other person in the relationship is expressing two orders of message and one of these denies the other.
3. And, the individual is unable to comment on the messages being expressed to correct his discrimination of what order of message to respond to, i.e., he cannot make a meta-communicative statement [Jackson, 1960, p. 374].

In other words, the child is punished for understanding correctly, for discriminating both accurately and inaccurately. Punishment can be avoided only by the child's preventing the parents from understanding his or her response. Eventually, the child is unable to discriminate meanings.

Weakland (1960) and others compare double-bind communication to the process of mystification described by Laing (1965b) and to the ways of driving someone else crazy described by Searles (1959/1965b). The conflicting messages in double binds can occur on the same level or on different levels: on a verbal level one means one thing, while on a nonverbal, empathic level one means something else. An example of a verbal double bind is a mother who tells her daughter, "Always be honest with me, tell me everything that is on your mind," but also says, "Never tell me anything bad about your father." An example of a mixed-level double bind is a mother telling her thirty-year-old son, "Stop acting like such a child—be a man," while scrubbing him in the bathtub.

The double-bind theory of schizophrenogenic communication has been examined by asking the schizophrenic's family members to plan an event jointly. The family's interaction is then observed through a one-way screen and taped for later analysis. Another experimental paradigm involves asking the parents to explain an ambiguous proverb to their child and comparing their performance with that of "normal" parents. Investigators of schizophrenogenic families agree that double-bind communication occurs, but some question whether this communication pattern completely explains the development of the disorder. In part this theory is criticized because it does not explain why schizophrenia develops in only one sibling.

A second major concept arising from Jackson's research is familial homeostasis, which operates in both normal and schizophrenogenic families. According to Jackson, family homeostasis is the tendency to establish and maintain an equilibrium. If the equilibrium necessitates the labeling of one family member as schizophrenic, then the hospitalization and subsequent improvement of that family member should lead to a series of changes in the entire family. According to this point of view, it is senseless to treat the schizophrenic without treating the family. Schizophrenia is considered to be not an individual's illness but rather part of pathological family interaction. If one cures the schizophrenic without treating the rest of the family, one would expect serious consequences for other family members. This resembles the assumption of symptom substitution in individual psychotherapy. The principle of homeostasis has proved useful in understanding and anticipating family realignments as one member begins to improve, and has prepared clinicians for familial "acting out."

Work that issued from the Palo Alto group has been collected by Jackson (1968a, 1968b).

Laing

Laing (1965b) has labeled the major type of miscommunication in families "mystification," the function of which is to maintain the family status quo and stereotyped roles. In mystification, one person denies the other's experience out of his or her own defensive needs because, in the context of the family, repression is insufficient for those who want to avoid their conflicts; consequently, group sanctions and defenses are developed. Mystification on the part of the parent serves to maintain such primitive defenses as projective identification and induces confusion in the preschizophrenic, whose confidence in his or her own experiences, emotional reactions, and perceptions is consistently shaken through invalidation and denial.

Bowen

Research on families of schizophrenics began by emphasizing the role of the mother, moved on in the work of Lidz and others to consider the inadequacies of the father, and was further extended by Jackson and others to include communication patterns in the total family system. Bowen (1960) went one step further, having studied mothers and daughters in 1954, and the rest of the family in 1957, he then found it necessary to include previous generations. He used naturalistic observation and, like other researchers, found an interlocking system of defenses within the family. Bowen theorized that schizophrenia is a process which takes three to four generations to develop. Although he does not clarify what he means by "a critical level of immaturity," he states that the schizophrenic's parents are the two least mature members of their own families of origin, and he predicts (actually postdicts) that they will have at least one child with a very high level of immaturity who will become schizophrenic. He states that people tend to choose spouses of identical levels of maturity but with opposite defenses. The families of schizophrenics studied by Bowen were characterized by emotional distance. Usually one parent denied his or her own immaturity and erected a façade of overadequacy, while the other parent, usually the mother, accentuated immaturity. In such a family, conflicts develop over dominance-submission, the "overadequate" parent complaining that he or she is forced to make decisions and take responsibility while the other parent shirks responsibility. In fact, both parents have a great deal of difficulty in making decisions.

The conflict between such parents is less intense in the presence of a third person, especially a child. With the birth of a child, the inadequate parent, usually the mother, acquires someone who is more inadequate than she and whom she uses to bolster her self-esteem. A mother of this kind also tends to be narcissistic and to use her baby to satisfy her social needs. In addition, she makes conflicting demands on the child: to remain helpless so that she can feel more adequate, but also to become gifted and mature. Bowen remarks on the degree to which the mother's fears are transmitted to the child, who gradually becomes exquisitely sensitive to her anxiety level. "As soon as the overtly anxious mother is in direct contact with the patient, the mother becomes less anxious and the patient more psychotic and regressed" (1960, p. 363). The functional helplessness of the preschizophrenic child allows a less anxious adjustment in the parents. The child, who desires a "good enough" mother, a less anxious mother, behaves so as to suit her needs (see also Searles, 1965a), a course that leads to an arrest in his or her own development. Bowen has found that when the relationship between the parents improves, the child too improves. He also suggests that the pre-schizophrenic child is the one most attached to the mother.

Wynne and Singer

I conclude this section with a discussion of the work of Wynne and Singer because, in my opinion, it is the most comprehensive, reflecting the last twenty years of research on schizophrenia and taking note of relevant findings from other disciplines. Their work can be divided into three periods:

1. Wynne's work in the 1950s on pseudomutuality and the development of a sense of identity
2. Work begun in the 1960s with Margaret Singer, defining two major types of thought disorder—amorphous and fragmented—both of which arise from the transactional thought disorder within the family
3. Current work with high-risk families combining genetic factors, cognitive and perceptual styles (most probably innate), and familial patterns of communication

The last two periods of research are grounded in experimental work.

The Early Period: Pseudomutuality and the Rubber Fence: Wynne's early work was concerned with the study of family role organization and its relationship to the offspring's developing sense of identity (Wynne et al., 1958). This work was based on the intensive examination of four families. While in the hospital, the schizophrenic member of the family was seen in intensive psychotherapy and the parents were seen twice a week in outpatient sessions. Data from other family members, friends, nursing staff, and the ward administrator were also included in Wynne's reconstruction of family patterns. The goal of this early research was to delineate tentatively the qualities and patterns of relationship in the families of schizophrenics and to formulate hypotheses concerning the effect of these relationships on ego development and identity formation. Wynne started with two premises about human development: (1) humans are object seeking and move toward relatedness; (2) humans strive both consciously and unconsciously to develop a sense of personal identity, which grows out of self-representations and gives continuity and coherence to experience. Wynne hypothesized that the need for relatedness on the one hand, and for a sense of personal identity on the other, allows for three different forms of relating: mutual, nonmutual, and pseudomutual. The pseudomutual form is critical in the development of schizophrenia.

Each person in a pseudomutual relationship brings to it a primary invest-ment in maintaining a *sense* of relating. This extreme need leads to falsifica-tion of experience, acting as though one's own and the other's behaviors mesh even when they do not. In such relatedness, people are absorbed in fitting together at the expense of differentiation of identities. While partici-pants in normal human interaction experience varying degrees of mutuality and relatedness, those involved in pseudomutual interaction do not tolerate these normal vicissitudes and deny all differences. In fact, the open acknowl-edgment and/or exploration of differences can actually deepen relationships. But that does not and cannot occur in the pseudomutual relationship, since it is founded on a *sense* of reciprocity rather than on the accurate perception of the other. People caught in the web of pseudomutuality are not allowed to change because any alteration or divergence in behavior is seen as disrup-tive and to be avoided.

While Wynne does not consider pseudomutuality a necessary and sufficient condition for the development of schizophrenia, he did hypothesize that "Within the families of persons who later develop a schizophrenic episode, those relations which are usually acknowledged as acceptable have a quality of intense and enduring pseudomutuality" (Wynne et al., 1958, p. 208).

Wynne also studied the relationship of family role organization to the development of a sense of identity in the offspring. He believed that the nature of this organization was critical because "it is precisely this big jump from roles and identifications to true identity that the schizophrenic fails to make" (Ryckoff, Day, & Wynne, 1959, p. 110). He found that schizophren-ics come from families in which a tendency to rigid roles and family mytholo-gies makes it difficult for any one member to change or grow without causing drastic upheaval in the family as a whole. Wynne pointed out that the adoles-cent should have a variety of roles to choose from and to try out while searching for his or her own adult identity. However, in families with stereo-typed communication patterns, pseudomutuality, and rigid organization, in-dividual flexibility of definition is impossible. According to Wynne, schizophrenogenic families are characterized by:

1. Grossly condensed and stereotyped family roles
2. Rigid organization of the family's conception of itself, with no deviation permitted

3. Collaboration among family members in enforcing adherence to roles defined by a shared conception of the family
4. Powerful repressive forces against deviance in family members and against attempts to modify or amplify rigidly defined roles

Although these families have a static quality, they do not provide consistency because the fixed roles can be exchanged among family members. These families also fail to provide a true sense of relatedness, since their primary investment in maintaining a sense of relatedness is at the expense of differentiation of identities and true recognition of each member's unique personality and potentialities. The members of these families do not perceive each other accurately because to do so would threaten the façade of reciprocity and mutuality. Accordingly, these families tend to be conservative, preventing members from diverging and growing. Consequently, the changing needs of family members are not adequately reflected in the structure of the family. In order to keep deviation out of awareness, the family as a unit has defenses, which may involve distortion of reality (e.g., projection) and often lead to cognitive and perceptual blurring. This extreme defensiveness and conservatism leads to an absence of humor and spontaneity.

In their effort to maintain their skewed sense of reality and conservative self-definition, these families cultivate an attitude of self-sufficiency, shunning outsiders and discouraging their members from forming external intimate relations. Wynne refers to this aspect of the schizophrenogenic family as the "rubber fence" because it is a shifting boundary that encompasses and excludes events as the demand arises. This rubber fence is maintained by a shared family myth of the catastrophic consequences of recognizing divergence—something which would doubtless occur if real access to outsiders existed. Such a family produces children who are fit to live only within the family and cannot succeed in the outside world.

Wynne summarized his early views as follows:

> . . . internalization includes the meanings a person finds attached to his position in the social structure of family and wider community. Also internalized are the ways of thinking and of deriving meaning, the points of anxiety and the irrationality, confusion and ambiguity that were expressed in the shared mechanisms of the family modal organization. The fragmentation of experience, the identity diffusion, the disturbed mode of perception and communication and certain other characteristics of the acute reactive schizophrenic's personality structure are to a significant extent derived, by processes of internalization, from characteristics of the family social organization [Wynne et al., 1958, p. 215].

Implicit in Wynne's theory is an assumption that humans strive for individuation. I think we must assume that if the family of the schizophrenic were not ambivalent in its demands, the child would simply remain at home. One would also expect the "well" sibling to be better able to form truly mutual relationships outside the home than was the schizophrenic sibling. Somehow, the rubber fence excluded the well sibling. The finding by Hoover and Franz (1972) and others that the well sibling moves away from home at an early age tends to corroborate this aspect of Wynne's theory.

The Middle Period: Transactional Thought Disorder: In his second period of research Wynne collaborated with Margaret Singer, an expert psychodiagnostician, in an effort to understand the "links between family patterns and the structural aspects of schizophrenic impairment, especially upon thought disorder" (Wynne & Singer, 1963, p. 191). Wynne and Singer saw their work as diverging from the earlier conceptions of Federn and other deficit theorists who assumed that an innate structural ego defect lay at the core of schizophrenia and hypothesized that this defect led to a thought disorder, although its specific content is environmentally determined. Workers of the late 1950s, including Lidz, focused on the attitudes of parents of schizophrenics, on the emotional climate and dynamics of the families, and hypothesized that schizophrenic thought disorder stems from familial patterns of interaction. However, transmission of the thought disorder was vaguely attributed to a process of internalization. Nor did early studies on families of schizophrenics differentiate and relate types of schizophrenia to different types of families. The hypotheses derived from these early exploratory studies required more systematic examination.

In 1957, NIMH began to use family sessions, involving all members of the schizophrenic's family, in their research. The entire family met twice a week with two therapists who focused on family transactions; these sessions were tape-recorded. In addition, all family members underwent individual psychological testing and were given two family projective tests. Comparison families with hospitalized, psychiatrically disturbed, nonschizophrenic children were similarly studied. In all, fifty families, approximately two-thirds of which had schizophrenic offspring, were studied intensively. In addition, psychological tests of eighty parents of child psychiatric patients were reviewed. "The constant feature [in these families] is the presence of a sick offspring, disturbed and disturbing" (Wynne & Singer, 1963, p. 194).

Observation of these schizophrenic and nonschizophrenic families led to a research focus on possible links between family transactions and types of thought disorder in the children. Wynne and Singer examined contrasting family styles of "focusing attention" and communicating. They found that "characteristically in the families of young schizophrenics, the degree of disturbance in family transactions is greater and qualitatively different from that found in the contribution of any individual family member. The fragmentation, disjunctive quality, and blurring of attention and meaning found in *sequences* of family transactions cannot be adequately described by mechanically adding up the degree of disturbance of individuals out of context" (1963, p. 194). Verbalizations that might appear normal to the casual observer are, in their family context, revealed to be part of a "transactional thought disorder" as severe as that found in the most disorganized schizophrenic. To illustrate:

> PATIENT: (complainingly) Nobody will listen to me. Everybody is trying to still me.
> MOTHER: Nobody wants to kill you.
> FATHER: If you're going to associate with intellectual people you're going to have to remember that still is a noun and not a verb [1963, p. 195].

After years of observing families, Wynne and Singer concluded that the parents' *styles of thinking* are more predictive of the type and degree of pathology in their offspring than are their individual pathologies. Also important for such prediction is the combination of parental styles. Wynne and Singer found that the interlocking parental styles can best be observed in family interviews and through standardized procedures such as family and individual Rorschachs. In general, they found that familial thought disorder becomes more apparent in less structured, anxiety-provoking situations than in fact-finding interviews, and is most striking when issues of separation or intimacy are discussed. Wynne and Singer's experimental work has borne out the often-cited clinical finding that blurring of meanings and loss of focus occur in sessions with schizophrenics' families.

Wynne and Singer also differentiated two subgroups of schizophrenia based on differences in the structural quality of the thought disorder, drawing on Heinz Werner's principle that development

> . . . proceeds from a state of relative globality and lack of differentiation to a state of increasing differentiation, articulation and hierarchic integration. . . . Differentiation and integration can be evaluated along a number of more specific developmental issues and are also highly pertinent to core formal disturbances in schizophrenic disorders:
> a. The capacity to differentiate self from non-self.
> b. The capacity to recognize and distinguish different kinds of feeling states, impulses and wishes.
> c. The delineation of distinctive, specialized skills—motor, cognitive, expressive and linguistic.
> d. The capacity to discriminate different parts of the object world, personal and nonpersonal, and to distinguish abstract and metaphorical representations from their literal and concrete counterparts [Wynne & Singer, 1963, p. 200].

Integration and hierarchical organization build on successful differentiation. Employing this theory, Wynne and Singer predict that more seriously impaired schizophrenics, whose cognitive style they describe as "amorphous," will show a profound disturbance in the capacity both to differentiate and to integrate information; less severely impaired schizophrenics, whose cognitive style they describe as "fragmented," will show primarily disturbances of integration in which their thoughts are intruded on by irrelevancies.

Wynne and Singer's efforts to validate the above hypotheses on transactional thought disorder included clinical diagnostic ratings made without knowledge of projective test data. Patients were ranked according to the quality (fragmented or amorphous) and degree of thought disorder. A predicting psychologist (Singer) 3,000 miles away, with no information about the patients and using only projective test protocols of family members, was able to predict the patients' diagnoses as well as the form and severity of thought disorder. In a related study (Singer & Wynne, 1965), Singer matched patients with their families of origin solely on the basis of projective tests. In both procedures, she achieved statistically significant results.

> Predictions about thinking disorders in patient-offspring from the tests of other members of the family were especially based on:
> 1. family patterns of dealing with attention and meaning
> 2. erratic and inappropriate kinds of interpersonal distance and closeness (usually seen in interaction with the examiner)
> 3. underlying feelings of pervasive meaninglessness, pointlessness and emptiness
> 4. psychologically encompassing, overall family structure which is confusingly organized around denial or misinterpretation of the reality of major, anxiety-provoking feelings and events [Singer & Wynne, 1965, p. 199].

Wynne and Singer believe that the structural, formal aspects of communication are relatively stable, related to character structure, and analogously intractable. Thus they are convinced that they have identified a trait that predates the hospitalization of the schizophrenic family member. They also believe their technique for studying thinking can be applied to other cultures.

The Last Period: High-Risk Research: In his most recent work, Wynne (1972a, 1972b) considers genetic and biochemical findings and tries to specify the intervening variables at work between genetic endowment and the recognized outbreak of schizophrenia. He cites Rosenthal's (1968) statement that, although genetics obviously contributes to the schizophrenia spectrum, not everyone with certain genes becomes schizophrenic. Etiological theories must also account for the time lag between birth and the development of the overt symptoms of schizophrenia in some genetically predisposed persons.

Wynne distinguishes two intervening variables: response disposition and environment. Response disposition is a very broad category that includes temperamental, psychophysiological, neurophysiological, and perceptual factors, which determine how a person receives, regulates, and modifies environmental and internal stimuli. Other relevant dimensions in those at risk for schizophrenia are individual differences in cognitive controls (field-dependence–independence, stimulus sensitivity, tendency to augment or reduce stimulation, scanning, perceptual leveling or sharpening, constriction or flexibility, and conceptual differentiation) and individual differences in psychophysiological arousal, sociability, and social responsiveness. Wynne hypothesizes that schizophrenics show extreme response patterns that are genetically determined (Wynne, 1972b).

Environmental variables such as specific psychological trauma and family environment and communication patterns, as well as precipitating factors, differentially affect people with differing response dispositions. Transactional patterns of intrafamilial communication may influence each child differently depending on his or her response disposition. In addition, the specific quality of parental thinking may be secondary to parental response tendencies. Wynne is currently investigating further the transactional nature of thought disorders and the communication patterns within clinical interviews. He is also involved in the high-risk studies described in the next chapter.

EXPERIMENTAL RESEARCH ON FAMILY THEORIES

Empirical studies of families of schizophrenics have suffered from diagnostic fuzziness, inadequacy of controls, and problems of motivation. They are also beset by a problem found in other psychological studies, namely, whether the experimental procedure affects the quality being measured and whether the procedure chosen is adequate to the task at hand. That is, if we attempt to study dominance in schizophrenics' families using a measure of verbal interruptions, we are making a number of assumptions about the nature of dominant behavior: for example, we are assuming correlations between verbal and nonverbal forms of dominance and between public and private activity; and we are assuming that dominance can be measured in terms of structural qualities without considering the specific content of the interruptions. In addition, experimental operational definitions of a quality such as dominance may not be equivalent to the theoretical definition of that quality.

Studies that rely on individual self-report are considerably influenced by the reporter's motivation and desire to present him/herself in a particular light. Observational studies of family interaction, on the other hand, are affected by the expectations and biases of the observer—there can be no "blind" observation when the schizophrenic is present—and, moreover, can never determine whether the behaviors observed are the cause or the effect of schizophrenia in one family member. The schizophrenic affects the family in several obvious ways: by requiring the attention of outsiders (professionals) and at times prolonged removal from the family; by subjecting the family to the curious stares of outsiders, requiring extra attention at home, often bringing the family in contact with the law (see Wilson [1968] for a firsthand account), and by subjecting family members to a barrage of primitive, frightening, and confusing utterances and actions. Some studies, seeking to control these factors, use control populations of families with children hospitalized for chronic physical illness or for nonschizophrenic psychiatric disturbances. However, one can still argue that the schizophrenic's distorted meanings have a profound impact on the rest of the family. Even trained professionals find the constant barrage of primary-process thinking draining and confusing, from which we can conclude that the effect of schizophrenic thinking on the family should not be underestimated.

Future family studies should utilize standardized diagnostic criteria and specify the length of hospitalization and the premorbid adjustment of each patient. In addition, researchers attempting to validate a specific theoretical postulate would be wise to contact the originator of that postulate to determine whether he or she considers the measures to be used appropriate.

It is beyond the scope of this review to discuss all the experimental literature on families of schizophrenics. Rather, I shall indicate the major forms that such research has taken.

Early family studies (1945–1960) were primarily descriptive, exploring the personality characteristics of family members and identifying the general patterns of familial interaction. They employed semistructured individual and family interviews aimed at eliciting patterns of child rearing, descriptions of child development, and personality characteristics of family members. Examples are the studies of Gerard and Siegel (1950), Caputo (1963), Laing and Esterson (1964/1970), Cheek (1965), Lidz, Fleck, and Cornelison (1965), and Alanen (1968, 1972).

Following the publication of the major family theories of schizophrenia, researchers set out to investigate more systematically the hypotheses and claims of Lidz, Wynne, Jackson, and others. Early studies focused on the parental dyad and tested Lidz's hypotheses regarding dominance, conflict, and sexual identification patterns in the parents of schizophrenics. Later studies included more family members, some comparing the interactions of families with their schizophrenic and nonschizophrenic children, others comparing families of schizophrenics with normal families and families of nonschizophrenic psychiatric patients, to determine whether patterns of communication differed. In addition to issues of dominance and submission, and conflict, researchers began to look at patterns of alliances and cognitive styles.

Studies of interaction patterns frequently devised conflict-laden experimental situations to study how family members attempt to resolve their differences. One such method is the Revealed Differences Test, which uses items from the WAIS, responses to a questionnaire on child-rearing attitudes, and/or responses to the Rorschach. After individual family members have privately responded to these items, they are brought together and asked to arrive collectively at a single response to items on which there was initial disagreement. The examiner is then able to analyze family interaction through observation of interruption patterns, the amount of time various members spend talking, whose responses win out, how often a new solution arises, and whether agreed-upon solutions are more or less adaptive and efficient than those arrived at individually. Another technique for analyzing communication patterns is simply to ask the family to plan an event together.

In *Family Processes and Schizophrenia,* Mishler and Waxler (1975) have collected several representative studies that have yielded contradictory findings. Structural qualities of interaction appear to be more enduring than specific content areas. To date, there is no convincing experimental evidence that schizophrenogenic families have more double binds than normals, or that the marital patterns of schism and skew sufficiently characterize these families to be considered etiologically significant in the development of schizophrenia. In addition, no consistent differences have been found between familial interaction patterns with schizophrenic offspring and with their "well" siblings.

THE WELL SIBLING

A major criticism of family theories of schizophrenia is that not all siblings in the family become schizophrenic. Even when heredity is the same and the environment is similar, as in the case of identical twins reared together, 20 to 70 percent of the pairs (depending on the study) are discordant for schizophrenia. Over the years, this finding has led to some very interesting research—the best examples of which are the NIMH twin studies conducted by Pollin, Stabenau, Mosher and Tupin from 1966 to 1974.

Early studies of sibling differences (Kempler & Brissen, 1962; Lidz, Fleck, & Cornelison, 1965; Prout & White, 1956), like early family research in general, used interviews and adjective checklists to describe the history and personality of the typical "well" and schizophrenic siblings. The aim of these studies was both to note the incidence of severe pathology in other siblings and to formulate hypotheses for future research on the nature of sibling differences.

Prout and White (1956) found that well and schizophrenic siblings did not differ in the incidence of childhood trauma, but they did differ in their reactions to these traumas. In general, the well siblings were able to use difficulties as opportunities for growth, whereas the preschizophrenics experienced these same difficulties as much more traumatic and were incapable of deriving anything positive from them. These findings are consistent with the later work on temperamental differences in children of Thomas, Chess, and Birch (1969), who found that slow-to-react and difficult children show more distress in novel and/or stressful situations throughout their lives, and with Wynne's recent work on the importance of response dispositions (1972b). Prout and White suggest that the temperament of the preschizophrenic may have elicited the often-noted overprotectiveness of the mother.

Using retrospective history, Pollack et al. (1966) report a greater incidence of pre- and postnatal complications, greater irritability in childhood, poorer school performance, and greater social isolation in the schizophrenics than in their well siblings.

Lidz, in his major work on schizophrenia (Lidz, Fleck, & Cornelison, 1965), suggests that male and female children require different "nutriments" for optimal growth. His division of schizophrenogenic families into those displaying marital schism—generating female schizophrenics—and those with marital skew—producing male schizophrenics—suggests a clear, testable hypothesis: same-sex siblings should show a greater incidence of pathology than opposite-sex siblings. Alanen (1968) and Lidz, Fleck, and Cornelison (1965) reported that this was the case, but Pollack et al. (1969), who found no such gender concordance in rate of schizophrenia, criticized the above studies for being nonstatistical and lacking clear diagnostic criteria.

Lidz suggested that the "choice" of the schizophrenic sibling may be determined by differences in the intrafamilial influences impinging on the siblings. He suggested (Lidz, Fleck, & Cornelison, 1965, p. 237) that the following critical factors need to be considered:

1. Changes in family circumstances and intrafamilial role relationships (across time)
2. The mother's varying capacity to provide nurturance during infancy
3. Different role allocations and assumptions of the children in the family dynamics
4. The ways in which parental personality and the configuration of their relationship lead children of one sex to be confronted by greater developmental problems
5. Idiosyncratic problems—e.g., fantasies about children before they were born
6. Influence of one sibling on the others

Lidz also claimed that most siblings of schizophrenics show severe psychopathology; only six of the twenty-four siblings he studied were considered "well." He noted two main defenses employed by the truly well sibling: constriction (including isolation of affect, repression, and denial) and flight. The well sibling was less involved in the parental fights of the schismatic family and received less attention in the skewed family. He or she was also able to leave home more easily than the schizophrenic sibling.

As we can see, research in the mid-1960s tested hypotheses put forth by major family theorists. In fact, Lidz's last finding, supported by Lu (1961) and Meissner (1970), corroborates Wynne's "rubber fence" hypothesis that the preschizophrenic is kept from intimate contact with the outside world. Actually, all theories of familial pathology implicitly suggest that the ability to seek and find outside relationships is critical, since it affords the child the opportunity to sample "normal," mutual, non-double-binding communication.

Day and Kwiatkowska (1962) as well as Lidz, Fleck, and Cornelison (1965) report a high incidence of severe pathology in siblings of schizophrenics. However, Day and Kwiatkowska's work is especially biased against the well sibling. They observe that the well sibling, in defending against both parental pathology and involvement in the schizophrenic sibling's hospitalization, is insensitive, impersonal, shallow, detached, and guarded. In addition, Day and Kwiatkowska attempt to prove, through structured and unstructured tasks, that the well sibling is in fact quite fragile and disturbed, falling apart on unstructured tasks and displaying an underlying psychotic core.

Hoover (1965; Hoover & Franz, 1972) criticizes Day and Kwiatkowska, Lidz, and Alanen, and stresses that the difference between schizophrenia and nonpsychotic pathology is not to be taken lightly. Hoover and Franz conclude their review of the literature by saying: "We are convinced family therapists, but unprepared to dispute the existence of schizophrenia as an individual reality, a phenomenon which can be present in one person and not in another, whatever role the family context may play" (1972, p. 335). They, like Meissner (1970) and Lu (1961), found that family entanglement is a critical discriminating variable. Well siblings tend to be less enmeshed in their families. Hoover, more than other researchers in this field (with the exception of Anthony, whose work will be discussed below), views well siblings as survivors and inquires into their specific survival strategies.

The concept of the well sibling as a survivor generates several questions that require further research:

> When does the well sibling first realize that the preschizophrenic sibling is in trouble?
>
> What, if anything, does the well sibling do about it?
>
> How does he or she feel about this?

What are his or her reactions to the sibling's hospitalization?

What form, if any, does the well sibling's sense of guilt assume?

What could mental health professionals be doing differently to help these well siblings? What should one expect in the transference-countertransference reactions of such patients?

TWIN STUDIES

Early work in sibling differences reflected a naïveté about genetic factors. Prout and White (1956) erroneously prided themselves on using siblings to control for hereditary factors, when in fact only workers using monozygotic twins can properly make this claim. In this regard, Mosher states: "In twin pairs, genetic, ethnic, and social class factors were identical and each twin experienced the impact of family crises at the same developmental stage— thus eliminating the investigative problem of weighing the age differential impact of such crises when ordinary siblings are compared" (1972, p. 61).

To date, the most thorough, controlled, and ambitious research project on twins to be completed is the study conducted at NIMH of twenty-four sets of identical twins, fifteen of which were discordant for schizophrenia (see below).

It has been my conviction throughout this inquiry that the truth about schizophrenia is interdisciplinary and that meaningful investigations must consequently be cross-disciplinary. Such projects are of necessity costly and limited in number. The NIMH twin research is testimony to the fruitfulness of such an approach. Over a period of eight years, in more than twelve articles, senior authors Mosher, Pollin, Stabeneau, and Tupin, with the help of many specialists, have published findings on all aspects of schizophrenic etiology.

Initially, they conducted a national search for families with identical twins discordant for schizophrenia. Those who met preliminary criteria were asked to undergo intensive observation for a two-week period in Bethesda. Those who were able to do so (of necessity a biased sample) were then subjected to strict tests of zygosity (see Pollin, Stabenau, & Tupin, 1965, for details). Diagnostic ratings of the identified patient and his or her siblings were based on strict criteria, applied to a mental status exam conducted by several research psychiatrists. In addition, hospital records were obtained and only those twins who had been previously labeled schizophrenic and unanimously diagnosed as schizophrenic by five psychiatrists were used as the patient population. In all, there were fifteen pairs of identical twins discordant for schizophrenia, three pairs of concordant twins, and four pairs of normal twins. Each twin and his or her family were interviewed intensively and given a standard battery of psychological tests, as well as the Minnesota Multiphasic Personality Inventory (MMPI), Embedded Figures, and various biochemical tests. The family members were interviewed conjointly and given family projective tests.

Although their study was reported in twelve separate articles, I shall summarize the conclusions across studies:

1. LIFE HISTORY DIFFERENCES

The preschizophrenic:
a. Frequently weighed less at birth
b. Became the focus of more parental worry, attention, and involvement
c. Developed slightly slower than the well sibling
d. Did less well and was perceived as less competent and weaker than the well sibling
e. Tended to be more docile, more compliant, and less independent than the well sibling

The rigid pattern [of perceived differences] appeared to derive in part from constitutional differences, and in part from rigidly "imprinted" role expectations, initiated at birth, determined by constitutional differences and subsequently reconfirmed by minor differences in development . . . It appears likely that there is a large measure of self-fulfilling prophecy in this role expectation [of weakness] [Pollin, Stabenau, & Tupin, 1965, p. 68].

Pollin et al. found that the preschizophrenic or vulnerable child had spent more time in the hospital, either because of low birthweight and prenatal complications or because of an early illness. Thus at the outset this twin was the legitimate focus of parental concern. Frequently the mother had had excessive death fears before the birth of her twins and became over cautious with the weaker twin. Pollin et al. hypothesized that this early training in dependency paved the way for later personality development.

Mosher, Pollin, and Stabenau (1971a) report that the vulnerable sibling, legitimately perceived as more fragile at birth, became identified with the more pathological, submissive parent (usually the mother), who characteristically evidenced a global, loose cognitive style. "It appeared that the negative side of the parent's self-image had a greater tendency to become projectively identified with the smaller twin than the larger twin" (Pollin, Stabenau, & Tupin, 1965, p. 74).

2. PRENATAL AND NEUROLOGICAL FINDINGS

a. Twelve out of fifteen index cases had lower birthweights than their well siblings.

b. Index cases had more signs of early physiological disequilibrium, e.g., anoxia, colic.

c. Because of birthweight and/or fetal position, circulation and/or crowding, one twin was born at a higher stage of physiological development than the other. Subsequent differences may be due directly to this physiological difference, or this difference may be an indication of some underlying process (see diathesis-stress theory), or it may set in motion differential patterns of parental identification (see above).

d. There were significantly more abnormal neurological signs in index twins than in co-twin controls.

e. Neurological signs were correlated with low birthweight and with later WAIS scores and indices of level of pathology.

f. Although phenothiazine usage was not controlled, there was no correlation between total phenothiazine intake and neurological signs (Mosher, 1972; Mosher, Pollin, & Stabenau, 1971b).

3. BIOCHEMICAL FINDINGS

Many previous reports of biochemical abnormalities were refuted:

a. S-19 macroglobulin level was related to sex rather than to schizophrenia. There were no significant differences between levels in schizophrenics and in their normal siblings.

b. Lactate/pyruvate (L/P) ratio was related to drug intake, rather than to the presence or absence of schizophrenia.

c. 3,4 DMPEA was found in both index and control twins and thus may be genetic, but it is not specific to or causal of schizophrenia.

d. In summary, no biochemical abnormalities are consistently associated with schizophrenia (Mosher, 1972).

This series of articles concluded that the primary feature that distinguishes the schizophrenic from his or her well sibling is the early pattern of parental projective identification based on the initially legitimate greater dependency of the index twin. The family of these twins was subsequently unable to alter its perceptions and role assignments, rigidly perpetuating the index twin's weaker and more dependent position, and thus leaving him or her vulnerable and unprepared for autonomous adult behavior. No significant biochemical differences were found. The finding of soft neurological differences does suggest some physiological difference in the schizophrenic, who was frequently clumsy as a child. However, neurological findings after the outbreak of schizophrenia may be secondary to the disease process.

The major criticism of these studies is that they remain retrospective, a problem avoided only by longitudinal high-risk studies (see Chapter 10).

<table>
<tr><td>

Social and Cultural Factors in the Etiology of Schizophrenia

</td><td>

Chapter Nine

</td></tr>
</table>

The sociology of schizophrenia is a relatively neglected area of study. The classic studies were conducted in the 1940s, 1950s, and early 1960s. In some ways psychologists' reactions to social and cultural explanations are as skeptical as their reactions to genetic and biochemical explanations. Traditionally, psychotherapists have been loath to believe that a given behavior is the consequence of social, cultural, or political realities. I think as a group we can be criticized for minimizing the influence of the body on the one hand and of society on the other. Both greatly influence one's experience, behavioral repertoires, and personality structure, even though one is not necessarily conscious of their impact.

The problems facing researchers interested in cultural and social factors are practically insurmountable. Just as experimental psychological research may seem soft to biochemists, so, too, does sociological research appear to psychologists. In epidemiological and sociological research, many compromises must be made regarding diagnostic and class indices, and the researcher must be resigned to the fact that many confounding variables cannot be controlled, eliminated, or measured. Such investigations are easy to criticize, but their combined weight points to interesting and important avenues of further research and possible intervention.

Social and cultural studies refer to incidence rates—that is, the rate of new cases of schizophrenia or mental illness within a given year—and prevalence rates—the number of people with schizophrenia or mental illness at a given time.

Although incidence rates are preferable, they are generally more difficult to ascertain than prevalence rates. Prevalence rates reflect the duration of illness which, as Hollingshead and Redlich (1958) have shown, is highly correlated with class. Upper-class neurotics receive treatment more often, and for longer periods of time, than lower-class neurotics, whereas the reverse holds, even more dramatically, for psychoses. Both incidence and prevalence rates are generally determined by the number of people receiving treatment in hospitals or other social agencies. This method of establishing incidence or prevalence rates is the most reliable one, although it does have its shortcomings. Social class and cultural factors affect one's willingness to enlist the help of outside social agencies; treated schizophrenics differ markedly from untreated schizophrenics (Srole et al. 1962). The alternative methods require the investigators themselves to check all members of the population sample for evidence of schizophrenia or mental illness. This technique, used in the Midtown Manhattan Study, (Srole et al., 1962), has the disadvantage of looser diagnostic indices—at least hospitalization is an objective indicator of serious debilitation. Diagnostic indices are more varied and less stringent in large-scale studies than in either laboratory research or standard psychiatric hospitalization. It is not possible to study the population of an entire county using a battery of tests and interviews that take several hours per person. Diagnosis based on self-report of specific symptoms can become biased, both by the respondent's willingness to report and by the symptoms chosen. For example, the Midtown Manhattan Study symptom inventory included many psychosomatic complaints. A later study by Crandell and Dohrenwend (1967) found that lower-class patients are more likely than upper-class patients to experience somatic complaints at the onset of psychotic symptoms. Lower-class patients are not as likely to discuss their difficulties in psychological terms as are upper-class patients.

Earlier in this book I referred to the universality of schizophrenia, a statement based on the International Pilot Study of Schizophrenia (IPSS) finding that, given standardized criteria for diagnosing schizophrenia, its rate is relatively constant throughout the world. Torrey (1973, 1979) is critical of this claim and offers several arguments against it. He points out that IPSS centers are located in cities, which represent the most Westernized and/or advanced parts of developing countries. People in these areas are likely to be undergoing stress owing to many significant changes in their way of life. It is more difficult to study people from rural areas in underdeveloped countries, and these people are less likely to be hospitalized if they are ill. Reports of serious mental illness or schizophrenia in underdeveloped "primitive groups" have been made, but only by anthropologists with little or no training in formal diagnosis. Diagnostic expertise is especially important in some parts of the tropics where several organic conditions can masquerade as schizophrenia. Torrey cites several prevalence studies that suggest a correlation between diagnosis and degree of European or Western influence. In the light of Torrey's review, one should perhaps be more skeptical about the universality of schizophrenia. However, one may certainly conclude that it exists in all developed and developing parts of the world. If it does not exist among some tribes in the interior of Brazil, Africa, or the Philipines the reason may be selective breeding, life style, diet, child-rearing practices, or life stresses.

SOCIAL FACTORS

The social variable most frequently and successfully studied is social class. Garmezy (1974a) notes that, aside from genetic studies, the most consistent finding in the literature on schizophrenia has been the correlation between class and rate of schizophrenia. Two major early studies posed the central problem: rates of first hospitalization for schizophrenia are highest in the inner cities, where low-status socioeconomic groups are concentrated, and diminish as one moves out to the periphery and high-status groups (Faris & Dunham, 1939); and rates for schizophrenia are highest for lowest-status occupations (Clark, 1948, 1949). Both findings have been frequently and consistently replicated (Hollingshead & Redlich, 1958, Kohn, 1968, 1973; Srole et al., 1962).

In his reviews of the literature, Kohn (1968, 1973) points out that these findings are significant only in large cities. The correlation between class and rate of schizophrenia diminishes in smaller cities, finally disappearing in rural areas. He found predictable patterns of distribution of schizophrenia for population centers of various sizes. Thus, rates of schizophrenia are distributed similarly by class in all cities of 500,000, whether they are in the United States or Europe, in a pattern that differs from that found in a town of 5,000.

The interpretation of these findings is subject to much dispute: What is the direction of causality? Do the conditions of lower-class life "cause" schizophrenia, or does schizophrenia lead to a reduction in status and social class? Before discussing this question, it is important to reiterate the methodological problems that consistently plague this form of research. Lower-class psychotics are more likely to be hospitalized, and if hospitalized, are diagnosed as schizophrenic more often than their upper-class counterparts. Srole et al.'s (1962) field investigation found that the people who seek treatment differ markedly from those who do not. Most research on incidence and prevalence rates is based on treatment by social agencies. Often only prevalence rates, which reflect the duration of illness and thus are greater for lower-class patients, are reported.

Despite these cautionary notes, research supporting class differences in prevalence of mental illness is too impressive to be ignored. Critics have argued that the schizophrenia-prone person drifts to the lower levels of society because of his or her cognitive and emotional deficits—class position then reflects the poor functioning of the preschizophrenic. Others, like Kohn, argue that this process might account for some, but not all, of the variance. This issue was researched by studying the social mobility of schizophrenics—what class they were born into and where they are at the time of illness (Goldberg & Morrison, 1963; Srole et al., 1962; Turner & Wagenfeld, 1967). In his review, Kohn was forced to conclude that the findings are inconsistent: some schizophrenics do suffer a loss in status, others remain the same, and some reach a higher level. Generally, he found that schizophrenics do not rise above their parents' level, although their peers do. Turner and Wagenfeld (1967) also reported that although there is a significantly higher percentage of patients from lower social classes, and also a higher percentage of patients whose fathers were lower class, these two groups do not coincide. Hollingshead and Redlich (1958) reported that 91 percent of the schizophrenic patients belonged to the same socioeconomic class as their parents. Where there was mobility, it was more likely in an upward direction. In fact, Myers and Roberts (1959) hypothesized that the stress of middle-class strivings and upward mobility contribute to severe mental illness among white-collar and skilled manual workers.

Researchers have been reluctant to suggest that class per se is pathogenic and have offered a variety of alternative hypotheses to explain the consistent finding of higher rates of schizophrenia among the lower classes. Some have argued that it is not class per se but rather social isolation and/or lack of social integration that is pathogenic. They point out that the lower classes often consist of minority groups living in neighborhoods where they are isolated or simply unintegrated into society. Thus, whites living in a predominantly black area of town have a higher rate of schizophrenia than blacks in that area or whites in other areas. First-generation immigrants generally have higher rates of schizophrenia than second and third generations; the higher rates may reflect the selective migration rates, the stresses of the new environment (e.g., isolation), or the specific conflicts between one's culture of origin and the culture of one's adopted land.

Clark (1948, 1949) reports that occupational status correlates with incidence of mental illness when corrected for age. However, despite his reassurances, it seems impossible to correct for age when one considers that schizophrenia generally appears in late adolescence and young adulthood. This timing limits educational and occupational advancement. It is highly unlikely that the preschizophrenic would achieve an occupational level that requires four or five years of postcollege training or experience before his or her first breakdown. Any who did would probably be diagnosed as reactive (good-premorbid) schizophrenics, or as suffering from affective psychotic reactions.

Ødegaard (1956) suggests the issue is not occupational status per se but whether one's occupation is shrinking or expanding. The question we must ask of all these hypotheses remains: What is pathogenic about social isolation or encroaching job obsolescence? Kohn (1973) argues that substantial evidence supports a class factor. He notes that class is related to how one is treated by others and to conditions at work; it reflects educational level, including style of thinking and perceiving; it influences social values, child-rearing practices, types of stress encountered, types of social services available, and one's sense of power or helplessness. Several research groups (Dohrenwend & Dohrenwend, 1969; Langner & Michael, 1963; Rogler & Hollingshead, 1965) have investigated the relationship between stress and class. They all report that the lower the class, the higher the stress. The Midtown Manhattan Study went further and looked at the three-way interacton of class, stress, and mental illness. Srole et al. (1962) found high correlations between level of stress and mental illness, between class and mental illness, and between class and stress. Stress alone was not a sufficient explanation, since, at all levels of stress, those in the lower classes were more likely to have mental illness.

Kohn points out that reward and opportunity are also differentially distributed according to class. Lower-class people have had fewer rewards and are less likely to have available alternative courses of action in times of stress. In addition, the educational and job opportunities of the lower classes are geared to a more concrete level of thinking, perhaps making these persons less adept at coping with abstraction and at handling ambiguity, unpredictability, and uncertainty. He suggests that lower-class patterns of childrearing, growing out of the constricted conditions of lower-class life, do not teach adequate coping methods for dealing flexibly and resourcefully with stress.

There are those who counter the above arguments by extending the drift hypothesis to include past generations. They argue that schizophrenia is the end product of several generations of poor adaptation, which leads to a drop in social class. According to this view, the schizophrenic has acquired inadequate coping skills from his inadequate, possibly schizophrenia-spectrum downwardly mobile parents, who are overconcrete and have a poor grasp of reality. In this view, social class is a by-product of generations of inadequate functioning.

CULTURAL FACTORS

Incidence, prevalence, and symptoms of schizophrenia have been studied in Asia, West Africa, Europe, and North America. Murphy (1978) notes that cultural factors are generally the last to be considered and gain credibility only after genetic loading, social selection by migration, stress of social change, adverse effects of low or minority status, and comparative diagnostic criteria have failed to account for significant differences in rates of schizophrenia in two or more populations.

Culture "consists of the values, beliefs, and patterns of behavior which a society teaches to its members with a view to equipping them better for the task of life" (Murphy, 1968, p. 137); it is somewhat analogous to the habits taught by the family. Culture grows out of specific life conditions and should gradually shift as these conditions change. Murphy hypothesizes that when a specific culture does not meet the real conditions of life—because times have changed or the person has migrated from one culture to another—the particular set of cultural beliefs may become pathogenic, or at least stressful. In addition, some cultures may be intrinsically more conducive to a specific form of mental illness than others. He describes three populations in which exceptionally high rates of schizophrenia appear to be related to cultural factors.

A study (Kadri, 1963; Murphy, 1959) was conducted at Singapore University, where all students' absences are reported, medical care is free, and doctor's certificates are required following any absences. Thus it was possible to keep track of students' serious mental problems. Indian students and Indians in the general population of Singapore had a significantly higher rate of schizophrenia than the Chinese students and residents of Singapore. Contrary to most social-class findings, the incidence was highest among upper-class Indians, the Tamils, who also had a higher-than-average incidence of schizophrenia in the Indian Army. Murphy hypothesized that the culture of the Tamils was especially maladaptive in situations in which they were accountable to an authority.

The second study Murphy cites (Crocetti, et al., 1964) is of the people of northwest Croatia, the most Westernized, autonomous region of Yugoslavia. This group's rate of rejection from the military because of schizophrenia is double that of the general population.

The impact of culture on incidence, prevalence, and symptoms of schizophrenia has been most thoroughly studied in relation to Irish Catholics. Since 1880, it has been noted (Malzberg, 1940; O'Doherty, 1965; Pollack, 1913, 1928; Spitzka, 1880; Swift, 1913) that Irish Catholics have significantly higher rates of chronic schizophrenia and new admissions for mental illness than do other immigrant groups, even after controlling for alcoholism. In Ireland, there are twice as many patients in mental hospitals as in England and Wales. The occupancy rate is double and the admission rate is double. Diagnostic criteria are similar since the psychiatrists have had similar training. The rate of schizophrenia among Irish Catholics in Canada is also higher than average, regardless of the length of time they have been in that country (e.g., second and third generations), whereas Irish Protestants have the lowest rate of schizophrenia in Canada.

Murphy reports that these findings cannot be explained by social selection for migration, by the stresses of immigration, by diagnostic criteria, or by genetic selection. If anything, the trend toward late marriage in Ireland decreases the likelihood that adult schizophrenics will marry and bear children. All things being equal, there should be a lower-than-average rate of schizophrenia in successive generations as a consequence of late marriages. Murphy asks whether cultural differences might explain this high rate of schizophrenia, especially among Catholic males. He suggests that Catholic values pose more conflicts than do Protestant values for men growing up in highly developed countries such as Canada. Catholism offers the priest as an important adult role model that excludes marriage and sexuality. Catholicism stresses communality, obedience, and the intangibles in life, whereas Protestantism stresses independence, private problem solving, working at one's calling, and, basically, the desirability of material acquisition. The Protestant ethic, as Weber noted, upholds the spirit of capitalism.

Murphy speculates that the elevated rate of schizophrenia among Catholics in Southern Ireland, especially in rural areas (again, counter to the general trend toward higher rates in urban areas) may arise from their specific culture. Ireland has been called the land of double-talk and doublethink. He hypothesizes that the genetically vulnerable person is severely stressed by the strange brand of sarcasm, punning, and ridicule endemic in Irish culture. He suggests that those in rural communities suffer more because of the unavailability of modifying influences and the inescapability of the stressful environment—an environment that shares much of the schizophrenic family's mystification processes described by Laing (1965b).

Murphy also discusses the increasing rates of schizophrenia among women in certain parts of Canada where traditional values of motherhood have come into sharp conflict with the values of education and independence. His point is that when one is reared and "programmed" to expect a certain way of life, and is later programmed in the opposite direction, one is caught in a deep-seated identity conflict. A person caught in such a conflict, lacking traditions integral to current life demands, lives under unusually great stress and requires very flexible, sophisticated coping strategies. Such a person is thus more likely to have serious mental problems. Kohn (1973) notes that while the poor of this country are told that this is the land of equal opportunity and honest pay for an honest day's work, they remain immersed in the culture of poverty where, owing to lack of jobs, the main way up is through crime.

Both Murphy (1978) and Katz et al. (1978) cite examples of cultural influence on symptoms. The Indians in Singapore presented a more hysterical picture; the Chinese seemed more schizoid. In Hawaii, Katz studied Japanese and Filipino paranoid schizophrenics, all from the same hospital and meeting the same diagnostic criteria. The Japanese seemed more suspicious and withdrawn, the Filipinos more manic and aggressive. Their respective communities, although recognizing signs of serious illness, viewed them differently than did the mental health professionals. The Filipino schizophrenics were seen as helpless, and the Japanese schizophrenics as overexpressive. Katz et al. suggest that the behaviors reflected cultural differences that were somewhat misunderstood by the professionals, who were themselves from a different culture. They hypothesize that schizophrenics tend to enact the negative side of the cultural coin during psychotic episodes; that is, they act out the forbidden, repressed wishes of that culture.

PROGRESS AND COURSE OF SCHIZOPHRENIA

For the most part, studies of outcome find that a third of first-admission schizophrenics are cured, a third have an intermittent course, and a third deteriorate. However, an interesting, unexpected finding has emerged from the International Pilot Study of Schizophrenia (Sartorius, Jablensky, & Shapiro, 1978): the course of illness is less grim and the prognosis better in underdeveloped countries than in developed countries. Although the reasons for this cannot be stated with certainty, it appears that cultural attitudes toward schizophrenia can influence course and prognosis. In cultures where schizophrenia is thought to be caused by an external agent—one outside the individual's control, a spirit that can also leave—the course is either brief or more intermittent than in cultures that view schizophrenia as a deteriorating, degenerative illness. Cultures that see schizophrenia as the product of a person's life style, subject to his or her own actions, often increase the likelihood of a deteriorating course as the person struggles to understand what he or she has done (Murphy, 1978). Life in a traditional society may be more structured, more predictable, and less stressful than a modernized existence, especially for those struggling with attentional or perceptual deficits and emotional and social isolation. At an international symposium on the diagnosis and treatment of schizophrenia throughout the world (held in 1974, sponsored by the Joint Committee on Schizophrenia, New York State District Branches, American Psychiatric Association), some relevant impressions were reported. In some parts of Africa, psychiatrists have enlisted cultural beliefs that schizophrenia in a tribe member is a sign that something is wrong with the community. The afflicted person is not ostracized but taken care of—this person is the messenger of the gods and thus is not at fault. Great care is taken by these societies in following the doctors' suggestions about medication and follow-up appointments. Kety (1976) reported an unusually low proportion of hospitalized schizophrenics in the People's Republic of China. Schizophrenics were briefly treated with a combination of Western medication and Maoist teachings and then discharged to communes where they worked in the fields in a structure not unlike a sheltered workshop or halfway house. A similar situation was observed in Cuba (S. Donaldson, 1977, personal communication).

Although no definitive conclusions can be drawn from these studies, they do point in a positive direction. Society cannot make up for schizophrenogenic families or faulty genes, but it can recognize the role society plays in making some of our members more seriously disturbed than others. If we face this fact, we can make progress toward preventing some cases and improving the prognosis of others.

High-Risk Studies	Chapter Ten

Almost all of the studies discussed so far in this book (and most research conducted before 1962, regardless of discipline) were retrospective and/or postdictive in nature. As Mednick, Schulsinger, and Schulsinger (1975) note, one reason for the difficulties in understanding the causes of schizophrenia is that we are always looking after the fact and thus are unable to separate cause from consequence. In a similar vein, Garmezy (1974a) notes that there have been two approaches to research on schizophrenia: structural and dynamic. We have made great strides in understanding the structure of schizophrenia—the symptoms and correlates of the schizophrenic state. We are much less certain about its dynamics—the course and development of schizophrenia. As noted in Chapter 8, descriptions of family interaction are based on observations made after the appearance of schizophrenia in one family member. As Anthony (1970) pointed out, families develop unusual behaviors around any chronic illness in a family member, and thus post facto observations yield no causal data. Zubin and Spring (1977) have emphasized that current neurological and biochemical findings may be state-dependent; such findings can usefully augment our knowledge of the schizophrenic moment, but they cannot significantly expand our understanding of etiology. Comprehensive longitudinal studies of biochemical, neurophysiological, behavioral, and communicational factors in persons before and during a schizophrenic episode are necessary to correct our ignorance.

Longitudinal follow-up on remitted schizophrenics and psychophysiological and biochemical testing of their relatives (as reported in Chapter 6) have made some contributions toward isolating enduring traits of pre- and postschizophrenics as distinct from state-dependent variables. By far the most promising and thoroughgoing efforts in this direction are the high-risk studies, which provide long-term follow-up of populations at risk for schizophrenia. The goal of high-risk research is to identify the biochemical, neurophysiological, psychological, and behavioral characteristics that distinguish the preschizophrenic child. This research strategy was developed by Mednick (Mednick & Schulsinger, 1965, 1968) and has since been adopted, with some modifications, by many researchers in the field. Most of the research is still in progress, but some tentative results are available. Garmezy (1974a, 1974b) has extensively reviewed high-risk research as well as summarizing earlier follow-back and follow-up studies. More recent reports can be found in Wynne, Cromwell, and Matthysse (1978), Garmezy (1978a, 1978b), Rieder (1980), and Erlenmeyer-Kimling, Cornblatt, and Fleiss (1979).

Garmezy (1974a) defines a child at risk "if there is a greater likelihood that he will develop a mental disorder than a randomly selected child from the same community" (p. 17). Two questions follow: (1) Who are the predisposed children? (2) What determines this predisposition? Most high-risk studies consider children with one or more schizophrenic parents as their population at risk. Ten percent of all children with one schizophrenic parent later develop schizophrenia. A problem with these studies is that the vast majority of schizophrenic adults did not have schizophrenic parents. Another difficulty with these studies is controlling for assortative mating—the other parent. In fact, only 10 to 20 percent of schizophrenics have schizophrenic parents.

Most high-risk studies are of children with one schizophrenic parent, usually the mother. Often the fathers of children at risk are either unknown or have not been diagnosed as part of the initial research strategy. This fact can confound the data significantly by raising the possibility that the child's pathology is a result of unknown inheritance from the father as well as inheritance from the mother. Kirkegaard-Sorenson and Mednick (1975) found that schizophrenic women tended to mate more frequently with sociopathic men than did women in the general population. This finding might account for the higher incidence of sociopathy among children at risk, an incidence previously thought to be related to the mother's schizophrenia (Heston, 1966). The presence of schizophrenia-spectrum disorders in fathers of children at risk may increase the genetic risk for schizophrenia in children. At present only Erlenmeyer-Kimling (1968, 1975) is studying children of dual schizophrenic matings. These children are doubly at risk; their morbidity rates are about 39 percent. This research strategy has the advantage of increasing the number of children in the risk group who will eventually develop schizophrenia. It also eliminates the problem of the father's diagnosis and its influence on children's outcome. However, these children of two schizophrenic parents, from an intact family, are atypical in that the family is intact (Robbins, 1966) and in the degree of environmental pathology to which they are exposed. Noteworthy in this regard is Mednick et al.'s (1978) finding that correlates of risk differ for male and female children. For males, a critical factor is the absence of a father. Absence of a father correlated with social class, and Rieder (1980) suggests that this fact might account for some of the difference in incidence rates in different social classes.

Another research strategy has been to consider at risk those children who have been referred to child guidance centers. The problem in these studies is that the early development of these children has already escaped the examination of researchers. Furthermore, children are generally referred to agencies for antisocial behavior. The more withdrawn, seemingly well-behaved, but equally disturbed child may escape attention.

Goldstein et al. (1978) did a follow-up study of adolescents seen at a clinic, looking at type of adolescent pathology and style of familial communication (see Wynne, Singer, & Bartko, 1975). They found that the adolescents who became schizophrenic had been actively hostile to their parents and were internally distressed but not delinquent; that they came from families with communication deviance; and that children from families without communication deviance clinically improved over time.

This study is useful in suggesting what the preschizophrenic male looks like as an adolescent, but it offers no primary etiological clues. It is suggestive of a useful preventive measure—namely, improving familial communication patterns or perhaps providing something along the lines of Anthony's (1974a, 1974b) proposed interventions.

After a population at risk is selected, several other issues must be resolved. A major problem in longitudinal research is the choice of measures that, it is hoped, will remain relevant twenty years after the inception of the research project. In addition, although behavioral measures must vary at different stages of development, they should be equivalent. Because motivation is also a factor, researchers must frequently compromise their desire for comprehensive information in order to get willing subjects. A final factor worth mentioning is the effect of social mobility on these studies. The Scandinavian countries have proved to be most suitable for longitudinal research because of the relative stability of their populations and the comprehensiveness of their records.

The criteria for inclusion in studies of this sort can significantly influence the results. For example, Erlenmeyer-Kimling (1975) uses only intact families, whereas Mednick (1978) does not. Garmezy (1978a) suggests that their findings differ because schizophrenics from intact families are less disturbed than those from broken families, whereas Erlenmeyer-Kimling thinks that their differences are a function of the age of the children, the severity of parental disorders, and situational variants (Garmezy, 1978a). If selection criteria favor one subgroup over another, assortative mating can influence one's results in unanticipated ways. For example, schizophrenic women frequently marry psychopathic men, who, according Mednick (1978), show distinctive neurological patterns that may affect those of the children. Children reared by schizophrenic parents have experienced different traumas from those reared away from such parents.

All of the above-mentioned factors can account for some of the discrepancies in the literature and make identification of causal factors difficult. Among children with one schizophrenic parent, only 10 percent will develop schizophrenia. Group data may therefore be confusing, and it is only after some of the cohort begin to "break down" that researchers can look for individual patterns that differentiate those who were *truly,* genetically, "at risk." Even then a major obstacle exists. As we know from the 50 percent of MZ twins who are discordant for schizophrenia, not all people with the schizophrenia genotype develop schizophrenia. Some are what Anthony calls invulnerable. The high-risk researchers will be including, in the 90 percent of high-risk children who do not develop schizophrenia, some who have the genes but do not manifest schizophrenia. In addition, if schizophrenia is indeed a heterogeneous syndrome, there may be no common manifestation of the predisposition to the disorder (Rieder, 1980). Thus searches for significant antecedents of schizophrenia would be doomed to failure.

Another problem in this literature is the ambiguity of terms because of their different usage by several key writers. For example, Zubin and Spring (1977) uses the term "vulnerability" as a second-order term that includes genetic and environmental factors. Anthony (1974a) means something similar by the term "total risk," and uses "vulnerability" to indicate a more specific attribute. Garmezy (1974b, 1974c, 1975) speaks of "competent" and "incompetent" children at risk. And more concretely, various investigators use different measures for studying similar attributes (Rieder, 1980), again making comparisons across studies difficult.

A relatively consistent finding in high-risk research is the higher incidence of low birth weights in the histories of schizophrenics (Pollin & Stabeneau, 1968). Less consistent have been the findings of increased incidence of pregnancy and birth complications (PBCs) in their histories (Mednick, 1970; Mednick & Schulsinger, 1968; McNeil & Kaij, 1978). However, the meaning of these findings, the direction of causality, is unclear. Sameroff and Zax (1973) found that women with the most psychiatric contacts and hospitalizations had the highest incidence of perinatal complications, regardless of diagnostic group. Low birth weight but not PBCs may be secondary to a genetic diathesis which leads to an early developmental disturbance (Rieder, 1980), whereas a high incidence of PBCs may be due to poor general health and prenatal care secondary to the mother's disturbance. McDonald (1968) suggests that PBCs could be secondary to anxiety and emotional upset during pregnancy. He hypothesized that the biochemical effect of the mother's anxiety disturbs the fetus throughout the pregnancy. In addition, during childbirth the mother's anxiety translates into increased muscle tension, which increases the duration of labor and the difficulties associated with delivery. And finally, the mother's anxiety level affects her relationship with her obstetrician and the kind of care she receives.

Thus not only genetic heritage but also the mother's nutritional and emotional state during pregnancy, the fetus's attachment and position in utero, and the birth process and its complications contribute to the infant's health at birth. This is in keeping with Pasamanick and Knobloch's (1961) idea of reproductive casualty.

Infants with low birth weight and more PBCs are more likely to experience physiological disequilibrium, as indicated by respiratory, sleep, and digestive difficulties (Pollin & Stabeneau, 1968). These difficult infants pose special problems for parents and elicit special feelings and behaviors. McNeil and Kaij (1978) conclude their review of conflicting reports on the presence of PBCs in those at risk for schizophrenia by saying that PBCs do increase an individual's risk for becoming schizophrenic and should be taken seriously. Sameroff and Zax (1978) propose a transactional model of risk for schizophrenia involving genetic factors in the infant, PBCs, and deviant mothering practices. In their project they found that the psychiatrically disturbed mother's interaction with her infant differed from that of control mothers and perhaps was responsible for differences in infant behavior observable by the age of four months. A given infant's vulnerability can be accentuated by its mother's deviant child-rearing practices. Sameroff and Zax found that while offspring of schizophrenics are not happy, tending to be more fearful, sad, sickly, retarded, and more socially maladjusted than the norm, this characteristic does not distinguish them from children of other psychiatrically disturbed mothers nor from normal children of low socioeconomic classes.

A possible consequence of PBCs and/or low birth weight is the infant's state of distress, disequilibrium, and neurological immaturity. This leads us to a second important finding in high-risk studies—early differences in response tendencies and neurological patterns of behavior. Reports on these specific differences are somewhat contradictory. I shall review several major studies.

Fish was a pioneer in the longitudinal study of children of schizophrenics. She began working with infants of schizophrenics in 1952 and has followed them through adolescence (1957, 1959, 1971, 1976, 1977). Starting when she did, her research strategy is not as sophisticated as that of later investigators. She used a small sample of twelve children of schizophrenics. At a ten-year follow-up, she found ten of the twelve index cases to be psychiatrically distrubed—an unusually high rate of pathology—including two childhood schizophrenics. This project focused on measures of developmental irregularities. She found that the two schizophrenic children showed a major disorganization of neurological maturation involving postural-motor, visual-motor, and physical development as early as the first month of life (1977, p. 1303). Despite what she calls "pandevelopmental retardation," she found a low rate of PBCs (as opposed to Mednick, 1978). However, her records of pregnancy and delivery were not complete. In addition to this early biological disorder, the two index cases who became most disturbed also had the most impoverished environments.

The classic work in this field is Mednick's (Mednick & Schulsinger, 1968; Mednick, Schulsinger, & Schulsinger, 1975), begun in 1962. He studied 207 "normal" children with chronically ill schizophrenic mothers and 104 matched controls. The average age of the children was 15.1 at the start of the study, and they have been followed up to the present. The age of these subjects poses several drawbacks that Mednick and others have attempted to avoid in subsequent work. This age was specifically chosen, however, to insure that the group would pass through the risk period for schizophrenia during the investigator's life span. Mednick's assumption was that, of the roughly 200 children of schizophrenics, 30 would become schizophrenic, another 70 would have serious disturbances, and 100 would be normal—at high risk, but well. Pairs of high-risk (HR) subjects were matched for age, sex, father's occupation, rural/urban residence, years of education, and institutional upbringing versus family life. A low-risk (LR) subject was matched on each variable and selected for each HR pair. This initial division of HR subjects into two groups is somewhat abstract; a true matching within the HR groups cannot take place until after the first wave of breakdowns. The LR group had been screened to ensure that they, their parents and their grandparents were free from mental illness. An artifact of this design was that many of the LR children in institutions had criminal fathers. This led to an accidental matching of LR and HR groups for criminality, since schizophrenic mothers often marry psychopathic men.

Mednick's group collected the following details on each child (see Mednick, 1970):

1. Physiological conditioning and extinction testing, continuous recording of heart rate, muscle tension, respiration, and galvanic skin response (GSR) during rest, conditioning, generalization, and extinction
2. Wechsler Intelligence Scale for Children (WISC)
3. A personality inventory based on the Minnesota Multiphasic Personality Inventory (MMPI)
4. Word Association Test
5. Continuous Association Test
6. Adjective checklist—used by professional staff to describe the subject, who also rated him/herself
7. Psychiatric interview for diagnostic purposes and to rate level of adjustment

8. Parent interview
9. School report
10. Midwife report

By 1970, Mednick could report on the first twenty high-risk subjects to exhibit serious mental illness. These "sick" high-risk subjects were compared both with a matched group of well high-risk subjects who had had an equal level of adjustment in 1962, but had since improved, and with a matched group of low-risk subjects. In comparison to the well high-risk group, the sick group had lost their schizophrenic mothers to psychiatric hospitalization earlier, and their mothers had been more severely disturbed (this might constitute either a genetic or an environmental factor affecting the sick high-risk group's development). Members of the sick group were reported by teachers to be more disruptive—quicker to anger and slower to calm down. On the continuous association test, the sick group showed two distinctive patterns: (1) extreme loosening of associations and (2) severe blocking. On electrophysiological measures, the latency of GSR was significantly faster for the sick group, and it did not show any signs of habituation. In fact, the "latencies of the sick group progressively decreased [over a series of trials], suggesting a negative habituation, or even increasing irritability" (Mednick, 1970, p. 55). The sick group also showed great resistance to extinction and unusually fast recovery rates. Seventy percent of the sick group had suffered one or more PBCs, compared with 15 percent of the well high-risk group. This finding, however, has been criticized by McNeil and Kaij (1978) in their review of the PBC literature. Mednick hypothesized that PBCs trigger a genetically predisposed anomaly; he further proposed that the specific problem arose from hippocampal damage secondary to fetal anoxia (See Chapter 5, this book).

Mednick finds support in this data for his conception of schizophrenia as a learned evasion of life. He interprets the psychophysiological data to mean that the sick high-risk children have an aptitude for learning avoidance responses which, in combination with a noxious environment, can lead to schizophrenia.

Mednick has described the twofold aim of high-risk research, which seeks first "to elucidate patterns of premorbid variables which distinguish the high-risk individuals who later become schizophrenic. Such a pattern must then be tested in an unselected population for its predictive value" (Mednick & Witkin-Lamoil, 1977, pp. 153–154). This second stage is addressed in the Mauritius Project (Mednick, Schulsinger, & Schulsinger, 1975; Mednick & Witkins-Lamoil, 1977). Mauritius is a small island nation with one psychiatric hospital. The chief psychiatrist there requested that the World Health Organization (WHO) initiate a mental health research project—and it was there that Mednick's group screened the entire population of three-year-old

(1,800) children. The assessment consisted of: "(1) Parent interview; (2) social behavior in a laboratory observation; (3) psychological and cognitive assessment; (4) psychophysiology tests (skin conductance, skin potential and EKG); (5) obstetric information; (6) pediatric exam; and (7) an EEG exam for part of the sample" (Mednick & Witkin-Lamoil, 1977, p. 161).

Mednick hopes to find long- and short-term behavioral correlates of psychophysiological measures. He also hopes to assess the impact of various strategies of intervention. Two hundred children were selected from the initial sample for more intensive study. Half of these children were in special nursery schools, and half remained in the community. Both the nursery school and community control groups contained 54 children with extremely fast recovery rates, 32 children with average recovery rates, and 14 who were nonrespondents. In all, three-fourths of each group showed deviant psychophysiological responses. Children with fast autonomic nervous systems (ANS) recoveries cried more during testing and showed more fear and anxiety; they were also more aggressive and disruptive in the nursery school. Ratings were made of the children's school behavior: at least once a year the investigators returned to assess the children's development. Present reports (Mednick & Witkin-Lamoil, 1977) indicate that the children in nursery schools have become more spontaneous and less fearful in their interactions with others, and their parents describe them as happier at home. Mednick hopes in the future to determine not only which children develop difficulties but whether the nursery school experience was a useful preventive measure. If it was, the specific preventive factor could be one of several: the separation from home, the impact of the school, the diet in school, the effect of being with similar children, or the effect of being selected for special attention. Mednick is also considering specific biofeedback techniques to alter ANS responsiveness and possibly break the cycle of avoidance learning.

Erlenmeyer-Kimling (1968, 1975; Erlenmeyer-Kimling & Cornblatt, 1978) is studying children of schizophrenic mothers, schizophrenic fathers, and dual schizophrenic matings. Using intact families, she has collected data on 205 children aged seven to twelve. Her study focuses on neurological, psychophysical, attentional, and distractibility measures. She hypothesizes that preschizophrenics have a defective filter (see discussion of Broadbent in Chapter 6), and she is looking for age-specific vulnerability. She reports that children of schizophrenics show greater developmental lag (as measured on the Bender Gestalt test and on a test of motor development), although neurological examinations failed to differentiate them from normals. Her data do not support Mednick's (Mednick & Schulsinger, 1968; Mednick, Schulsinger, & Schulsinger, 1975) findings of faster ANS recovery in children at risk. As described above, selection criteria may account for this difference.

A very different approach to high-risk research is best illustrated by the

St. Louis project, headed by Anthony. Anthony (1968, 1971a, 1974a, 1974b, 1977) is attempting to prevent schizophrenia in children at risk with a combined program of cognitive training and emotional support. This approach derives from his earlier theoretical work (Anthony, 1970, 1971b) on the nature of vulnerability.

Anthony distinguishes between risk and vulnerability and observes:

> Two children from the same stock, the same womb, the same propitious or unpropitious environment, may end up quite differently with one falling psychologically ill and the other apparently blossoming. . . . By what mysterious process of psychological selection is the one destroyed and the other preserved? . . . [Anthony suggests that the vulnerability is related to the degree of] harmony between internal and external environments and to a capacity to accommodate flexibly to change . . . to the capacity to cope and to master . . . and to competence. . . . Competence is the ability to construct an internal representation of an external event, that is, the capacity to conceptualize and order the manifold incoming data so that they become sufficiently meaningful for the individual to act upon [1974a, pp. 533–536].

Anthony concludes that while risk is a function of the actual physical and psychological environment, vulnerability is a state of mind induced by exposure to risks. He found that children of schizophrenics who did not become schizophrenic showed a curiosity about their parent's illness and had been aided in an objective appraisal of the illness by the "well" parent, who also fostered autonomous behavior. It is this "gift" of the well parent that Anthony hopes to provide in his preventive groups for children psychologically at risk.

Anthony investigated 193 children at risk for schizophrenic or manic-depressive illness. At the start of his project, 30 percent of the children seemed normally adjusted, 30 percent showed minor adjustment problems, and 40 percent showed significant maladjustment. He found an inverse relationship between severity of disorder in the child and malignancy of the disorder in the parent. Schizoaffective and pseudoneurotic types of schizophrenia in parents produced the most immediately debilitating effect, and the younger the child, the more noxious the relationship. The child suffered more if he or she was involved in the parent's psychotic symptoms. Anthony concluded that, for high-risk subjects, environmental aspects of psychosis influence maladjustment during childhood, whereas genetic factors exert their influence later on. He found that separating the child from the reactively ill parent immediately improved the child's condition. However, "antecedent disturbances," such as micropsychotic episodes in children of parents with chronic psychoses, continued to increase in intensity and frequency regardless of separation from the ill parent.

In his research, Anthony (1977) further differentiates children at risk by rating them along four dimensions:

1. *Risk:* those factors external to the child that affect his or her psychological organization. They include genetic, prenatal, constitutional-developmental, and traumatic events, as well as physical environment.
2. *Vulnerability:* the child's disposition to psychosis. He studies this from two vantage points: (a) psychiatric evaluation to assess suggestibility, submissiveness, and involvement or identification with the psychotic parent; and (b) psychological evaluation by a battery of tests to determine current pathology.
3. *Competence:* the child's capacity to master difficulties, solve problems, and overcome obstacles. This is seen in terms of school performance, social skills, and ability to represent what is happening within the home.
4. *Maladjustment:* the child's current problems.

Anthony (1977) then predicts outcomes, which he tries to alter through various forms of intervention. Specifically, he offers four types of intervention:

1. *Compensatory:* aimed at building the ego, strengthening self-confidence, and offering benevolent figures and organizations to interact with.
2. *Classical:* individual and group psychotherapy.
3. *Cathartic:* aimed at eliciting feelings during acute and relapsing phases of parent's illness. This he found especially helpful within the family group.
4. *Corrective:* aimed at improving specific predisposing cognitive deficits; for example, self/nonself discrimination and reality testing.

He found that when the quality of therapy was constant, there was a significant correlation between the quantity of treatment and the amount of change in vulnerability and maladjustment. When quantity was held constant, classical interventions were most effective, followed by corrective measures. There was more change in the most disturbed children on all measures; there were no gender-based differences.

These findings fail to offer hope of efficient, inexpensive interventions with children at risk, but they do suggest that interventions can be effective at least in the short run. We must await future data to ascertain whether these children are able to overcome their genetic risk status by showing a significantly lower incidence of schizophrenia than those in nonintervening high-risk studies.

I have described two high-risk studies in some detail to give a feeling for this work. At present, several major projects are following children at risk. Many, like the Mauritius project, start with children at an early age. Some (e.g., Garmezy and Anthony) focus on determining which factors enable those at risk to survive without the disorder; others aim at identifying predisposing factors. These studies are still in their infancy. Not enough time has yet elapsed for most index cases to pass the age of risk for schizophrenia. Clearly high-risk studies are the path for the future with, it is hoped, increased attention to identification of subgroups at risk through biochemical markers, e.g., low MAO (Buchsbaum et al., 1978; Meltzer, 1979; Wyatt & Murphy, 1976) or neurophysiological indicators (Bellak, 1979; Bellak & Charles, 1979; Mednick, Schulsinger, & Schulsinger, 1975; Spring & Zubin, 1977).

General Organizing Principle, Integration, and Treatment Implications

PART 3

3

| A General Organizing Principle Based on an Integrative Theory of Development | Chapter Eleven |

Most researchers in this field have worked only within a specific discipline; there is an increasing need for an integrative, unifying theory of schizophrenia. Zubin and Spring (1977) have made such an attempt in their work on "vulnerability." Corbett (1976) has noted the need for a unified theory. I am attempting to formulate an integrated theory of emotional and cognitive development that bridges the gaps between the hard and the soft sciences and between the individual or family and the larger social context.

I believe that efforts to integrate what is known about schizophrenia into a "metatheory" will lead to a new, more textured conception of normal and pathological development. What follows is a beginning in this direction. But first an apologetic note of caution. There is a danger in applying models from other fields of science (e.g., physical, mechanistic, linguistic, or information-processing) to the study of human behavior. At present I have found it necessary to follow this course in order to make sense of the diverse forms of data on schizophrenia. Perhaps in the future a more lively, human language will suffice. For a more formal version of the integrative principle discussed below, see Shapiro (1978).

Our starting point is the belief that schizophrenia is a complex disorder, a syndrome that manifests itself through disturbances on many levels of functioning. Schizophrenia has been approached by many different disciplines. Unfortunately, significant findings from one discipline are often unknown to or unintegrated by other disciplines. This is due partly to parochialism and partly to the inadequate language for "the boundary regions of science" (Wiener, 1965).

Schizophrenia is a particularly human disorder. As Lidz (1973) says:

> Human adaptability, in contrast to that of all other organisms, depends upon the ability to use language and to think—but it contains an inherent vulnerability. The brain permits thinking but does not guarantee its rationality. Meanings alter in the service of emotional needs; and when a person's acceptability to himself and others is threatened, when no way out of an irreconcilable dilemma can be found, and when all paths into the future seem blocked, there is still a way. One can simply alter his perceptions of his own needs and motivations and those of others; one can abandon causal logic or change the meanings of events; one can regress, retreating to a period in childhood when reality gave way before the wish, when one felt central to the parents' care, or even to a time when one was not fully separated from the mother—and thus regain a type of omnipotence and self-sufficiency. In short, one can become schizophrenic. *Indeed, this path is so clearly open to man that if we did not know of a syndrome such as schizophrenia we would have to search for it as an anticipated anomaly of the developmental process* [p. 10, italics mine].

Schizophrenia involves disturbances in the use of abstract symbols and in the capacity to form meaningful interpersonal relationships. These capabilities can be viewed as complex adaptive behaviors that are ontogenetically linked. If we look at evolution, we see that the more complex the organism and the wider its range of adaptive behaviors, the greater its dependence on learning for survival (Sagan, 1977).

The drawback to extragenetic learning is that the young of the species are not born with all the information necessary for adaptive behavior. That knowledge is not as simply or inexorably transmitted as it is in the lower animals. When nongenetic learning replaced simple instinctive behavior, the young of the species required time to learn necessary survival techniques. This time, known as childhood, was prolonged as the expectable adult behavior became more complex. Even within a species, namely, Homo sapiens, childhood and adolescence were prolonged as culture became more complex (see Ariès, 1962).

The more complex organisms often have longer periods of infancy during which time the young are dependent on the ministrations of the mothering one—both for ongoing survival and for education or training in order to become self-sustaining. The mothering one is in turn dependent on the help and protection of other members of the species. Cooperation and socialization among mammals is adaptive both for the care and training of the young and for protection of all members from predators.

As far as we know, only humans have developed the capacity to store information extracorporeally. That is, they have developed written language and have elaborated it into a vast system of culture. This system holds more information than any single human being can know or encompass, but it is stored and thus available, and belongs to the species as a whole. This extracorporeal information capacity has greatly increased our ability to survive. It has expanded our adaptive capacity, which in turn has required (1) an increased reliance on education, not only within the family—which was sufficient in simpler, agrarian societies—but also in specialized institutions of learning, and (2) a prolonged period of childhood and adolescence—a longer period of preparation for adult functioning.

The ability to communicate and store information that is not directly observable, requires a symbolic, abstract level of thinking. Although this capacity may not be uniquely human, it does appear to be most highly developed by humans, who, in contemporary society, have both broadened the individual's personal access to information and parceled out the storage of information to specialists on whom the rest of society must rely. Such specialization greatly increases the adaptive potential of society and its individual members. For each specialty, we depend on experts and machines, and through them we increase our own survival capacity. However, this system works only when we can communicate with, understand, and trust other members of the species. To this end we have developed complex social organizations and rules of interaction. As we become increasingly dependent on the various specialists, we assume more social roles and our lives become more complex.

A critical idea begins to emerge from this discussion, namely: cognitive and social-emotional development cannot be separated because they are dependent on each other. On the one hand, socialization requires language, which in turn increases our cognitive (abstract and symbolic) capacities; on the other hand, language needs to be learned, and this learning takes place through social systems. Emotions can be intrapersonal or interpersonal signals that register the discrepancies between expectations and reality; they may provide the social glue, or be socially divisive; they also serve as signals for critical life-threatening situations.

HUMAN ADAPTATION AND DEVELOPMENT

On the basis of the work of Miller, Galanter, and Pribram (1960), Ashby (1965; Conant & Ashby, 1970) and Beck (1971), it is possible to formulate principles of human development.

The goal of physical, cognitive, and emotional development is both individual and species survival through increasingly adaptive behaviors. Development itself consists of successive, approximate adaptations to the environment.

As Conant and Ashby (1970) have attempted to prove, and Beck (1971) and others have stated less formally, adaptation requires the development of an internal model. The process of adaptation requires the recognition of redundancy in the environment: there must, therefore, be some way of *re-cognizing.* In fact, most attempts at understanding human development and human psychology place considerable emphasis on the description of an internal model. But such a model, while intuitively and introspectively available to us, is difficult to prove.

The significance of internal models is increasingly being noted, for example, in Anthony's paper linking psychological invulnerability in children to greater than average competence. Anthony defines competence as "the ability to construct an internal representation of an external event, that is, a capacity to conceptualize and order the manifold incoming data so that they can become sufficiently meaningful for the individual to act upon" (1974b, p. 536).

It is important to note that an internal model is not merely a cognitive-perceptual apparatus but also has emotional and social significance. Feelings about people and the means of expressing these feelings develop over time. Later experiences with feelings resonate with earlier ones. In addition, as Beck (1971) points out, models play a critical role in socialization. The ability to work, communicate, and plan with others requires the internalization of shared meanings, values, and plans. The content of one's models and plans must be reasonably congruent with those of other people, at least to the extent that one can distinguish congruent models from incongruent ones.

Complex adaptation proceeds in stages and proceeds optimally when most of the environment—all but the to-be-adapted-to part—is held constant. This can occur in several ways:

1. The rest of the environment can be removed. This course is usually not possible, since the environment and its stimuli surround us.
2. Some intervening variable can act as a wall between the organism and the environmental variables, thus protecting the organism from impingement by keeping these variables constant. For the time being, the intervening variable is making the adaptation to the environment for both itself and the organism under its wing. Obviously the organism's adaptation to the environment is, during this period, only as good as the intervening variable's adaptation. In reality, this role is often taken by the mother. However, if we shift perspectives, we see that it occurs on a larger scale as well. In the traditional family, the father serves this function in relation to some variables, the mother serves it in relation to others, and the parents in turn depend on a host of specialists and agencies to take care of certain functions.
3. The third way of keeping most variables constant is through recognizing redundancy in the environment. It is the task of human development to increase our recognition of redundancy. For example, the one-and-a-half-year-old who is learning to walk must devote considerable attention to the

process of walking and may not be able to watch TV and walk at the same time. As the child becomes more "secure" in the ability to walk, walking becomes habitual and little or no attention is paid to it unless some novelty, either in the form of an external obstacle (e.g., a pothole) or an internal change (e.g., physical injury, earache, dizziness) intrudes. Walking, with all of its attentional and proprioceptive cues, becomes sufficiently learned to become routine, redundant, and therefore more or less constant.

If the flow of new information proceeds at an optimal rate, normal adaptation occurs and adequate internal models of the environment are formed. These models hold ever-larger portions of the environment constant while the organism adapts to the next variable. If the pattern of input is not "good enough," adaptation does not proceed normally, and the developing organism either fails to make an internal model or makes a defective model of the environment, affecting future adaptations and the value of future internal models. Such defects can be due to failures of "hardware"—biochemical or neurophysical problems—or failures of "software"—poor programming, inadequate or invalid models.

In human development optimal adaptation proceeds radially outward in stages. This radial development provides successively more complex data for adaptation. This principle is illustrated in Figures 1 and 2.

Figure 1 represents the early movement from undifferentiated self-mother to separation of the two. Figure 2 represents later development, encompassing an ever-widening range of experiences. Although I cannot present a complete picture of development, I shall present a tentative elaboration of this diagram.

In utero, the physiological needs of the fetus are met continuously, apparently with no "need tension." The task of the fetus is "simply" to unfold—to enact its genetic material, developing the species-specific structures necessary both to maintain its life and to learn more complete adaptation. Several failures of adaptation are already possible, including:

1. The specific genetic makeup may not be good enough, and the fetus will abort.
2. Even when a viable fetus develops, the genetic makeup may be sufficiently anomalous to cause visible birth deformities and/or an absence of specific sensory modalities.
3. Even when there are no clearly visible genetic defects, there still may be genetic deviation that will interfere with later development, e.g., temperamental differences (Thomas, Chess, & Birch, 1969), abnormal hedonic capacity (Meehl, 1975), unusual sensitivities (Bergman & Escalona, 1949), or neural integrative deficit (Fish, 1971; Mednick & Schulsinger, 1968; Mednick, Schulsinger, & Schulsinger, 1975; Meehl, 1962).

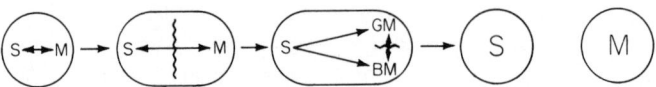

FIGURE 1. The Separation of Self and Mother

Key: S = Self; M = Mother; GM = Good Mother; BM = Bad Mother

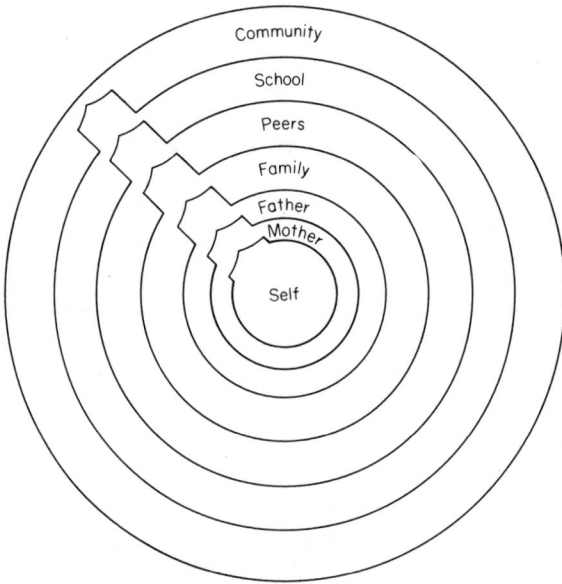

FIGURE 2. Adaptation Proceeding Radially Outward

4. When the intrauterine environment has not been "good enough" or constant enough, it can pose premature challenges to the unborn fetus, possibly leading to spontaneous abortion, deformities, or prematurity.

Once born, the infant must be physically sustained. During the birth process, the baby must be protected by a wall of constancies; the mother, father, midwife, and/or doctor work to minimize the infant's upset and change and to keep the essential variables (EVs; Ashby's [1965] term for life-sustaining functions) within critical limits.

Following birth, the mother no longer involuntarily provides physiological protection for the infant. Instead, the infant is dependent on the conscious, motivated responses of the parents, responses that are subject to and a product of the parents' own personal histories, past and present environments, and the prevailing cultural norms. Thus, although governed by clear limits if the infant is to survive, the satisfaction of the infant's physical needs is subject to significant variations in its parents' behavior.

Initially, the infant cannot do much to actively sustain itself, having a vocabulary of only three cries—pain, pleasure, and hunger (Wasz-Höckert et al., 1968)—and several reflexes—sucking, grasping, motor, etc. (Wolff, 1966). From this basis the infant will develop the primitive schema of the world that will eventually mature into the complex cognitive inner world of the adult. However, the infant/child is still dependent on the ministrations of adults for biological survival, the avoidance of physiological trauma, and phase-appropriate cognitive and emotional stimulation.

For the infant to move beyond this stage of helplessness, two things must occur:

1. The infant must continue to grow. Physiological development must proceed. The unfolding of a relatively normal genetic heritage is a prerequisite for future independent adaptation.

2. The infant must be provided with adequate "phase-related" stimulation, which is comparable to what Winnicott (1963/1965c) called the gradual failure of adaptation. Assuming an optimum rate of stimulation at each successive stage, the developing child must not be overstimulated, understimulated, or confused.

   a. *Overstimulation:* receiving more information than can be absorbed by the infant's inadequate internal structure. Some theories suggest that a stimulus barrier provides some innate protection during the first months, but this soon disappears and its function must be assumed by the mothering one. An infant who receives more information than it can successfully decode or adapt to is likely to experience fear or persecution. Such experiences not only cause present discomfort but may also impair the formation of schemas and structures to cope with subsequent stimuli.

   b. *Understimulation:* receiving an amount of information insufficient for making internal models of the world, thus retarding the child's development. Just as the child whose legs are bound has weakened muscles and difficulty learning to walk, so, I contend, is the infant who does not experience some phase-appropriate challenges to his or her current experience and conception of the world, prevented from exercising the capacity to make internal models. In Piaget's terms, if the infant is not forced to accommodate his or her schemas to new data, the quality of the schemas will suffer.

   c. *Confusion:* a variant of overstimulation is the presentation of confusing or conflicting data, for example, double-bind communication. Although adults must be capable of recognizing the subtle, often conflicting, levels of meaning in a message, this adaptive behavior is a later development. For a toddler to learn the denotative meanings of words, the idiosyncratic connotative meanings distinguished by the parents must be minimally interfering during the early stages of language acquisition.

The infant, provided with simple reflexes and means of communication, and the mother, who can satisfy the infant's needs but also has her own history of associations to nurturant behavior, meet in what seems to be an interaction of the "simplest" kind but is in fact very complex. Subsequent development, which is at least as complex and more difficult to tease apart, will not be described as thoroughly.

When development proceeds adequately, the infant, through successive experiences of tension and relief, develops what Erikson (1963) calls a sense of basic trust. It also begins to discriminate itself from others.

The first two categories of experience, namely, good-bad or pleasurable-unpleasurable, at first correspond almost entirely with the infant's physiological state. These dichotomous categories aid future discriminations, acting as reinforcers or means of discriminating among events. The pleasure of satiation experienced after a good feed but not after self-stimulation (thumb sucking), aids in the differentiation of self from other, which is the first fully learned nonmotoric category and quite possibly the basis for all future categorization and structuring of experience.[1] Self–not-self is a definite dichotomous category whose clarity affects the sharpness of future categorizations.

As the infant interacts more with the world around it, the other members of its family and its physical surroundings become more important. Certain basic distinctions begin to emerge, e.g., mother/father, parents/all other people, male/female. Mother is different from other people because she alone has a feeding breast; father holding baby smells, sounds, and feels different from mother holding baby. On the social level, certain nonverbal gestures acquire meaning, e.g., the smile, and there is the beginning of language acquisition.

Normally, adaptation proceeds radially outward: the infant, having adapted to certain critical features of mother, thus establishing some constancies in its environment, can then move on to father. When the infant has achieved a stable distinction between self and other in relation to mother, it can transfer that distinction quite quickly to father and attend to his distinguishing features. When the young child understands the mother's language (assuming her language is within normal limits), then it can adjust quickly to the father's language. Minor changes in pitch, inflection, etc., should not interfere with this transfer of knowledge of denotative language. The child can then attend to the subtler connotative differences in the parents' use of language. The child whose mother spoke autistically and gave the child no stable sense of the denotative meaning of words will have to learn language anew with the father.

The child with some schema of mother greets the father and other

---

[1] For different reasons, Freud believed that thought derived from this period of development. He considered the prototype of thought to be the fantasized breast.

members of the nuclear family with a primitive mental representation of the world and of people in the person of mother. The concept of people (not yet in generic form) begins to be hierarchically organized as data from other persons—first members of the family and then others in the neighborhood—become integrated. Notions about things are sorted into people and nonpeople, animate and inanimate, mother and others, as the child begins to categorize the surrounding world.

A similar process of increasing differentiation and integration occurs in the developing child's sense of self and his or her own actions. In addition to forming a representation of the external world, the child develops a representation of self that is at first relatively concrete and tied to the body image, but later takes a more complex and abstract form (Sandler, 1962).

During the jumps or shifts in orbit of early development, it is of critical importance that the previously adapted-to parts of the environment stay relatively constant. This constancy affords the child the opportunity to attend more thoroughly to novelty, e.g., school, and gives the child faith in his or her models of previous events or experiences, in his or her capacity to recognize redundancies in the environment, and in the ability to relegate portions of adaptation to "automatic pilot."

If the mother, on seeing her child interact more with others, becomes hostile, withdrawn, or even psychotic, then the child's relationship with and understanding of mother no longer serve as a constant backdrop to life. Rather, the child must readapt to mother. As a further consequence, the child may be more cautious in ventures into the world, since such movement can have cataclysmic effects on the significant others in the environment. Furthermore, this experience can create a generalized sense of the impermanence and untrustworthiness of prior experience. Parents affect their children not only through specific stimulation but also as role models; they demonstrate how to handle the changing demands of people and situations, as exemplified by their responses to the changing demands and impingements initiated by their children.

As the child grows, his or her world and internal representations of it expand. The child's conceptual capacities differentiate and integrate at different levels. This growth, like the growth of the embryo, can be stunted at each level in various ways.

SCHIZOPHRENIA

Let us now return to the subject of this book and review what is known about schizophrenia.

1. Schizophrenia, as the term is currently used, refers to a psychotic state whose

primary feature is a "formal thought disorder." In most cases, the disorder first becomes clinically evident in late adolescence and early adulthood. Researchers have come to view schizophrenia more as a syndrome than as a specific disease entity. Because its etiology remains uncertain, no valid core definition or definitive diagnostic criteria exist. There are probably different forms of schizophrenia, with differing etiologies, genetic and otherwise.

2. As reviewed in Chapter 3, considerable evidence suggests that a genetic predisposition exists in at least some forms of schizophrenia. Although reported concordance rates vary considerably, even the lowest figure of 33 percent in monozygotic twins is significantly higher than the 12 percent reported in fraternal twins. This finding strongly suggests a hereditary factor, although the precise role of this factor is not clear. A genetic predisposition might work through intermediate variables, such as sensory thresholds and temperamental variables, that would make the person more prone to developmental difficulties. Or it might work directly, by providing the blueprint for an abnormal enzyme or autotoxin.

3. A genetic predisposition seems to act through biochemical and/or neurophysiological alterations, which may become manifest in attention and arousal difficulties.

4. When this psychological deficit exists at birth, the infant cannot adequately regulate the flow of information (stimulation) that impinges on it. This deficit can be overcome by a caretaker who is sensitive enough to function as an auxiliary stimulus barrier and who can aid in the infant/child's gradual adaptation to the world and to his or her own extrasensitive sensory apparatus.

5. Environmental extremes of over- or understimulation similarly affect the infant/child's capacity to adapt and develop internal models of the world. Environmental extremes can lead to extreme deficits, which in turn affect arousal level and create a situation quite similar to a genetically initiated process.

6. An inadequate model of the environment does not allow adequate adaptation and/or information regulation.

7. Thus there is a rather complex interaction between the infant's genetic, biochemical, and neurophysiological endowment—its hardware—and the quantity of stimulation in the environment, the quality of caretaking or mothering, and the information-regulating capacity. The interaction is such that the less adequate the information-regulating capacities of the infant, the more adequate must the caretaker be in order to compensate for the information load of the environment. Furthermore, the more diverse and/or phase-inappropriate the stimulation in the environment, the more the information-regulating capacity is taxed. I propose that *inadequate adaptation occurs when caretaker inadequacy and environmental information overload combine to overtax the information-regulating capacity of the organism.* At first, this capacity is almost entirely a function of hardware; later it is based on past experience and the adequacy of internal models, or "software."

8. When an inadequate internal model of the environment is formed at a given stage of development, the information-regulating capacity of the organism at the next stage of development is effectively lowered.

9. Thus an organism with a genetic predisposition to an attentional/arousal deficit will suffer a cumulative informational overload unless an adequate caretaker compensates for the deficit. Such an overload may also occur in an organism without genetic defect that is subjected to unusual amounts of environmental stimulation during critical periods of development and is thus unable to create successful models of the environment. At some point in development, during periods of great internal or external stress, the capacity for information regulation will be exceeded, and the organism will be unable to assimilate and adapt to the current situation. A regulatory failure and a breakdown will occur. Life crises are prototypical of external information overloads; adolescence and menopause are prototypical of internal overloads.
10. The breakdown constitutes a return to earlier models of the environment in an effort to reconstruct and organize the chaotic input.

Schizophrenia, a psychosis whose cardinal feature is a thought disorder, with, according to experimental findings, an attentional/arousal deficit, is the specific end point of various maladaptive processes. These processes have in common the characteristic of significantly stunting, limiting, or deforming the internal representations of the world and/or the capacity accurately to construe and conceptualize the world. Since perception is a function not only of sensory data but also of memory and expectation, such a deformation will lead to perceptual discrepancies.

Inadequate models of the world or a defective capacity to form models provides a shaky foundation for future adaptation by interfering with and detracting from one's ability to attend selectively and, more important, to shut out stimuli. This poor foundation increases anxiety and lessens the capacity to create adequate future models.

A schizophrenic episode is precipitated by an unassimilable incident that paralyzes the schizophrenic with anxiety. The inability to cope further interferes with the normal flow of stimulation. Extreme anxiety interferes with perceptual processes, an interference that in turn increases anxiety. Inadequate or discrepant models and perceptions increase social alienation.

Novel situations act like Ashby's (1965) step functions: there is a critical moment that triggers the breakdown. Each person's critical point is unique in both content and quantity of arousal, since it is based on his or her unique biochemistry, particular history, and set of internal models and their flexibility, as well as on the current situation—whatever supports or environmental constancies exist.

One critical feature of our theory merits emphasis: cognitive and emotional development go hand in hand. One's first internal representations and constructions of the world occur in the context of the mother-child dyad in the pleasurable-painful aspects of nursing and nurturant care. In that context the infant develops the first schemas, refines the capacity to suck, and begins to distinguish good from bad, self from nonself, fantasy gratification from reality, animate from inanimate, male from female, mother from others. To the extent that a person's constructions of the world are similar to and congruent with those of society, he or she can interact in a reasonably predictable, not intolerably anxious, way with others. When a person's constructions, models, or expectations of events are too "off," too discrepant, too quirky, he or she will not only relate incorrectly to all manner of things but will also become increasingly isolated from others who could provide corrective experiences. In the normal course of events, relationships with others tend to modify and correct the maladaptive, untrue expectations that evolved in relation to a single set of humans—one's parents. As Sullivan (1953) pointed out, the juvenile period can exert a corrective influence, but only on children who are not so weird that they are already shunned by their peers. The studies of the "well" siblings of schizophrenics support this view through the finding that these "survivors" often left home early and formed attachments with nonfamily members (see Chapter 8).

Early experience is critical, in providing both an emotional basis for connecting with people and cognitive basis for developing reasonably reliable categories of experience. When all else fails, we come back to the question: Is this me or is this "not me"? This distinction is modified throughout our lives, moving from the concrete "breast is not me" to the subtle differentiations made in the therapeutic encounter between transference and countertransference, resistance and counterresistance, anxiety and counteranxiety (Wolstein, 1967).

If the above theory is correct, one could predict an increase in acute, situational psychoses or reactive schizophrenia as more communities enter the postindustrial age—that is, as fixed roles and traditional means of coping are lost and the rate of social novelty increases (see Toffler, 1970). Cross-cultural and longitudinal epidemiological work using standardized diagnostic criteria and including acute as well as "core" schizophrenics (the latter most likely have a genetic disorder and thus a relatively constant rate) is needed to test this hypothesis.

It also follows from this theory that a given society's stability and success rest on its capacity to "hold" its members by providing them with constancies in the form of rituals, rites of passage, structured role expectations, and institutions, all of which lessen the amount of novelty its members will have to adapt to in their lifetimes. As freedom of expression increases and traditional models collapse, the number of choices one makes in the course of defining oneself increases tremendously. In such times, one no longer knows clearly the limits of one's experience—much more is possible and much more is demanded than in more structured, static times. Criteria for evaluating the quality of one's life alter within a lifetime, as do the moral standards of the community. Society's task of providing some constancies and stability is more difficult in such changing times. Rates of mental illness, especially suicide, do seem to climb during periods of social change. As yet, however, the rate of acute reactive schizophrenia has hardly been studied.

The theory developed here has important preventative implications. If it is correct, psychophysical assessment of infants and children should enable us to identify temperamental differences that lead some children to be more at risk than others. Such identification would enable professionals to aid parents in their efforts to adapt to and care for these infants. In addition, special education could be provided for these children to strengthen their ability to filter stimuli, to attend selectively, and to develop appropriate constructs of the world. To prevent early trauma and inadequate care, we might begin to provide counseling and education for parents and children at potentially traumatic times. Our definition of education can be broadened to include training in flexible, adaptive modeling of the world around and inside of us. This new education for the future would emphasize process (rather than content), individual growth, emotional security, and the capacity to exchange information effectively. Steps have already been taken in this direction on an experimental level by Anthony (1974b) and on the level of social policy by the Scandinavian countries (Kahn & Kammerman, 1977).

In this chapter I shall temporally organize the theories and experimental data presented in the first ten chapters in light of the theory presented in Chapter 11. The purposes of such an organization are: (1) to illustrate the varying forms of vulnerability to excessive stimulation as they occur at each successive stage of development; (2) to identify various etiologies within the schizophrenic spectrum; (3) to provide a developmental diagnostic schema that is useful in understanding and rating the depth or intransigence of a particular instance of the disorder; and (4) to provide a framework for prevention.

Although I cannot claim to induce specific etiologies of schizophrenia from my general principle, since that principle is itself deduced from what is known, it is still useful to state what would be expected from and consistent with that principle.

Schizophrenia is a specific maladaptive behavior that occurs as a consequence of a serious inability to attend selectively or maintain an awareness of constancies in the environment. Normally, the use of internal models leads to the recognition of redundancy in the environment, which allows for temporary independence of parts. The loss of this independence impairs current and future concept formation and adaptation, further diminishing one's capacity to maintain temporary independence. This diminished capacity makes negotiating one's way in the world difficult and anxiety-provoking; such anxiety further impairs the potential for adaptive behavior.

Throughout development, there is an optimum neurophysiological/biochemical state of the organism—we can consider this the hardware of the model. There is, concurrently, an internal model of the environment capable of handling or adapting to a specific range and rate of new information—this is the software of our model. Whenever major new information must be assimilated, something can go wrong in either the hardware or the developing software.

Chronic aberration in a person's hardware would make progress along consensual lines difficult, if not impossible. Sudden or acute changes in the neurophysiological or biochemical hardware would lead to temporary disruptions, possibly quite flamboyant but not usually as serious as those due to chronic aberrations, since underlying structures or programs developed under normal conditions are retained during acute disturbances. When hardware is defective, adaptation may be faulty or information may be stored in erroneous ways, thus leaving an area of vulnerability even after the hardware returns to normal.

Faulty programs or models can be caused either by erroneous informational input or by too much information coming in too quickly. Faulty programs affect future adaptation and create areas of greater vulnerability. Failures in the fundamental or organizing adaptations affect the person more seriously than failures in less basic adaptations. Thus a traumatic experience with one's father, the prototypical male and authority figure, is likely to have a more far-reaching impact than an equally traumatic and disturbing event with bridges, since more later events and adaptations will be built on the initial one with father. Failures or maladaptations in the critical tasks of maturation have more serious consequences than those in the less essential areas.

In Table 5 I have summarized the major tasks of each stage of development from conception to maturity. This Eriksonian organization of data is an attempt to form a unifying model of the diverse literature on normal development. This will serve as a background for understanding pathological development.

Table 6, a description of pathways to schizophrenia, highlights stage-specific maladaptations corresponding to current theories and includes speculations about the person's subsequent life course. Frequently, several major maladaptations occur in the history of a given person. The piling up of maladaptations increases the likelihood of a schizophrenic episode. Biochemical and neurophysiological theories of schizophrenia cross temporal lines and therefore do not show up in the tables; however, current research in these areas will be discussed after the table has been explained. Briefly, I believe that biochemical and neurophysiological aberrations may be viewed as either continuous or step functions that play a critical role in the development of schizophrenic symptoms, whether in a primary or a secondary way.

Despite my earlier criticism of the vague use of the term "schizophrenia," I am falling into similar usage. This usage is invoked deliberately, however, to include all forms of mental illness that have been called schizophrenia. In this I am implicitly stating my belief that at the present time all efforts at

NOTE: Table 5 summarizes the critical components of normal development and the requisite achievements at successive developmental stages. The material is divided into thirteen columns, which are to be read vertically.

TABLE 5: Critical Aspects of Normal Development

Genetics	Intrauterine	Birth	Infant's Temperament
Within normal limits.	Within normal limits.	Within normal limits.	Within normal limits, including the three temperaments identified by Thomas et al. (1969) as: easy, difficult, and slow to warm up.
	Adequate supply of oxygen and nutrients.	Normal Apgar.	
	Protected from physical trauma and illness.		
	Not subjected to harmful drugs and/or alcohol.		
	Mother is in good health and good spirits—wants the child.		

Mother's Temperament	Parents' Family Style	Infant Dev. 0–6 Mo
Within normal/neurotic limits.	Father, if not directly involved in infant care, is sufficiently supportive of mother to maintain her nurturant capacities during this period.	Normal repertoire of cries and reflexes.
Sufficiently similar to infant's or sensitive enough to adapt to infant's temperamental needs.	As a family there are clear generational boundaries.	Infant moves from *total dependence* on caretaker with no clear awareness of self or other to *dawning awareness of separation.* Increased awareness of faces/people.
Capable and desirous of being depended on and caring for a child, but not needing the childd's dependence to make her life meaningful or bolster a shaky sense of self-worth.	Neither parent has a thought disorder.	
	Most of the time there is an atmosphere of hope, optimism, and a belief that life is worth living; achievement and intimacy are possible.	*Maturation* of perceptual and motor systems.
	Parent's relationship is good enough so that they do not seek inappropriate gratification of needs from children.	Development of a sense of basic trust.
	Attention paid to impact of crises on children.	Has moved through the stage of *normal autism* to *normal symbiosis.*
		Begins to experience *stranger anxiety.*

TABLE 5: Critical Aspects of Normal Development *(Cont.)*

"Mother":Infant 0–6 Mo	Infant Dev. 6–24 Mo	Mother/Father: Infant 6–24 Mo
Mother has successfully recognized infant's cries and needs and has been able to meet them.	Normal physiological maturation —crawling, walking, beginning of speech.	Parents able to adapt to growing independence of child. They can appropriately set limits and also delight in the curiosity and autonomy of their child, balancing support and availability with respect for the child's growing autonomy.
She has adjusted to and welcomed the necessary and normal symbiosis.	Critical stages of separation-individuation process achieved.	
She was not overly depressed by the physical separation and/or exhaustion of the birth.	Able to learn from and integrate disappointments, separations, and buildup of need tension.	They consistently communicate love and support while maintaining boundaries and limits.
She was not made over anxious by dependency of the infant.	By the end of this period has a reasonable sense of self-other differentiation.	Parents stimulate and encourage child's curiosity —do not get over anxious at the "freshness" of the toddler.
Her own environment has held her securely during this period— she has not had to sustain trauma.	Has passed through the period of separation anxiety.	They are sensitive to the child's reaction to birth of siblings, to separations, to illness, etc.
	Has the beginnings of permanency of objects.	
	Is ready for toilet training and is not traumatized by recognition of sex differences.	

Juvenile Stage	Adolescence	Maturity
Growth continues with an increase in balance, strength, and coordination.	Successfully copes with the abrupt physical changes of puberty.	Able to make a career or job choice and successfully hold a job.
Toilet training is the first of many activities the juvenile successfully masters.	Has a clear sense of sexual identity, thus can survive the first difficult moves toward sexual relations.	Able to leave family of origin and form intimate relations with others, creating own family of generativity.
Begins to move out of the family and into the neighborhood. Begins to learn to decenter.	Is able to welcome the capacity for abstract thought without getting lost in it.	These moves arouse anxiety, but the normal adult can withstand anxiety and persevere.
Is able to leave home and to go school.	Begins to make plans for future away from family.	Is able to trust and depend on others and in turn be trustworthy.
Separateness becomes more real as child develops own life.	Becomes self-conscious and reflective and also more aware of others' feelings.	Is flexible enough to adjust to changing times.
Learns the basic physical laws of the world, e.g., conservation, concrete and functional categories of things, a moral sense.	Parents, not too threatened by sexual and/or ambivalent autonomous strivings, are able to support budding adulthood.	
A sense of competence emerges; the first real friendship develops—chums.		

strictly defining or diagnosing schizophrenia, though useful for empirical research, run the risk of excluding some members of the same class and of including members of different classes with similar symptoms. As researchers learn more about the specific etiologies of disorders currently considered part of the schizophrenic spectrum, we will be able to break down the large, heterogeneous grouping into several discrete disorders: some that are inherited, others that derive from biochemical aberrations or psychophysical disorders, and still others that stem from family communication patterns. At present, schizophrenia can be thought of as a cluster of symptoms. We can then ask when these symptoms started, what purpose they serve, and so forth. To this end, I am presenting in table form the possible starting points of schizophrenia, which is defined as a psychosis, the primary feature of which is a formal thought disorder. I shall then show how these starting points— each representing one or more major theory—mark an impairment in the organism's capacity to create adequate internal representations, to maintain temporary independence of parts, and to attend selectively to stimuli.

Table 6 illustrates the various starting points for the development of schizophrenia. These points correspond to the various etiological theories discussed in Chapters 3 to 10. They are sequentially organized along a time dimension, starting with genetic factors and proceeding through infancy, childhood, adolescence, and adulthood. Each starting point in the table has been given a number, and in the following discussion these starting points are correspondingly numbered.

1. *Diathesis-Stress Theory:* One specific form of diathesis-stress theory maintains that a genetic predisposition to schizophrenia in the form of an intrauterine metabolic disorder leads to structural changes in the central nervous system. These changes cause a deficit in neural integration and become manifest in personality problems that start in childhood and lead to an increased vulnerability to stress throughout life.

In my terms, the structures for selectively tuning in, for integrating sensations into perceptions, and for construing the world are abnormal. There is defective hardware in the form of extreme sensitivities or unusual patterns of arousal. The infant's capacity to flourish in the normally "good enough" environment is diminished because of a seriously impaired capacity for integration and filtering. This person's capacity to adapt is limited from the beginning, and it seems logical to assume that the greater the complexity of the environment, the more the person will fall behind. However, a better-than-average caretaker can help the infant overcome this early hardware defect. The greater the environmental stress during such a person's development, the more vulnerable he or she is likely to be as an adult. The intrauterine disorder may also be responsible for the lower birth weight reported by Mosher (1972; Pollin & Stabenau, 1968) in preschizophrenic monozygotic twins. The parents' reactions to a difficult child such as this are greatly affected by their own personalities and situations at the time of the birth. In addition, one or both parents, even if not schizophrenic, might also have the diathesis for schizophrenia. If so, they may show signs of this diathesis in as yet unknown ways, which have an effect on their children.

2. *Monogenic Bioamine Theory:* This theory suggests a genetic metabolic disorder in which the afflicted person produces an abnormal metabolite that causes schizophrenic symptoms. According to this theory, a discrete difference exists between schizophrenics and those who will never be schizophrenic. The abnormal metabolite is a step function that is not operative in most people. The person's development before the outbreak of schizophrenic symptoms is not stipulated by this theory, which views schizophrenia as appearing from out of the blue because of an autotoxin. According to this theory, increased arousal is a consequence of change in the perceptual world. Perceptual changes caused by an endogenous psychedelic make it impossible to utilize many previous adaptations because constancy in the environment is no longer recognized as such. Thus, the person is confused by a new world, which initially may seem more intense and exciting than the old, but which disrupts previously organized routines. One regresses to a period before those adaptations, which further increases anxiety and social isolation.

3. *Defective Hedonic Capacity:* According to this view, some people have a genetic impairment in the form of a defective capacity to experience pleasure (Meehl, 1975), which makes discrimination of the first dichotomous category (pain/pleasure) especially difficult. I would further hypothesize that the early development of the infant is seriously disturbed by the lack of internal reinforcers for adaptive behaviors and by the defective signaling and reinforcing of the mother. These factors make the first learned experiences less secure and interfere with future attempts at adaptive behavior.

4. *Slow Virus:* The only current evidence for this theory is that (1) a disproportionate number of schizophrenics are born in the winter and summer months; (2) schizophrenics have an unusually high number of abnormal fingerprint patterns (Torrey & Peterson, 1976). Some viruses, such as encephalitis, can produce symptoms similar to those of schizophrenia, suggesting that a virus attacking the central nervous system might lead to schizophrenia. This would represent a sudden defect in the hardware.

5. *Abnormal Intrauterine Experience:* This is a less specific abnormality than that hypothesized in the diathesis-stress model, one which leads to an inadequate transmission of nutriments and the potential for premature or difficult birth. The extent of damage from pre- and perinatal complications

NOTE: Table 6 presents a summary of critical developmental deviations that *may* lead to schizophrenia. The origin of schizophrenia is represented in the table at the point of the primary defect as postulated by a specific theory. The table is divided into nine sections (A–I), each representing either a critical stage in the individual's development or a critical component in the environment. Within each section the major problems that can arise during the period specified are shown in boldface. I then hypothesize the subsequent course of development for an individual with that problem. The subsequent course can be read horizontally, through maturity and outcome. Thus, for example, in Table 6A three hypothetical genetic deviations are shown in boldface and the consequences are followed horizontally through the life cycle. In the subsequent sections of Table 6, as I summarize problems starting later on in development, the point of onset (shown in boldface) moves to the right.

TABLE 6: Pathways to Schizophrenia
A. Genetic Factors

Genetic Factors	Intrauterine Experience	Birth Complications	Infant Temperament
(1) Diathesis stress.	Possible abnormal metabolic digression leading to structural anomaly in CNS in the form of a neural-integrative defect.	Probably none. Possibly low birth weight secondary to diathesis.	Probably more difficult than normal, exhibiting some avoidance behavior and anxiety.
(2) Monogenic bioamine abnormality.	?	Probably none.	?
(3) Defective hedonic capacity.	?	?	Infant will experience less than normal amounts of pleasure and possibly unusual amounts of pain as well.

Mother's Temperament	Parental Family Style	Infant Dev. 0–6 Mo
Anything from normal to schizophrenic. 10% chance that mother is schizophrenic.	Anything possible, but it is likely that one of the parents has some of the diathesis.	Probably somewhat more difficult and sensitive to stimuli, or not as responsive to mother as most.
10% chance that mother is schizophrenic. Otherwise unspecified.	Unspecified. 10% chance that father is schizophrenic.	?
Mother may or may not have similar difficulty with hedonic capacity.	Unspecified, although father may have defective hedonic capacity.	Difficult because of lowered experience of pleasure leading to faulty reinforcement of infant and mother— possibly weakened bond.

TABLE 6: Pathways to Schizophrenia *(Cont.)*
A. Genetic Factors *(Cont.)*

Mother:Infant 0–6 Mo	Infant Dev. 6–24 Mo	Mother/Father: Infant 6–24 Mo	Juvenile Era
Mother may or may not be able to cope with difficult infant.	Should show physiological signs of deviance (e.g., over-arousal).	If one or both parents also deviant they may be inconsistent in child rearing and communication.	The more diathesis exists, the more "off" the child is, and the more environmental failures compound its difficulty.
Unspecified.	?	Unspecified.	?
Mother may or may not be able to get enough satisfaction from infant who is unable to respond positively. May compare infant unfavorably with siblings.	Given the difficult beginnings, may have trouble separating; may not get enough pleasure from new situations to offset anxiety about novelty.	Parents may or may not be able to get enough satisfaction from infant who is unable to respond positively. May compare infant unfavorably with siblings.	Child remains out of synch— may have trouble making friends and enjoying self.

Adolescence	Maturity	Outcome
The more diathesis exists, the more "off" the child is, and the more environmental failures compound its difficulty.	Very fragile. Prone to break under stress.	Depending on the degree of genetic diathesis and the amount of stress, will be schizophrenic, or borderline, or creative, or ?
At this point, if not before, faulty metabolism becomes expressed in schizophrenic symptoms.	At this point, if not before, faulty metabolism becomes expressed in schizophrenic symptoms.	Schizophrenia.
Child remains out of synch— may have trouble making friends and enjoying self.	Lower than normal tolerance for anxiety; nothing good offsets it; weak bonds to others.	Somewhat schizoid; schizophrenic break possible.

TABLE 6: Pathways to Schizophrenia *(Cont.)*
B. Intrauterine Experience

Genetic Factors	Intrauterine Experience	Birth Complications	Infant Temperament
Normal/unknown.	**(4) Slow virus.**	None.	Normal.
Normal, although poor fetal attachment might occur as a consequence of abnormal genetic heritage.	**(5) Poor fetal attachment.** Inadequate supply of oxygen, etc.	Birth probably premature, with low Apgar.	Probably initially slow, neurologically immature. Possibly oversensitive, lacking adequate stimulus barrier.
? Let's assume no genetic predisposition.	**(6) Mother actively psychotic while pregnant.**	Unknown effects on fetus and birth; possibly difficult labor.	?

Mother's Temperament	Parental Family Style	Infant Dev. 0–6 Mo
Normal.	Normal.	Normal.
(a) Good enough or superior. Able to tune in to infant's needs.	(a) Good enough. In no need of a scapegoat or a weak member.	Somewhat fragile and/or sickly. Possibly slight developmental lag.
(b) Feels weak and helpless and projects feelings, along with death fears, onto infant.	(b) One or both parents feel weak and helpless and project feelings, along with death fears, onto infant.	
(c) Irritable—unable to tolerate and rejects infant's needs.	(c) Irritable—unable to tolerate and so rejects infant's needs.	
Mother actively psychotic at times, often has a thought disorder, likely to have trouble with symbiosis.	(a) Father compensates.	(a) Possibly normal.
	(b) F ignores M's problem.	(b–d) if separated from mother or exposed to inconsistencies, may lack adequate symbiosis and bonding.
	(c) F leaves M.	
	(d) F blames child for M's psychosis.	
	(e) If F denies M's difficulty, then family is "skewed."	

TABLE 6: Pathways to Schizophrenia *(Cont.)*
B. Intrauterine Experience *(Cont.)*

Mother:Infant 0–6 Mo	Infant Dev. 6–24 Mo	Mother/Father: Infant 6–24 Mo	Juvenile Era
Normal.	Normal.	Normal.	Normal.
(a) M tolerant of infant's extra needs and dependence. Not overprotective. (b) M tolerant of and encourages dependence; in fact, overprotective. (c) Unable to meet infant's needs—rejection leads to failed symbiosis.	(a) Slightly slower than normal development of autonomous skills, but catching up. (b) Slow to grow, separate, and become independent. (c) Lacking appropriate symbiotic stage; toddler is clingy.	(a) Foster autonomous activity without rejecting dependent needs. (b) Foster dependence, not autonomy. (c) Push autonomy too quickly.	(a) Normal. (b–c) In either case, child likely to have trouble leaving home, going to school, and having relationships outside the home. Socially inept and fearful.
(a) M good at this stage. (b) Out of house—in hospital. (c) Unable to adapt and be available to infant's needs.	(a) Normal. (b-c) Trouble separating due to M's fear of separation or inadequate earlier attainment of symbiosis.	(a) Parents adjust well. (b) Dread infant autonomy, which threatens their stability. (c) Not consistently there for critical rapprochement.	Child either copes by using premature ego development or is immature and dependent. Cognitive skills suffer from M's fuzzy thought processes unless child gets skills from F.

Adolescence	Maturity	Outcome
At some point virus breaks out.	At some point virus breaks out.	Schizophrenia.
(a) Normal.	(a) Normal.	(a) Normal.
(b–c) Trouble achieving mature functioning; trouble at home. One solution is romantic-symbiotic relationship.	(b–c) Trouble achieving mature functioning; trouble at home. One solution is romantic-symbiotic relationship.	(b–c) May break with additional pressure. Possible schizophrenia.
Cognitive skills suffer from M's fuzzy thought processes unless child gets skills from F. In addition, if F rejected and blamed child, added trouble with sexual identification can be expected.	(a) Normal. (b–c) Neurotically depressed or prone to psychotic break, depending on the combination of factors.	(a) Normal/neurotic. (b–c) Neurotically depressed or more seriously disturbed and prone to psychotic break.

TABLE 6: Pathways to Schizophrenia *(Cont.)*
C. Birth Complications and Infant Temperament

Genetic Factors	Intrauterine Experience	Birth Complications	Infant Temperament
Normal.	Normal.	**(7) Premature.** Low Apgar and/or hospital care required.	Neurologically slightly immature. May have weak stimulus barrier. Possibly difficult.
Normal.	Normal.	None.	**(8) Difficult, oversensitive,** inadequate stimulus barrier.
Normal.	Normal.	None.	**(9) Slow to warm up.**

Mother's Temperament	Parental Family Style	Infant Dev. 0–6 Mo
Unspecified. Can either: adapt; project helplessness; reject infant as defective; resent infant's neediness.	Unspecified. Can either: adapt; project helplessness; reject infant as defective; resent infant's neediness.	Somewhat fragile and/or sickly. Possibly slight developmental lag. Or too much stimulation. Symbiotic and nurturant needs unmet, inadequate stimulus barriers. Or predominance of good experience; infant achieves normal symbiosis.
(a) M unable to tune in to infant's special needs. (b) Super M tunes in to and even treasures unusual sensitivities.	(a) M and F irritated with child, might scapegoat; or F understands. (b) If F does not understand, parental conflict may ensue.	(a) Too much stimulation. Symbiotic and nurturant needs unmet, inadequate stimulus barriers. (b) Predominance of good experience; infant achieves normal symbiosis.
(a) M an extravert, loves novelty, can't tune in. (b) M understands.	(a) F tunes in, good adjustment possible; or F rejecting, might scapegoat. (b) Relationship of M and F good enough to tolerate child's special needs.	(a) Much fear of novelty; possibly persecutory feelings; slow to make affective connections. (b) Same as above, but environment adapts to infant's needs.

TABLE 6: Pathways to Schizophrenia *(Cont.)*
C. Birth Complications and Infant Temperament *(Cont.)*

Mother:Infant 0–6 Mo	Infant Dev. 6–24 Mo	Mother/Father Infant 6–24 Mo	Juvenile Era
(a) Tolerant of extra needs and dependence of infant. Not overprotective. (b) Tolerant of and encourages dependence; in fact, overprotective. (c) Unable to meet infant's needs—rejection leads to failed symbiosis.	(a) Slightly slower than normal development of autonomous skills, but catching up. (b) Slow to grow, separate, and become independent. (c) Lacking appropriate symbiotic stage; toddler is clingy.	(a) Parents foster autonomous activity without rejecting dependent needs. (b) Foster dependence, not autonomy. (c) Push autonomy too quickly.	(a) Normal. (b–c) In either case, child is likely to have trouble leaving home, going to school, and having relationships outside the home. Socially inept and fearful.
(a) M becomes increasingly irritated and frustrated by infant. (b) M has her hands full but valiantly adjusts.	(a) Has trouble separating because inadequately connected. Has trouble isolating relevant stimuli in environment. (b) Relatively normal despite idiosyncratic sensitivity.	(a) Parents probably rejecting, irritated, and hostile. (b) M's goodness continues, but may have difficulty separating. Might be marital tension.	(a) Good father may help child recoup; if father bad, child is isolated, has many peculiarities. Peers may be helpful if child not too peculiar. (b) May have Oedipal struggle, school difficulties. Hopefully teacher/others encourage and use sensitivity.
(a) Confusion and anger that her child is different. Disappointment. (b) Tunes in to and might even identify with infant's needs.	(a) Has great trouble growing and separating, since senses rejection. (b) Slow to move on but gradually matures.	(a) Parents pushy and rejecting, or danger of parental overprotection and caution. (b) Parents able to encourage appropriately.	(a) Child fearful in school. Boy might be seen as "sissy." Has trouble getting along. (b) Child has some interpersonal difficulties, but is more able to tolerate them because of good basis.

Adolescence	Maturity	Outcome
(a) Normal. (b–c) Trouble achieving mature functioning; trouble at home. One solution is romantic-symbiotic relationship.	Dependent on both parental reaction to prematurity and extent of actual physical frailty, vulnerability, and time spent (if any) in hospital.	Dependent on parents' response, and can range from normal to schizophrenic.
(a) Good father may help child recoup; if father bad, child is isolated, has many peculiarities. Peers may be helpful if child not too peculiar. (b) May have Oedipal struggle, school difficulties. Hopefully teacher/others encourage and use sensitivity.	(a) World of abstract thought difficult, since primary concepts unclear. (b) Relatively normal, though probably introverted.	(a) Poor interpersonal relationships. Prone to schizophrenia. (b) Normal, or even creative.
(a) Scared of heterosexuality, competition, and achievement. (b) Somewhat slow and cautious, but has friends.	(a) Extremely fearful. Unable to achieve or make friends. (b) Introverted slightly cautious, but able to make good contact.	(a) Schizoid. (b) Mildly neurotic.

TABLE 6: Pathways to Schizophrenia *(Cont.)*
D. Mother's Temperament

Genetic Factors	Intrauterine Experience	Birth Complications	Infant Temperament
Normal.	Normal.	None.	Normal.
? Let's assume does not have genes for schizophrenia.	Normal.	None.	Normal.
Normal.	Normal.	None.	Normal.

Mother's Temperament	Parental Family Style	Infant Dev. 0–6 Mo
(10) Mother has postpartum psychosis.	(a) No compensation. Family in turmoil. (b) Father and family compensate for mother.	(a) Lacks adequate care and might experience excessive anxiety. (b) Normal, but might have trouble greeting mother.
(11) Mother is ambulatory or chronic schizophrenic. Family skewed. Mother actively psychotic at times, often has a thought disorder, likely to have trouble with symbiosis.	(a) Father denies mother's difficulty. Skewed family. (b) Father acknowledges and seeks to compensate.	If father or outside caretaker takes over/helps out, needs might be met; otherwise not.
(12) Mother is borderline, very seductive, and uses primitive defenses: splitting and projective identification.	Family polarized by M's intense moods and primitive defenses. Considerable covert manipulation. ? Marital schism.	Might be subject to extreme variation and inconsistent handling. Unpredictability.

TABLE 6: Pathways to Schizophrenia *(Cont.)*
D. Mother's Temperament *(Cont.)*

Mother:Infant 0–6 Mo	Infant Dev. 6–24 Mo	Mother/Father: Infant 6–24 Mo	Juvenile Era
M unable to cope with birth and separation and/or extremely dependent; pushed into adult maternal role. Easily overwhelmed by needs.	Might have trouble relinquishing symbiosis; either clingy or superficial, premature autonomy.	Mother has trouble tolerating child's autonomous strivings. Overprotective and infantilizing.	If mother improves or if family compensates for mother, environment may be good enough for child to benefit from school; otherwise fear of autonomy gets worse.
(a) M good at this stage. (b) Out of house —in hospital. (c) Unable to adapt and be available to needs.	Language and concept development might be off. Trouble separating due either to M's fear of separation or inadequate earlier attainment of symbiosis.	Difficulty tolerating autonomy. Might give conflicting messages and be engulfing. Not consistently there for critical rapprochement.	Child might cope by using premature ego development. Cognitive skills suffer from M's fuzzy thought processes unless child gets skills from F. Child may have social problems with peers. Possible folie à deux.
M alternately delights in and resents infant. Might project bizarre qualities onto child.	Some difficulty achieving stable self-other differentiation and stable construction of world since mother is unpredictable.	Inconsistent reaction to autonomous strivings, at times encouraging, at other times infantilizing.	Oversexualization and rivalry. Argumentative home. Child has some trouble concentrating in school.

Adolescence	Maturity	Outcome
If mother improves or if family compensates for mother, environment may be good enough for child to benefit from school; otherwise fear of autonomy gets worse.	If normal, may have depressive quality.	Will not achieve autonomous adult activities if father did not act as buffer.
Juvenile problems increase unless father, school, or other external supports can correct them.	Females have trouble with feminine identity, males with masculinity. Both may have mild thought disorder.	Prone to breakdown unless father successfully compensated for mother and/or outsiders were available.
Could have trouble with world of ideas and sexuality. Shaky sense of identity.	Very confused about who he or she is and who parents really are. Sexual problems and trouble with impulse control; possible thought disorder.	Schizophrenic, borderline, or highly tuned in and sensitive to others.

TABLE 6: Pathways to Schizophrenia *(Cont.)*
E. Parental Family Style

Genetic Factors	Intrauterine Experience	Birth Complications	Infant Temperament
? Let's assume does not have genes for schizophrenia.	Normal.	None.	Normal.
Normal.	Normal.	None.	Normal.
Normal.	Normal.	None.	Normal.

Mother's Temperament	Parental Family Style	Infant Dev. 0–6 Mo
(a) Passive and acquiescent. (b) Independent, see clearly F's difficulty. (c) Might separate.	**(13) Father psychotic.** Family skewed.	(a) May be somewhat less "held" because of family irregularities. (b) Normal.
?	**(14) Marital schism.** Probably one or both parents have character disorder; passive-aggressive, hostile-dependent, or borderline.	Possibly difficult (e.g., colic) in response to underlying family tensions.
?	**(15) Pathological family communication.** M and F may not be psychotic when alone, but together they create double binds, mystification, transactional thought disorder.	Normal.

TABLE 6: Pathways to Schizophrenia *(Cont.)*
E. Parental Family Style *(Cont.)*

Mother:Infant 0–6 Mo	Infant Dev. 6–24 Mo	Mother/Father: Infant 6–24 Mo	Juvenile Era
(a) M somewhat tense in response to F, also not adequately "held" by F. Can't cope with infant.	(a) Too close to M and/or subject to bizarre appeal of F. Beginnings of faulty language.	(a) Bizarre language, inappropriate sexual and generational boundaries, confound infant development.	(a) Child might start showing strange behaviors leading to social isolation. Difficulty with language.
(b) Somewhat tense in reaction to F, but adapts.	(b) Subject to some of (a).	(b) M tries to compensate for the above.	(b) Might have trouble leaving home, wanting to protect M.
(c) M is secure in decision to leave and adapts to infant.	(c) Normal.	(c) Normal.	(c) Normal.
M anxious, withdrawn, not adequately available for nurturance.	Might have difficulty separating because, sensing underlying tension, inadequate symbiosis and rapprochement.	M and F have difficulty accepting child's activity and negativism. Might scapegoat and/or violate sexual and generational boundaries.	Poor sexual and generational boundaries and inappropriate seductiveness leave child preoccupied, unable to concentrate at school.
Normal—unspecified.	Begins to have trouble learning limits and clear meanings.	M and F unable to set clear limits since decision-making processes are disordered.	Child subject to confusing communications, might withdraw and/or develop linguistic peculiarities, which isolate socially and lower IQ.

Adolescence	Maturity	Outcome
(a–b) Cannot cope with abstract thought. Might have trouble with sexual identity. Females might have escaped. Males have more trouble. (c) Normal.	(a–b) Depending on external compensators, prone to schizophrenia. Thought disorder. Females might have trouble marrying. Males troubled by success and intimacy. (c) Normal.	(a) Possible schizophrenia. (b) ? Normal—depending on adequacy of mother and outsiders. (c) Normal.
Socially isolated, or inappropriate acting out of sexual tensions stimulated by parents. Trouble separating.	Has difficulty leaving home and becoming gainfully employed and/or successfully completing school. Socially isolated, incapable of intimacy.	Possible schizophrenia.
Further disturbed by development of abstract thought. Socially isolated.	At best, a mild thought disorder; isolated by peculiarities. At worst, schizophrenic.	Possible schizophrenia.

TABLE 6: Pathways to Schizophrenia *(Cont.)*
F. Infant and Mother During First Six Months

Genetic Factors	Intrauterine Experience	Birth Complications	Infant Temperament
?	? Normal.	? None.	Very difficult; does not respond to mother's ministrations.
Normal.	Normal.	None.	Normal.
Normal.	Normal.	None.	Normal.

Mother's Temperament	Parental Family Style	Infant Dev. 0–6 Mo
Normal.	Normal.	**(16) Unable to achieve symbiosis.**
? Normal, but not sensitive to what constitutes an impingement.	? Normal, but unable to form stimulus barrier.	**(17) Overimpinged on.**
Normal.	Generally normal.	Might be colicky, tense, unable to achieve peaceful, reliable symbiosis.

TABLE 6: Pathways to Schizophrenia *(Cont.)*
F. Infant and Mother During First Six Months *(Cont.)*

Mother:Infant 0–6 Mo	Infant Dev. 6–24 Mo	Mother/Father: Infant 6–24 Mo	Juvenile
M frustrated by lack of infant response.	Isolated and withdrawn. No language development.	Parental concern and anxiety lead to outside intervention.	⟶
M cannot or will not buffer infant.	Might show premature and/or false self-development.	Rapprochement phase probably inadequate; infant has difficulty integrating good and bad objects.	False adjustment.
(18) Mother and/or family under extreme stress and therefore anxious and preoccupied.	Has difficulty separating since symbiosis not "good enough," or develops "false self."	Unspecified.	May have trouble leaving home and trying new things; clingy. Or false adjustment.

Adolescence	Maturity	Outcome
		Early infantile autism.
(a) False adjustment.	(a) Prone to break.	Adjustment likely to range from borderline or schizoid to schizophrenic.
(b) Behavior disorder.	(b) Lower than normal tolerance for anxiety; nothing good offsets it; weak bonds to others.	
Juvenile difficulties continue. Outcome depends on friends and parents during these stages.	Lower than normal tolerance for anxiety; nothing good offsets it; weak bonds to others. Or good experiences balance things out and has normal/neurotic life.	Ranges from normal to severely disturbed, depending on subsequent adequacy of parents and outsiders.

TABLE 6: Pathways to Schizophrenia *(Cont.)*
G. Infant and Parents: 6–24 Months

Genetic Factors	Intrauterine Experience	Birth Complications	Infant Temperament
Normal.	Normal.	None.	Normal.
Normal.	Normal.	None.	Normal.
Normal.	Normal.	None.	Normal.

Mother's Temperament	Parental Family Style	Infant Dev. 0–6 Mo
? Normal, but M overinvolved with child because of her own personality, the child's temperament, or nature of marriage.	? Normal, or (like mother) views this child as special.	Normal.
Normal.	Normal.	Normal.
Normal.	Normal.	Normal.

TABLE 6: Pathways to Schizophrenia *(Cont.)*
G. Infant and Parents: 6–24 Mo *(Cont.)*

Mother:Infant 0–6 Mo	Infant Dev. 6–24 Mo	Mother/Father: Infant 6–24 Mo	Juvenile Era
Normal.	**(19) Overprotected, engulfed.** If autonomous strivings exist, they are unrewarded. Won't leave symbiosis.	Parents overinvolved and protective, possibly in a seductive manner. Infantilize and cling to child.	Child has trouble leaving home and becoming "one of the gang." Probably "picked on."
Normal.	**(20) Premature motor development.**	(a) M is overeager for child to be autonomous, is not supportively available for rapprochement. (b) M aware that despite precocity, infant still needs nurturance and support.	(a1) Child reacts to pushing by regressive clinging. (a2) Attempting to please, continues to appear precocious, denies needs. (b) Normal.
Normal.	Difficult period, inadequate rapprochement phase and/or separation anxiety. ? Rejection of absent parent.	**(21) Untimely separation** (e.g., illness, war).	Without compensation: (a1) Child reacts to pushing by regressive clinging. (a2) Attempting to please, continues to appear precocious, denies needs. (b) Other parent adjusts during crisis of separation; normal development follows.

Adolescence	Maturity	Outcome
Troubles of juvenile stage continue and increase. Fearful of heterosexual contact. Unable to rebel and differentiate.	Overdependent, inadequate personality. Delayed movement toward autonomy.	? Might be underemployed or work in family business. Unable to form new family. If pressed to separate, prone to breakdown.
(a1) Difficulty with added demands for separation. (a2) Pseudoindependence, denial of fears. (b) Normal.	(a1) Overdependent, inadequate personality. Delayed movement toward autonomy. (a2) Brittle overachieving, denies dependency needs. (b) Normal	? Psychosomatic problems. ? Hypochrondriacal or prone to break under unusual stress.
(a1) Difficulty with added demands for separation. (a2) Pseudoindependence, denial of fears. (b) Normal.	(a1) Overdependent, inadequate personality. Delayed movement toward autonomy. (a2) Difficulty forming trusting, intimate relations. (b) Normal.	(a1) Prone to breakdown or severe depression. (a2) Unable to form deep ties with others. (b) Normal, with overreaction to separation.

TABLE 6: Pathways to Schizophrenia *(Cont.)*
H. Juvenile Era and Adolescence

Genetic Factors	Intrauterine Experience	Birth Complications	Infant Temperament
Normal.	Normal.	None.	Normal.
Normal.	Normal.	None.	Normal.
Normal.	Normal.	None.	Normal.

Mother's Temperament	Parental Family Style	Infant Dev. 0–6 Mo
Normal.	Normal.	Normal.
Normal.	Normal.	Normal.
Normal.	Normal.	Normal.

TABLE 6: Pathways to Schizophrenia *(Cont.)*
H. Juvenile Era and Adolescence *(Cont.)*

Mother:Infant 0–6 Mo	Infant Dev. 6–24 Mo	Mother/Father: Infant 6–24 Mo	Juvenile Era
Normal.	Normal.	Normal.	**(22) One or both parents become bizarre, thought disordered.**
Normal.	Normal.	Normal.	Normal.
Normal.	Normal.	Normal.	Normal.

Adolescence	Maturity	Outcome
Becomes ashamed of family; may become socially isolated. Might have a situational, temporary psychosis.	Depends on adequacy of early years. Probably will fear loss of control.	More prone than normal to psychotic experiences.
(23) Adolescence under very perverse conditions (e.g., concentration camp).	Might have pockets of psychotic thinking as well as underlying depression and cynicism.	Prone to psychotic depression, hypochondriasis.
(24) Early and/ or extensive use of psychedelics.	Overloose categories of thought; has difficulty in maintaining "secondary process."	Possibly ambulatory or character schizophrenia.

TABLE 6: Pathways to Schizophrenia *(Cont.)*
I. Maturity

Genetic Factors	Intrauterine Experience	Birth Complications	Infant Temperament
Normal.	Normal.	None.	Normal.
Normal.	Normal.	None.	Normal.
Normal.	Normal.	None.	Normal.
Normal.	Normal.	None.	Normal.

Mother's Temperament	Parental Family Style	Infant Dev. 0–6 Mo
Normal.	Normal.	Normal.
Normal.	Normal.	Normal.
Normal.	Normal.	Normal.
Normal.	Normal.	Normal.

TABLE 6: Pathways to Schizophrenia *(Cont.)*
I. Maturity *(Cont.)*

Mother:Infant 0–6 Mo	Infant Dev. 6–24 Mo	Mother/Father: Infant 6–24 Mo	Juvenile Era
Normal.	Normal.	Normal.	Normal.
Normal.	Normal.	Normal.	Normal.
Normal.	Normal.	Normal.	Normal.
Normal.	Normal.	Normal.	Normal.

Adolescence	Maturity	Outcome
Normal.	**(25) Prolonged illness, hospitalization, or surgery, causing profound regression and/or disturbance of body image.**	Depressive or unspecified situational psychosis.
Normal.	**(26) Toxic reaction to exogenous or endogenous substance** (e.g., hormones, chemicals).	Transient psychosis.
Normal.	**(27) Extreme social changes** (e.g., in status or in values; cognitive dissonance).	Increased likelihood of acute situational psychosis.
Normal.	**(28) Sensory deprivation, sleep deprivation. Social isolation for prolonged periods.**	Increased likelihood of acute situational psychosis.

varies from temporary developmental lags to a permanent neurological deficit. The premature infant is likely to have difficulty in following the normal developmental pattern since it is neurophysiologically immature and especially vulnerable to the influx of novel stimuli, therefore requiring a greater degree of auxiliary ego functioning by the parents. This assumption of auxiliary functioning is necessary to keep the new world within "reasonable to adapt to" limits. The premature infant is vulnerable to parents who cannot compensate for the deficit and therefore subject the infant to extreme impingement. Or the parents may initially care for the infant properly but later insist on maintaining him or her as helpless and dependent. The NIMH twin study (Mosher, Pollin, & Stabenau, 1971a) found that the smaller or sicker of the discordant monozygotic twins became schizophrenic and hypothesized that this development was caused by the parent's need to have a helpless child. The maintenance of a person in the role of "the helpless-dependent one" denies that person access to the cognitive "exercise" required to adapt to the world on one's own. It also fosters an internal representation of oneself as someone incapable of being on one's own and of the world as a terrifying place that one cannot manage by oneself. Although this is very damaging, it is probably less serious than the effects of overimpingement.

6. *Maternal Psychosis during Pregnancy:* It is not known whether maternal psychosis during pregnancy affects the infant, assuming that the infant is genetically normal. Biochemical metabolic alterations in the mother (if there are any) may be transmitted to the fetus, affecting its own development or its experience in utero. This is an uncharted area, although recent work on neonatal response to tape recordings of uterine sounds suggests some memory traces of sensory experiences during this period, experiences that could be distorted by an endogenous psychedelic. If a biochemical alteration occurs during psychosis, and if the substance passes the placental barrier, it might interfere with the wall of constancies necessary for early physiological regulation of the fetus. The subsequent ramifications of this early impingement are unclear. Psychosis during pregnancy interferes with prenatal care in many ways detailed by Sameroff and Zax (1973). Use of phenothiazines during pregnancy affects the fetus in unknown ways. Torrey and Peterson (1976) report a higher rate of fetal deaths among schizophrenic women.

7. *Premature Birth:* See 5.

8. *Temperament:* Infants with unusual sensitivities (Bergman & Escalona, 1949) are more sensitive than normal in one or all sensory modalities and must adapt to changes in those modalities. They are thus robbed of the average expectable wall of constancies by their precocious awareness of change. In order to develop normally, such an infant requires parents with

a capacity to tune in to such sensitivities to eliminate them or to buffer the infant from these special impingements. Mothers who have successfully adapted to their own inheritance of unusual sensitivities are able to provide such care, whereas mothers with more blunted sensitivities, or those who never adequately adapted to their own unusual sensitivities, cannot. Thus a tone-deaf mother will not be able to distinguish the particular sounds that distress her infant. If the mother is the main caretaker, the infant will suffer even if the father is more sensitive. If the mother has the same high awareness of smells, touch, or taste as the infant, but cannot cope with her own awareness, she may sympathize but be too disorganized to provide a valuable model for coping; or she may project her own hatred of that part of herself onto the infant. The mother who can successfully meet her baby's unusual sensitivities is able to hold the environment constant while the infant gradually develops the skills to do this for itself.

An infant's inborn regulatory system may also cause temperamental difficulties (Thomas, Chess, & Birch, 1969). Thus, some infants seem to be sleepy, alert, hungry, active in relatively clear sequences from an early age and are easy for their mothers to adapt to because they are regular and predictable. Their mothers can then build on or alter the infants' patterns slightly so that infant and mother can know what to expect from each other. The mothers of less regular infants—those who wake up or experience hunger at odd times—are less able to predict their needs, less able to leave them in the care of others, and more subject to frustrating, anxiety-provoking, trial-and-error efforts to meet their infants' needs. Maternal anxiety not only makes the mother's learning more difficult but is also communicated to the infant.

The "regular" infant is less likely to experience a long delay before need tensions are satisfied than is the irregular, unpredictable infant. A difficult infant will more frequently become "disorganized" by intense needs and be unable to enjoy a good feed when the mother finally figures out what the baby wants. Once there is some pattern to hunger, both mother and infant are free to explore other aspects of the situation, safe in the knowledge that their need-satisfying systems are productively interlocked.

9. *The Slow-to-Warm-Up Child:* Like the extrasensitive or colicky child, the slow-to-warm-up child is likely to arouse some anxiety in the mother who is trying to be "good enough." By not following the expected sequence of development in the usual time frame, the infant disturbs the mother's expectation of predictable behaviors, causing her anxiety and reducing her ability to alleviate the infant's tensions. An alternative difficulty occurs when the mother either overidentifies with the child's difficulty or uses the child as a vehicle for projective identification of her own insecurities (Bowen, 1960); she thus protects the young child from too much anxiety but never moves

back enough to foster autonomy. Instead she provides training in dependence (Mosher, Pollin, & Stabenau, 1971a; Pollin et al., 1966).

Children with difficult temperaments require a greater flexibility and tolerance for uncertainty in caretakers than do easygoing infants. In the course of developing autonomy, difficult children will also need to adapt to their own peculiar needs and limitations—but this is possible only after a period of helplessness in which the onus is on the parents.

10. *Postpartum Depression:* The mother who has a postpartum depression is probably reacting to the loss of physiological symbiosis with the infant—a physical state which reinforces an emotional identification with the infant and minimizes her role as *mother.* Such a woman might unconsciously view the infant as her infant self and panic at the thought of having to separate and *mother* her infant. As a consequence of her depressive reaction she is physically and/or emotionally unavailable to her infant in its first weeks of life, and normal mother-infant bonding is disturbed. Often a substitute bond with a surrogate mother (grandmother, nurse, father) is formed. The father might respond to his wife's depression with anger toward his child, blaming his wife's condition on the child, who is then further burdened. When the mother does recover she might form an intense attachment to her infant, a reaction to compensate for her initial absence. This new attachment might lead to further problems when the infant seeks to individuate in its second year. It is probable that issues of attachment and separation will remain sensitive ones to the child born to this mother. The degree of sensitivity or difficulty will be related to its own temperament (capacity to adapt to new situations) and the behavior of significant others (like the father).

11. *Chronically Schizophrenic Mother:* The mother who is chronically schizophrenic may have a child genetically prone to schizophrenia. Even a genetically normal child is, for several reasons, at risk for later psychosis. The schizophrenic mother will, in all likelihood, have difficulty in identifying the infant's needs as distinct from her own and/or have difficulty in meeting those needs. If she successfully meets these needs at an early symbiotic stage, she may have difficulty in perceiving the infant as separate and allowing it to perceive itself as separate.

The schizophrenic mother may be hospitalized and absent from home for long or short periods that may coincide with critical points in the infant's developing sense of separation and permanence. Even in remission, the chronic schizophrenic may have a subclinical thought disorder with some concreteness or loss of attentional boundaries that will profoundly affect the young child's efforts to understand the world around him or her. The meanings of the mother's messages and of the child's own messages are thus unclear.

If mother is to be seen as loving and lovable, respectable and intact, the child may have to distort his or her own experience. It is not uncommon to find situational psychoses or folie à deux in the children of schizophrenics (Anthony, 1971b). The child's exposure to and imitation of primary-process thinking when secondary-process thinking is most fragile and newly formed can be devastating to him or her.

The effect of an occasionally psychotic mother on the growing child is mediated by the quality of the father and any other significant caretakers. The father who has an accurate assessment of the mother can diminish her potentially detrimental effect by assuming the necessary auxiliary ego role for the growing child and by helping the child to understand the peculiarities of the mother's behavior. A father who ignores and/or tacitly goes along with the mother's psychotic world view (Lidz's skewed family) educates the child in pathology because he insists that insanity is sanity.

A psychotic upbringing not only alters the flow of new information to the young child—allowing either too much or too little at any given moment—but also gives erroneous information and erroneous models of what to anticipate in life. Thus the child who successfully adapts to the psychotic mother may be at a disadvantage in relating to nonpsychotic others. This leads to social isolation, depriving the child of potentially corrective experiences and keeping him or her locked in a pathological system of meanings.

A similar, but usually less pathological, outcome results from a psychotic father, because the father is usually less directly involved in the care of the young. A psychotic parent of either sex is likely to provide a poor model for identification for the same-sex child and a poor model for heterosexual relating for the opposite-sex child.

The specific content of the parent's pathology may lead to specific areas of psychosis in the child—areas that the child never adequately construed. Anthony is currently studying the possibility of preventive work with children of schizophrenics. This work is aimed at both cognitive strengthening and emotional understanding of the parent's pathology.

12. The Borderline Parent: A critical feature of borderline patients is their reliance on the primitive defenses of projection and splitting to maintain their equilibrium. It is very difficult to adapt to this equilibrium because it is so inconsistent. As parents, these people are extremely temperamental and unpredictable, shifting from intense, loving relatedness to hostile rejection. Frequently they relate to people through manipulative interpersonal strategies: "I'll love you if . . ."; "I'll kill myself if . . . ." The reliability, meaning, and seriousness of these pronouncements are questionable. In addition, this manipulative style is likely to pit family members against one another in an enactment of the borderline parent's internal pathology. Since members of these families constantly vie for the right position in the projective split, they cannot trust one another and home becomes a place of secret warfare and individual isolation. One or more children may serve as a buffer between the pathological parent and other family members.

The borderline or psychotic parent may attribute magically powerful qualities to the acts and words of the child, which can make development toward a realistic appraisal of personal power very difficult. Such parents are too erratic to provide the constancies necessary for the child's adaptation. The family is so chaotic that all the child's energy is spent adjusting to it or fleeing from it. Hope may exist in the person of the outsider who somehow remains apart from the system. However, this role is exceedingly difficult to maintain, as anyone who has treated borderlines can affirm.

According to most theorists, the borderline parent has had his or her own problems with nurturance, separation, impulse control, and integration of good and bad objects, and consequently has a limited capacity to help the child deal with these issues.

The family with marital schism (Lidz) is likely to include at least one borderline parent. The pathological effect of the schism is more in its misrepresentation of reality than in the actual disagreement and hostility between the parents. To the extent that such parents misrepresent themselves and insist that others, including their children, support this misrepresentation, they bury clear thought: in such a system truth is subversive. Double binds, mystification, and a transactional thought disorder become the rule, and the child is forced to walk a tightrope between its inner experience of truth and the interpretation foisted on it by those who are most important to it and on whom it is dependent—the parents. This discrepancy violates one of the culture's basic expectations: that parents can be equated with safety and well-being. This places the child in conflict and denies it the constancy of a benign parental model. It is noteworthy that parents who are consistently abusive and rejecting tend to raise antisocial, rather than schizophrenic, children. Such parents are not confusing; they are simply bad (J. Gunderson, personal communication, 1974).

In families with marital schism, siblings tend to line up on opposite battlefronts, often in defiance of generational or sexual boundaries. The lack of parental unity may later be reflected in a basic split in the child's internal representation of the world.

Faulty familial communication trains the child in irrational, nonadaptive modes of thought and traps the child in the chaotic home. Even if the child successfully adapts to the family of origin, he or she cannot translate any of this information for use with the rest of the world.

13. *Psychotic Father:* See 11.

14. *Marital Schism:* See 12.

15. *Faulty Familial Communication:* See 11 and 12.

16–21. *Early Developmental Difficulties:* Most psychoanalytic theories of schizophrenia postulate some difficulty in the early mother-child interaction, especially during the infant's first two years of development.

These theorists would agree that during this period, the infant normally moves from a state of undifferentiated autism and then symbiotic oneness with the mother to a state of recognized separation of self from mother. Simultaneously, the infant's sensorimotor equipment matures to increase perceptual awareness of the world. It is hypothesized that during the early stages of infancy, the infant is equipped with a stimulus barrier shielding him or her from direct exposure to the world; when this fails, the mother assumes auxiliary ego functions to replace or supplement the failing stimulus barrier. These auxiliary functions are then gradually assumed by the developing child.

The normal infant develops what Erikson calls a sense of basic trust in the benevolence of self and environment as well as a beginning sense of autonomy and mastery. This is evident in the toddler who succeeds in perceiving and tolerating separation from mother, takes over some of his or her own ego functions, and delights in their exercise.

Winnicott claims that the critical developmental task for the infant-mother dyad is the maintenance of a "good enough" environment in which the infant's "true self" can emerge and flourish. Fairbairn and Klein stress the importance of a prevalence of good over bad early experiences so that the infant is not too full of rage to successfully integrate an idea of good and bad into the figure of the mother, who is then experienced as separate and beyond the infant's omnipotent control. The Freudians speak of the need for adequate, but not oversatisfying, oral experiences as preparation for the later anal, phallic, and genital stages. Mahler speaks of the infant's initial stable sense of symbiotic oneness with the mother, followed by separation from the mother. Each of the above theories can be viewed in the light of our general principle.

Infantile autism is the most extreme form of psychopathology. Autistic infants, children, and adults dramatically attest to how developed and sophisticated a person must be before becoming schizophrenic. The autistic child is as far from the schizophrenic as the schizophrenic is from normal peers. In Mahler's (1968) terms, the autistic infant failed to use the mother as an "orienting beacon of light" and is stuck in the moment before even the dimmest awareness of the other, before even a symbiotic joining of functions with the mother. Perhaps autism is a fixation at that moment before the breaking of the stimulus barrier. It probably results from a genetic-organic impairment in the development of certain normally innate triggering mechanisms—those that maximize mutual gazing and conforming to the body of the person holding the infant, activities which normally reinforce the nurturant activities of the caretaker. Or these infants may have seriously disconnected or pathological pleasure-pain centers. The autistic person seems oblivious to all abstract categories and discriminations, existing solely in momentary contacts. Autism is too complicated a subject to discuss in depth here; I mention it solely to describe the pathological outcome of the earliest and most severe failure of experience.

Winnicott's (1958, 1965a, 1965b) views on early infant development are, more than any other psychoanalytic theorist's, easily integrated into the present schema. He describes the extreme helplessness of the infant and the need for the mothering one to prevent the premature awareness of this helplessness by providing the illusion of the infant's omnipotence. According to Winnicott this experience, which leaves the infant relatively free from internal and external impingements, is a prerequisite for the growth of the "true self."

Winnicott describes the mother's role as the maintainer of a wall of constancies. As the infant matures physiologically and adapts to the fundamental state of extrauterine existence, the mother must gradually cease to adapt to its needs. She must provide the infant with novelty at a pace to which it can adapt, so that it can gradually increase its capacity for adaptation.

An infant who has experienced too much impingement develops a "false self" and, through imitative or otherwise false behavior, appears to have mastered situations. In fact, he or she has never developed an autonomous internal model or set of processes. This inadequately adapted person can "go by the rules" but cannot generate them.

Winnicott and others believe that the infant requires some preparation in the form of omnipotent primary narcissism before facing the aloneness and fragility which will continue to be a source of pain and anxiety intermittently throughout life. During this protected period, the infant can focus on adapting to the extrauterine state, can regulate or recognize the experiences of hunger, pain, and satiation. Thus some form of internal, physiological adjustment, including the development of visual focusing, depth perception, perceptual constancies, and increased motor strength and coordination precede any adaptation to the state of separateness. One who lacks solid experience in these early body-regulatory adaptations has a fragile sensoriperceptual consensual experience of external reality and may regress to this early adjustment period. Until the infant develops a neuronal capacity for selective attention and inattention, an "other" is required to perform this critical ego function.

The infant cannot adapt to critical moments in life, e.g., crawling and walking, the birth of a sibling, the first day of school, without successfully having adapted to a series of smaller changes first.

Melanie Klein's (1948; Segal, 1973) description of the infant's ego as striving for integration and alleviation of anxiety is consistent with my position, which basically equates the ego with the adaptive capacity, including internal representations of the world. As Beck (1971) notes, anxiety is experienced when adaptive strategies fail. Klein states that the ego disintegrates in the face of intolerable anxiety, creating a circular reaction in which failure of adaptation leads to anxiety, and anxiety further limits one's adaptive capacity. Klein defines the earliest infantile anxiety as persecutory and ascribes it to the fear of the projected death instinct. I would agree that dread of a physiological state of disequilibrium is a core anxiety. This disequilibrium cannot be changed directly by the infant; rather, it can be altered only through the manipulation of external variables, e.g., by the mother, who thus assumes ominous significance.

Klein's (1945, 1952) description of the splitting of the world into good and bad parts through projection and introjection is similar to my statement concerning the organizing influence of the basic pleasure-pain dichotomy. The defense of splitting confuses the distinction between inner and outer, and self and not-self, but maintains the initial dichotomy of pleasure and pain. In order for the infant to move beyond the paranoid-schizoid position, the breast must be seen as more good than bad. When good and bad parts can be integrated, there can be a self and an other. Thus a pathology in the pleasure-pain experience can seriously impair the earliest movement away from infantile persecutory anxiety.

According to Klein, a predominance of good experiences not only makes possible the integration of objects but also strengthens and prepares the infant for the difficulties of the depressive position. Klein postulates that strong feelings of guilt and mourning attend the resolution of the splits and are concomitant with the perception of whole objects.

According to our principle, the infant who has never adequately achieved biological adaptation and/or has not had sufficiently good "holding" by the mother has acquired neither the most basic models of self and others nor a consistent internal equilibrium, and is thus incapable of attending to the expanding world around him or her. Inconsistent early mothering cripples both the development of a positive sense of self and a belief in the goodness of others. The model of all later social interchanges is distorted by the expectation of evil, by a lack of basic trust. In this pathological outcome, separation is seen as a threat because the environment is perceived as malevolent.

Fairbairn (1952a) states that, in favorable conditions, the "reality principle matures as experience expands" (p. 168) and the pristine unitary ego adapts to the world in ever-widening circles. He also states that internalization results from frustration. This view is similar to Ashby's (1965) statement that much is learned through failure. Fairbairn says these frustrating experiences are internalized by the infant in an effort to control its world.

According to Fairbairn (1952a), the parents' basic task is to love the child on the child's own terms and in his or her own right; that is, to respond to the infant-child as separate and distinct from the parents. Like Mahler, Fairbairn stresses the duration of the separation process and the vacillation during this extended transitional period between experiences of separation and those of oneness. In summary, Fairbairn states that the quality of mothering and of environmental responses to the infant affect the ability both to acknowledge separation and to adapt to the world. For Fairbairn, introjection and projection are reactions to frustration that confuse the distinction between inner and outer worlds and interfere with a stable sense of reality.

Mahler (1968; Mahler, Pine, & Bergman, 1975), somewhat more empirically, describes the infant's movement from symbiotic attachment to separation from the mother, during which time subtle differences in each infant's development interact with maternal personality and expectations in unique ways. Thus the mother who is eager to stop "mothering" assumes that her child with precocious motor development is ready to be on its own—neglecting to give the additional support necessary during the rapprochement phase. In other words, she inappropriately speeds up the rate of adaptation, perhaps impairing its quality. At the other extreme, a mother who needs to infantilize her child will not permit the autonomy necessary for separation, thus slowing down the rate of adaptation. In the above examples, the mother's own unresolved separation issues and limited adaptive capacities limit her child's achievement of separation. If mother is in equilibrium only when she is either symbiotically joined or totally withdrawn and unrelated to the infant, then the infant cannot find the behaviors necessary for mature, separate relatedness. As a result of such a pathological system, the child is unprepared for other people who can tolerate, and indeed demand, more mature forms of relating.

Mahler's descriptions suggest that as one proceeds radially outward to more complex forms of adaptation, one must be able to refer back to the level just achieved to insure its continuing stability.

It is critical for species survival that parents accept and encourage the greater adaptive capacity of their children. However, the parents' anxiety and conscious or unconscious envy all too often lead them to sabotage the growth of their children. Since parental approval and anxiety are critical influences on developing children and their conceptions of themselves and others, efforts at educating the young must involve "holding" the parents and diminishing their anxiety. Winnicott (1965b) states this quite directly in discussing the father's role with the mother of the newborn. The father must "hold" the mother by providing a wall of constancies and security, so that she can adapt to her new role and safeguard her infant's development. It is

the task of society and its institutions to provide a similar functio..
lies.

When psychoanalytic theorists speak of introjection, incorporatic.
identification, they are describing the construction of an internal represe..
tion of the world (Sandler, 1962). To the extent that one's introjects and
identifications represent reliable, consistent, and accurate views of the world
and the self, they greatly increase one's adaptive capacity. According to
Bychowski (1952), the preschizophrenic has conflicting, contradictory introjects that lead to faulty internal representations and therefore to faulty
expectations of oneself and of others. Similarly, Rapaport (1951) states that
adaptation requires reliable, consistent, and accurate introjects with which to
judge incoming stimuli and current behaviors. Thus a faulty set of introjects
leaves the schizophrenic with poor reality testing and other maladaptive
behaviors.

Hartmann (1939/1951) stated that a defect in primary autonomous ego
functions decreases the capacity to neutralize aggression; this lowered capacity further interferes with functioning. Hartmann's theory can be restated as
an innate deficit in the capacity to withstand and adapt to novel stimuli and
their attendant anxieties; such an incapacity further limits successful adaptation. Thus the ego of the schizophrenic is in conflict with reality because it
does not have adequate or valid models for adapting to reality; it must
therefore either deny it—molding reality to fit its erroneous constructions—
or experience excessive, even incapacitating, anxiety.

Arlow and Brenner's (1969) theory, which states that schizophrenia is a
regressive alteration of reality testing as a defense against anxiety, is consistent with Beck's (1971) description of anxiety as a reaction to a break in
programs caused partly by faulty, unrealistic models and leading to regression.

Easily integrated with our approach is Sullivan's early description of the
conservative aspects of schizophrenia as "attempts at regression . . . successfully to re-integrate masses of life experience which had failed at structuralization into a functional unity" (1924/1962e, p. 20), and his later view that
schizophrenia is a failure of the self-system to reserve attention to those
referential processes that can be consensually validated (1944/1964).

Sullivan ascribes the development of faulty internal models of the world
and the self to the infant's dissociation of those parts of experience which
aroused extreme anxiety in the mother, led to her disapproval, and resulted
in the infant's cataclysmic anxiety. The infant's anxiety and dissociation of
experience into the "not me" can be seen as an effort to remain adapted to
the mother, who is critical for survival. If she changes—becomes inconsistent,
unloving, anxious, hostile, or rejecting—the infant's capacity to adapt
is seriously disturbed by this loss of constancy. Furthermore, infants in
the above situation, motivated by the survival value of maintaining good

relations with the mother, will repress, deny, or otherwise rid themselves of behaviors that disturb her. Thus two things occur: (1) this behavior becomes dissociated; and (2) it is never sufficiently or validly represented and adapted to because it would alter previously constant adaptations.

During the juvenile period, the survival need for mother's approval diminishes somewhat and is replaced by an extreme preoccupation with peer regard and evaluation. According to Sullivan, this is a time when the preschizophrenic child can make up for deficiencies through the relatively simple adaptation to a juvenile, same-sex peer.

Sullivan describes the schizophrenic breakdown as a consequence of an event that is so much a part of the "not-me" system, so discrepant with one's sense of self, that it throws all the structures of the self-system into chaos. Sullivan suggests that an extreme confrontation with dissociated elements leads to extreme anxiety and the collapse of more recently socialized adaptations. In the midst of the ensuing chaos and panic, the person may entertain new models of the world which diminish anxiety, but are gross distortions of reality, for example, delusions.

Sullivan considers the failure of selective inattention to be critical to the development of schizophrenia. This failure is what I referred to as a loss of the constancies that normally enable us to form a barrier between ourselves and the myriad stimuli in the environment so that we may focus more clearly on the critical, novel elements.

22. The Juvenile Period: Although the basis for future cognitive and emotional development is laid very early, the child still has a great deal to master. For example, children must adapt to sexual and generational differences, accepting that they are not entitled to or capable of some of the pleasures that adults enjoy. Children must learn to communicate with peers and authorities outside the home. They must acquire the basic skills of their culture before they can truly separate from home and become independent. To this end, children play games, imagine themselves in various adult roles, go to school, and become apprenticed to masters. Children who are deprived of culturally appropriate training will be at a loss to communicate and commune with their peers and will be unable to support themselves.

Parents frequently teach children inappropriate modes of interaction. For example, they may seek to instill a Victorian morality in their pubescent girls, succeeding only in raising stilted, schizoid teenagers who, when finally away from home, cannot cope and at best react with extreme rebellion against their clearly inadequate, misleading parents. As illustrated by the above example, family mythologies can be seriously out of synch with the times and leave offspring both with an inadequate model of the real world and with a dilemma expressed by Sullivan's use of the "not me." If the child adapts to reality, as seen in the school and the world at large, he or she is becoming that which the parents deny or detest. The child cannot adapt to the discordant realities of both new and old experiences without a superordinate model that explains the discrepancy. Therapy may provide such a model, but it is usually unavailable.

Usually, this extreme discrepancy between the reality of the home and the reality of the rest of the world is not apparent until late adolesence, but in severe cases the child may notice it as soon as he or she ventures outside the immediate family.

When the child first goes to school or to a doctor, the absoluteness of parental authority is challenged and the child's capacity to adapt to this critical shift is influenced by the parental capacity to tolerate the shift from absolute to relative authority. The nature of this transition can be seen in the difficulty some children have in understanding that their parents may disagree with their teachers over disciplinary issues, ways of problem solving, etc. This difficult transition is also poignantly evident when children go to the hospital and are faced with their parents' reactions to doctors—frequently an anxiety-provoking surprise to the child.

Wynne et al. (1958) describe how some pathological families use what they call the "rubber fence" to prevent the child from seeing and experiencing other views of the world. In our terms, Wynne's rubber fence means that the radius of the sphere of successful adaptation is finite and includes only the immediate family. Relating to outsiders leads to parental hostility and rejection as well as to the child's fantasized destruction of the parents.

During the juvenile era, the child must learn the basic skills necessary for adult membership in society. These skills, be they hunting and fishing or reading and writing, are best learned in atmospheres in which all else, e.g., food and shelter, is held constant. Each achievement or successful adaptation not only forms the basis for the next adaptation but also increases the child's sense of well-being and competence.

Often the child who is incapable of learning because of retardation, subtle perceptual-motor difficulties, or preoccupation with problems at home is also alienated from his peer group. Perhaps the most pathological development during the juvenile period occurs when the child is subjected to a transactional thought disorder in the family of origin. Language—especially verbal expressions of approval or disapproval—becomes meaningful parts of the child's experience. The examples provided at home greatly influence the child. Learning to communicate and interact with unpredictable and irrational people provides training in maladaptive thought and communication. Since parental approval is more clearly linked to survival than is peer approval, it is generally a more powerful reinforcer. In addition, the child who adapts to the thought-disordered family is simultaneously ostracized by and disarticulated from peers, thus being denied the only possible corrective to the faulty education provided by the parents.

23-24. *Adolescence:* The adolescent must suddenly adapt to a great deal of novelty, e.g., changing body image and bodily sensations, new feelings, new ways of thinking, and new parental responses. Toward the end of adolescence, he or she must also adapt to physical separation and the achievement of an autonomous identity. Adolescence is an exceedingly difficult time at best, and it is often the last straw for the preschizophrenic.

I would argue that, even as late as adolescence and adulthood, the seemingly intact person can become schizophrenic. This disturbance can occur when the discrepancy between one's expectations and one's actual conditions persists long enough in the absence of support from parents or others critical to early development.

People who were sent to concentration camps while in their early teens experienced puberty under the most perverse conditions; some of these survivors became psychotic after liberation. One explanation for the psychosis is that the victims experienced a developmental stage of great novelty against a background of extreme social chaos. In a sense, those who survived this experience had successfully adapted to it; however, when they were freed at the end of the war, they experienced guilt not only over the loss of family and friends but also over their own departure from both their previous ideas of proper behavior and their previous expectations of the world as a whole.

Accounts of survivors of crashes, of hostages under siege, of prisoners of war, and even of people experiencing culture shock often suggest that the reactions of people both during and after these crises are greatly affected by the presence or absence of personal and ideological allegiances, which, I suggest, serve as an anchor or wall of constancy. Thus, the members of a soccer team stranded after a plane crash were able to adapt to the brutal reality of their situation by integrating the eating of human flesh into the ritual of the sacrament in Catholicism (Read, 1974).

During adolescence and adulthood, psychotic, schizophrenialike disturbances can be precipitated by the injection of toxins, by allergic reactions to medications, and by some diseases that apparently destroy or weaken the normal hardware of conceptualization (the central nervous system), altering perceptions and disrupting the recognition of patterns and constancy in the environment.

25-28. *Extreme Disturbances during Adulthood:* Serious illnesses involving prolonged bed rest and enforced regression can precipitate psychoses, possibly because of the sensory deprivation or the generalization of regression. Similarly, puberty, pregnancy, childbirth, marriage, surgery, and menopause can all precipitate psychotic episodes if the disruption of body image or self-image threatens the core of one's adaptation.

Social upheavals, threats to one's personal religious or ethical values, and extreme instances of misunderstanding can also precipitate psychoses. "The Marquise of O . . . ," by the nineteenth-century writer Kleist (1960), describes how a relatively sane adult can be forced by circumstances to a near-psychotic state. In this story, a respectable widow is raped at night while remaining asleep. Several months later she develops a peculiar feeling of nausea and dizziness, which both concerns and confuses her since she is aware that if someone else described these same complaints she would say that the person was pregnant, but that cannot be the case for her. At first her family is quite sympathetic and concerned, banishing a doctor who says that she is pregnant. But when a midwife confirms the diagnosis, the parents cease to believe their daughter and condemn her for her sinful behavior and attempts at deception. Ejected from her parents' home, the young woman feels deprived of their love. Convinced that she is not pregnant, she believes that she is going mad. Although she does not go crazy, one can imagine that others might since, in such circumstances, one is entirely alone with unassimilable data, deprived of a former basic, stable connection—the tie to one's family.

Adults who have had secure relationships with people critical to their early development seem better able to endure changes in the world around them than those who have lacked such relationships. This capacity to endure is due both to the actual buffering such critical others provide at times of stress and to "good enough" experiences that provide a wellspring of hope and faith in the reliability and applicability of one's strategies for survival—a memory of crises endured and overcome.

As mentioned at the beginning of this chapter, neurophysiological, experimental psychological, and biochemical findings are not specifically represented in Table 7. That is because they are generally viewed as secondary phenomena—possibly core symptoms, but nonetheless secondary to genetic, traumatic (CNS), or life-stress etiologies. For example, diathesis-stress theories of schizophrenia propose a genetically based neural integrative deficit (Meehl, 1962) or ANS anomaly (Mednick, Schulsinger, & Schulsinger, 1975) leading to perceptual and coqivitive disturbances. The monogenic bioamine theory of schizophrenia postulates a specific metabolic defect in the schizophrenic. Perhaps the low MAO found by Wyatt and Murphy (1976) is more than a genetic marker. Low MAO is consistent with both the dopamine hypothesis of schizophrenia and the endogenous hallucinogen model. This abnormal biochemistry may be evident throughout life, causing aberrant subjective experiences and subsequent problems of interpersonal relatedness, or it may be a latent propensity triggered by the physiological changes/disequilibrium of puberty, certain illnesses, or critical levels of stress. This biochemical change might in turn provoke neurophysiological change. An excess of dopamine, a neurotransmitter found in the deep limbic system of the brain, affects cortical activity in not fully charted ways. On the other hand, neurophysiological theories indicate an alteration in the schizophrenic's level of arousal, which may have unknown effects on brain metabolism. In cybernetic terms, the neurophysiological and biochemical systems are each parameters of the other; each represents a set of stimuli or conditions to which the other must adapt. In addition to continuous feedback and minor adjustments to each other, each system may change dramatically when a certain "last straw" is added, functioning, in Ashby's (1965) terms, as a "step function."

Neurophysiological and psychological studies of schizophrenia have indicated deficits in arousal, orienting and habituating responses, and the ability to maintain major sets. Whether a change in arousal response is primary or secondary to a cognitive deficit, each disrupts the other, and we would expect to find them together.

Biochemical theories of endogenous psychedelics do not explain the origin of the chemical, which might well be a secondary manifestation of a more fundamental disorder, thus accounting for secondary, rather than primary, signs of schizophrenia. Such an endogenous chemical may be a step function, secondary to a critical state of arousal. The dopamine hypothesis suggests that dopamine increases in schizophrenics until too much is transmitted, hypothetically causing deficient inhibition or selection of neuronal messages. Matthysse (1976b) has pointed out how this increase might be translated on a cognitive level into loosening of associations. NIMH twin studies suggesting that low MAO level is inherited point to a genetic basis for the increase in dopamine. As mentioned above, one can view alterations or defects in biochemistry as deviations in the person's hardware. The effect of these defects on behavior is a function of the extent of the hardware aberration and the comprehensiveness and flexibility of the programs, or software, available to the person at the time of a disruptive, novel event. Minor alterations in psychophysical, psychological, and biochemical processes can be assumed to exist throughout development, as described in Table 7, interacting with stage-specific deficits to produce, at times, major alterations. These changes, in turn, increase the person's level of tension, rate of experienced novelty, and social alienation.

| The Treatment of Schizophrenia | Chapter Thirteen |

Thus far, I have reviewed theories and research on the nature and possible etiology of schizophrenia at great length, while scarcely mentioning its treatment. A thorough discussion of the treatment of schizophrenia clearly requires a book of its own; this chapter is merely an introduction.

Just as there appear to be many pathways to schizophrenia—a disorder with a complex symptomatology—so there are many different approaches to its treatment. Some of these approaches arise from different etiological theories; others address themselves to specific symptoms and deficits. The schizophrenic has a thought disorder, shows poor reality testing, is socially isolated, and has a poor self-image, problems relating to his or her family, and difficulty at work. Regardless of what one believes causes these impairments, ideally treatment should alleviate all of them. Conceivably, intensive treatment that results in improvement in one sphere will have a general ameliorative effect even if it has not altered the "core" disturbance. For example, intensive family treatment might significantly reduce the stress contributed by the family and improve the patient's reality testing and capacity for appropriate behavior within the family. In so doing, this treatment might reduce the overall level of stress the patient is experiencing to the point where other schizophrenic symptoms abate. New skills acquired in the family therapy context may become generalized. Such a course is more likely to occur with acute schizophrenics who have been overwhelmed by precipitating events and have suffered a sudden alteration in functioning—a breakdown. Such persons already have a repertoire of complex and sophisticated skills. In more chronic cases, the patient seems to need less rehabilitation than habilitation.

The psychotic process or its precursors have probably impaired cognitive, emotional, and social functioning and development over a long period of time. These deficits, incurred over the years, require compensation.

The most optimistic claims for various treatment strategies arise from studies of the first group of patients—acute, good premorbid schizophrenics. In this section I shall review the major treatment modalities—what they do best and what role they take in multidisciplinary approaches to schizophrenia. The multifaceted nature of schizophrenia is reflected by the team approach. Ideally, the team consists of people with various skills and areas of specialization, all simultaneously involved in evaluating and treating the schizophrenic.

Although not all schizophrenics require hospitalization, generally the most complete evaluation and treatment plan can be made during an inpatient stay. The mere act of separating the patient from his or her usual environment can have serious implications. Currently there is considerable debate about the legitimacy and value of involuntary commitment. Preventive detention is unconstitutional in the United States, but people are frequently detained in hospitals against their wills. Using the hospital in this manner conflicts with the stated objective of hospitalization—treatment. Hospitalization in general has been criticized by Goffman (1961), Laing (1960/1965a), Szasz (1961), Foucault (1965), and others. There is also debate in this country about the patient's need for treatment versus his or her right to refuse treatment. The medically ill patient has a right to refuse surgery—in fact, the patient's permission is required for an operation. The psychiatric patient is often uninformed about the risks of treatment; only recently has informed consent been required for some treatments, such as electroconvulsive therapy (ECT).

The hospital setting itself may or may not be therapeutic. As described in Chapter 2, throughout history societies have isolated persons with serious mental disorders. At times this was done in a punitive, self-protective way; at other times an effort was made to soothe and rehabilitate disturbed people. Some contemporary hospitals are the total institutions described by Goffman (1961) in *Asylums.* They "strip" entering persons of all individual identity, insisting from the moment patients are admitted that all self-initiated behavior is symptomatic of the illness—a sign that the patients are crazy. "Healthy" behavior consists of bowing to the rules of the hospital bureaucracy.

Patients in total institutions eventually lose their will to initiate action, regress to states of extreme dependency, become isolated and uninterested in the outside world, and show signs of "institutionalization." It can be difficult to distinguish between the consequences of long-term hospitalization and a prolonged psychotic process. Recent work with chronic patients in state hospitals suggests that much of the behavior observed in people who have been hospitalized for twenty or more years is due to the lack of stimulation and social isolation produced by the hospitalization. Growing awareness of these ill effects, the development of effective antipsychotic medication, as well as economic considerations have caused a shift from long-term hospitalization to brief hospitalization followed by outpatient care. Now that the pendulum has swung, it seems that professionals may have lost sight of the benefits of hospitalization and milieu therapy.

MILIEU THERAPY

Early pioneers in the intensive treatment of schizophrenics believed it necessary to separate the patient from the home environment. Some dedicated therapists even took patients into their own homes in order to provide a safe therapeutic environment (Winnicott, 1965b; Sechehaye, 1951a, 1951b). Others, seeking to expose schizophrenic patients to several "healthy" professionals as role models, sought to create a therapeutic hospital environment. Sullivan (1931/1962a) started an all-male ward for six patients on which only male staff were allowed. He believed that heterosexual relations were too complex and demanding during this stressful period. An environment that recreated the chumship stage afforded a better hope of restitution.

Earlier, Simmel (1929) identified the critical feature of a therapeutic environment: it aimed to replace the family or society with a new reality. The hospital would be a better family that would limit acting out without reinforcing a primitive superego through punitive measures or infantile gratifications. Main (1946) and Jones (1953) developed the idea of a therapeutic community in which patients' initiative, autonomy, and judgment were fostered by lessening their dependence on authoritarian structures.

At Chestnut Lodge, attention was paid not only to the individual treatment of schizophrenics but to the psychiatric hospital as a whole. Overt and covert events on a specific ward and in the hospital as a whole were the objects of analysis in Stanton and Schwartz's (1954) study, *The Mental Hospital*. Regardless of the stated goals of a hospital, certain consequences follow from the intensity of the hospital environment and the pressures of working with very disturbed patients. One of these was best described by Stanton and Schwartz: the patient's behavior deteriorates as a consequence of covert staff disagreement. They found that when this disagreement was unearthed, the patient's behavior improved.

At present there is less interest in intensive hospital treatment of schizophrenics than in the 1940s and 1950s. However, some of the approaches used during this period have been incorporated into current work—the community meeting, activities therapy, skills for daily living, and rehabilitation counseling. Evaluating the role of the milieu in patients' improvement is difficult since it is not used in isolation, and comparison of patients treated in different milieus involves other variables as well (patient selection, staff sophistication, morale, etc.). Private psychiatric hospitals and wards in teaching hospitals tend to select voluntary patients who functioned at a relatively high level before their illness and who have spent less total time in hospitals. Patients in state hospitals tend to be persons with poor premorbid adjustments and chronic illness, impoverished, poorly educated, socially alienated, and with more prenatal and postnatal trauma. A recent comparison of patients randomly assigned to a community mental health inpatient unit and to a community residence that did not use traditional therapeutic approaches found that in both programs those patients who relapsed most quickly were the younger, less educated ones with poor job histories (Matthews et al., 1979).

Milieu approaches that are therapeutic with one group of patients should not automatically be applied to another. For example, there is reason to believe that a high staff/patient ratio and an active milieu can be a regressive environment contraindicated for borderline patients but therapeutic for acute and chronic schizophrenics. Many acute patients need an initial period free from external stimulation, whereas chronic patients need a stimulating environment.

Another cautionary note is in order in this context: patients may adapt well to the hospital environment only to face a rude awakening on leaving the hospital. A highly structured environment does not prepare a patient for the social isolation and total freedom of living on one's own in a welfare hotel. Thus, the optional hospital milieu depends on the specific patient's need and the available discharge plans. In addition, most people need some transition from the hospital environment to the family home or an independent living situation. Unfortunately, there are too few halfway houses available for people who no longer require full-time observation but are in need of some external structure and supervision. Ideally, there should be a graduated system of total care, three-quarter care, halfway care, and quarter-way care. With each successive step there would be slightly less staff supervision of behavior and more individual responsibility (see Almond, 1975).

Group Therapy

Various forms of group therapy have been used in hospital and outpatient settings. Traditional group therapy requires a more permanent membership than today's hospitals generally permit. On the other hand, patients on a hospital ward form a natural group with certain common interests, e.g., hospitalization, medication, rules, parties. Group or community meetings are the logical place to discuss these issues. Group therapy with schizophrenics generally focuses on more concrete problems (e.g., medication, meeting people, getting a job, staying out of the hospital) and on more concrete activities (e.g., having coffee, planning a meal) than does group therapy with neurotics. The group therapist encourages patients to interact among themselves, directing their comments and questions to each other rather than to their therapists. Using verbal and nonverbal means, the therapist tries to increase patients' social skills and reliance on peer support. A special advantage of group therapy with schizophrenics is that the patients generally have more experiential knowledge of schizophrenia than do the therapists, and once they are able to express themselves freely, they can give meaningful advice and support to one another. Group therapy improves patients' social functioning and can be especially valuable for withdrawn patients (O'Brien, 1975).

Occupational and Rehabilitational Therapy

One of the schizophrenic's major handicaps is the absence or loss of occupational and social skills. Here are two very different examples: (1) the college student who is exceptionally bright but who, after several psychotic episodes, seems incapable of pursuing earlier career hopes, and (2) the unskilled, semiliterate person who, although by no means retarded, has done poorly in school and has never held a job for more than three days because of intense suspiciousness of coworkers. This person is particularly suspicious of the written word and feels humiliated by his or her total dependence on others to explain written material. Both people are unable to support themselves and suffer from the low self-esteem inherent in such a position. Ideally, activities therapy, vocational counseling, and occupational therapy help the person to acquire the skills of daily living (e.g., meeting people, behaving appropriately in groups) and specific job skills, as well as providing sheltered job opportunities. Recent advances in obtaining rights for mental patients (they must be paid the minimum wage) have ironically lessened their chances of employment during their hospitalization.

Dance and Art Therapy

Dance and art therapy are generally used in conjunction with other forms of treatment. Frequently they are group activities that encourage interaction and communication around a common task. They offer nonverbal means of evaluating and communicating with patients who are either not used to verbal expression of emotions or are currently in a nonverbal, highly regressed state. Some patients are better able to communicate their feelings and concerns via drawing or movement. Frequently art and dance therapists are the first to make contact with, or notice differences in, regressed patients.

INDIVIDUAL PSYCHOTHERAPY

For many years, individual therapy and milieu therapy were the only treatments available for schizophrenia. Hannah Green's (1964) account in *I Never Promised You a Rose Garden* testifies to the effectiveness of psychotherapy with a severely disturbed girl who did not receive medication. This therapy was conducted by an exceptional therapist, Frieda Fromm-Reichmann, before neuroleptics were available. The place of individual psychotherapy in the treatment of schizophrenia has become more controversial since the introduction of neuroleptics. At present it seems unwise to attempt to treat most schizophrenics without the aid of medication. Individual psychotherapy nevertheless does have a significant place in the optimal treatment of most schizophrenics, although the preferred form of this therapy may differ depending on the particular patient and the particular therapist. I shall compare and contrast some forms of individual therapy.

The first goal of psychotherapy is to establish a relationship with the patient. With schizophrenics, this task is often a very difficult one because of the person's suspiciousness, withdrawal, and denial of problems. Though different therapists use very different techniques, they all share the strong desire to understand the patient and to connect with him or her. Therapists who are afraid of bizarre behavior and thoughts will find it difficult to make this first step. The therapeutic relationship is a prerequisite for any further work, be it supportive, confrontational, or interpretive. The therapist must become someone the patient is interested in, willing to talk to, and at times able to listen to. The relationship between therapist and patient can never be taken for granted—the therapist's willingness to hear and be part of the patient's experience is especially taxed with seriously disturbed patients whose behavior can be shocking, revolting, confusing, and frightening. It was in the context of such extreme schizophrenic behavior that theorists like Fromm-Reichmann (1959c) first noted the constructive use of countertransference as a signal that therapist and patient might have similar anxieties or wishes that impeded the treatment. Searles (1965a) has eloquently and courageously described how difficult it can be for the therapist to allow the patient to separate and leave the symbiotic transference.

The short-term goals of psychotherapy are to improve reality testing and to strengthen the person's adaptive coping capacities. Some therapists have a present-day, reality-based supportive approach. These therapists may actively model and teach new behaviors to the patients. Others see such an approach as superficial and infantilizing, and prefer to work toward long-term goals of autonomy and independent behavior. In one version of the first model, the individual therapist is an adjunct to chemotherapy and rehabilitation counseling—coordinating the "case," supporting the use of medication and various treatment modalities, and confronting the patient when his or her behavior is inappropriate. At the other extreme are long-term regressive treatments in which the patient is maintained with little or no medication through a lengthy hospitalization; he or she is permitted to behave in extremely infantile and deviant ways for as long as the therapist and patient feel is necessary (Foster, 1975).

Rosen has worked very intensively with acute psychotic patients. He emphasizes confrontations, such as "direct" interpretations of sexual and aggressive material, in the hope of establishing contact with patients and diminishing their psychotic symptoms to a point where more traditional therapy can be started (Rosen, 1947).

Most people who work individually with schizophrenics use some combination of the approaches mentioned here. Antipsychotic medication is often used during much of the treatment. The therapist tends to be more active and "real" than he or she might be with a neurotic patient. The therapist who works with outpatient schizophrenics may find it necessary to have some contact with patients' family members to help take care of daily-life crises as they arise.

Individual psychotherapy offers the schizophrenic the possibility of a long-term relationship with a reliable and concerned other who is willing to meet the patient on his or her terms and to live through the intensely emotional journey from illness to possible health. Not every therapist is willing or able to make such a commitment, and most cannot make it to very many seriously disturbed people at a given time.

FAMILY THERAPY

In Chapter 9, I reviewed major family theories of the etiology of schizophrenia and described how these theories arose specifically from therapists' experiences in interviewing and working with families of schizophrenic patients. During the 1940s and 1950s it was common practice to separate the patient from the family—the family was viewed as pathogenic. A growing interest in the communication patterns of schizophrenics' families shifted the emphasis toward work with families. Family therapy is rarely the sole treatment approach; generally it is used in conjunction with other forms of therapy.

Living with a schizophrenic can be a very frightening and disruptive experience, arousing extreme ambivalence in family members. They may want the schizophrenic person out of the home, but also feel guilty and frightened about his or her prospects in the community. Therapists and institutions that do not involve family members in planning for and treating the schizophrenic often find that their plans seem to be sabotaged by family members. Family members frequently need help in learning how to cope with patients before they can follow a treatment plan. In addition, family members can provide therapists with information regarding the schizophrenic's behavior outside the hospital and may be the first to notice the signs of decompensation. Often the patient's family or therapist wants the patient to separate from the family before the patient is ready. Separation from home is normally a long, difficult process; it is especially difficult for the schizophrenic. Beels (1975) argues against a view of the family as pathogenic and in most cases prefers to engage families in the patient's treatment because they are in the position to be the most helpful. Families may either distrust hospitals and professionals or have unrealistic expectations and demands for help—both attitudes require exploration and clarification for treatment to be effective.

When the schizophrenic is living at home or in frequent contact with family members, it is important to help family members learn to set limits and communicate their wishes clearly without infantilizing the schizophrenic or ignoring his or her real difficulties. It is important to keep in mind that all families experience great stress when one of their members is ill or hospitalized. Anxiety and uncertainty are high, and the family needs to be encouraged to ask important questions, which staff should try to answer. The family has a right to know about its member's illness. If such questions are avoided or reflected back, the family members will become even more anxious, distrustful, and confused. Imagine having a family member hospitalized for an unknown physical ailment and, on asking the doctors for an explanation, being met by silence or "What do *you* think it's about?" Regardless of the therapist's view of the etiology of the schizophrenia, the family is entitled to some explanation of the disorder in terms that it can understand. Thus a first step in family work is for therapist and family members to exchange information. The primary goals are to keep communication open and to increase the range of behavior that can be enjoyed by family members. For example, before an adolescent patient can successfully move out of the house, other family members must be helped to find new definitions for themselves.

BEHAVIORAL THERAPIES

Formally and informally, the techniques of behavior modification have been integrated into work with schizophrenics, whose behavior is often very disturbing to staff, patients, and family members. Often the patient must stop a specific disruptive behavior before staff or family members are willing to spend much time with him or her. Very assaultive patients are generally avoided by staff except when they are assaultive—which only serves to reinforce their assaultive behavior. The basic strategy of behavior techniques is to select certain behaviors for positive reinforcement and others for negative reinforcement. Although this strategy sounds like common sense on a busy ward it is often difficult to respond positively to a patient who is doing nothing inappropriate (sitting quietly) and to avoid reinforcing the patient who is very disruptive. The most ambitious behavior modification programs are the token economies. In a token economy, the entire psychiatric unit is run along behavior modification lines and aims to change disturbing behavior through a system of indirect (token) reinforcement. For this system to be effective, all staff members must be involved in accurately reporting behavior. Some staff and patients find a concrete objective system like this far easier to work in than the less structured, more subjective atmosphere of the psychodynamically run ward.

MEDICATION

The antipsychotic (neuroleptic) drugs discovered in the early 1950s are the mainstay of modern psychiatric treatment of schizophrenia. The biochemical action of these drugs was discussed in Chapter 4. They are characterized by "their effect on the ascending reticular formation which results in reduced reactivity to external and internal stimuli and in decreased spontaneous activity. Furthermore, their effects on the limbic system lead to a blunting of emotional arousal, their effects on hypothalmic regulations result in a variety of autonomic symptoms, and finally, their effects on the caudate-striate system may be manifested in different extrapyramidal symptoms" (Lehmann, 1975, p. 28)

Many different neuroleptic drugs are in use today (see Table 7). The therapeutic effectiveness of all neuroleptics is identical, although a specific patient may respond better to one drug than to another for reasons unknown. The neuroleptics do differ in their side effects and in their milligram potency.

Aliphatic phenothiazines and piperidine derivatives induce more locomotive and autonomic side effects than do the piperazine derivatives, which cause less drowsiness and more extrapyramidal side effects. Haloperidol, a butyrophenone, is very potent and causes few autonomic, but often intense extrapyramidal, side effects.

Acute schizophrenics are generally treated with 500–1000 mg/day of chlorpromazine (or its equivalent). Sometimes daily doses of two or three grams are required. Arousal symptoms (irritability, restlessness, aggressiveness) are generally controlled within two to three weeks, whereas symptoms related to perceptual and cognitive functioning may take six to eight weeks of treatment to disappear. Chronic patients generally require lower levels of medication than acute patients do and may not need neuroleptics at all. In general, patients should be maintained on the lowest possible dosages of

TABLE 7: Generic Names, U.S. Trade Names, and Conversion Factors for Doses of Neuroleptic Drugs in Relation to Chlorpromazine

Generic Name	U.S. Trade Name	Conversion Factor[1]
Phenothiazines		
Aliphatic		
Chlorpromazine	Thorazine	1:1
Promazine	Sparine	1:1
Triflupromazine	Vesprin	1:4
Piperazine		
Acetophenazine	Tindal	1:5
Butaperazine	Repoise	1:10
Carphenazine	Proketazine	1:4
Fluphenazine	Permitil	1:50
	Prolixin	
Perphenazine	Trilafon	1:10
Prochlorperazine	Compazine	1:6
Thiopropazine	Dartal	1:10
Trifluoperazine	Stelazine	1:20
Piperidine		
Mesoridazine	Serentil	1:2
Piperacetazine	Quide	1:10
Thioridazine	Mellaril	1:1
Butyrophenones		
Haloperidol	Haldol	1:50
Thioxanthenes		
Chlorprothixene	Taractan	1:1
Thiothixene	Navane	1:25
Dihydroindolone		
Molindone	Moban	1:5

1 Estimated dosage ratio in relation to chlorpromazine. For example: A dose of 10 mg of perphenazine (Trilafon) is equivalent to 100 mg of chlorpromazine (Thorazine) since it is 10 times as potent.

SOURCE: Table 1 from "Psychopharmacological Treatment of Schizophrenia," by H. E. Lehmann, in *Schizophrenia Bulletin,* No. 13, 1975.

medication. (This can be achieved after symptoms have disappeared by gradually reducing medication until symptoms reappear and then going back to the next highest dosage.)

Intramuscular injections are two to three times as potent as the equivalent dose by mouth. If a patient is suspected of hiding or "tonguing" tablets, liquid forms of medication should be used. Another option is the injection of long-acting neuroleptics: Prolixin enanthate or decanoate. A single injection remains active for about two weeks and is two to three times as potent as daily oral doses. For example, 25 mg Prolixin decanoate injected every other week is equivalent to 50 to 75 mg Prolixin taken orally per day. Injections bypass two major problems of medication: the patient's reluctance to take medication consistently and the difficulty of monitoring how much medication the patient actually receives.

Once a medication regime has begun, the patient can receive his or her entire daily dose once a day. Psychiatrists now recommend drug-free weekends or longer drug holidays to lessen the chance of tradive dyskinesia. Since neuroleptics remain in one's system for several weeks, the impact of discontinuing medication (i.e., the return of symptoms) cannot be seen immediately. Because of this delayed impact, it is often difficult to impress upon patients and their families the importance of continued medication.

The neuroleptics are not a cure-all. Some patients seem relatively untouched by large doses of medication; others do not respond as quickly as the staff would like. Some of these differences appear to be due to varying metabolic rates of absorption of the drugs. The plasma levels of some patients indicate that very little medication is being absorbed. Recent research suggests that a subgroup of acute schizophrenics may respond better to treatment without antipsychotic drugs (Matthews et al., 1979).

Staff frustration with disturbing behavior may lead to a premature change in medication or to the institution of polypharmacy. There is little justification for prescribing two different neuroleptics. The primary exception is when a daily oral medication is used in addition to Prolixin given parenterally. The main differences between these drugs are their side effects. Thus polypharmacy increases the likelihood of side effects without increasing therapeutic action.

The major problems caused by neuroleptics are the short- and long-term side effects. Familiarity with these side effects is important for anyone closely involved with someone receiving neuroleptics. Some side effects are acutely dangerous (e.g., agranulocytosis, hyperthemia, severe hypertension) or distressing (e.g., oculogyric crisis) and need to be treated immediately. Other side effects are psychologically very disturbing (e.g., inhibition of ejaculation, enlargement of the breasts and lactation). Some side effects interfere with normal activities: for example, blurred vision makes reading difficult, and akathesia makes sitting still almost impossible. (The latter is often misperceived by staff as agitation.) All these side effects can increase patients' discomfort, awkwardness, and alienation—they feel peculiar, not like themselves. Often patients have difficulty in articulating what is wrong. One woman told me that she had diamonds on her tongue and that her skin felt as if things were crawling on it. In her struggle to explain unusual physical sensations, she relied on vivid metaphors. Fortunately, she had a strong conviction about these changes in her body and persisted in her complaints until the medication was changed. All too often patients experiencing side effects like akathesia are seen as agitated and given more medication.

Side Effects

The different classes of neuroleptics have different side effects and should be chosen accordingly. For example, one might prescribe an aliphatic phenothiazine with sedating powers for a newly admitted, agitated patient. Such a neuroleptic would be inappropriate, however, for a patient who attends school.

Akathesias: These are the most common extrapyramidal side effects and are characterized by motor restlessness and muscle discomfort. The patient complains of an inability to sit still—something "made me get up and start moving." This side effect is dose-dependent and occurs within 72 hours. It may be related to increased medication. These short-term extrapyramidal side effects can be treated by administering antiparkinsonian drugs (Cogentin or Artane) and by lowering the dosage of neuroleptics.

Autonomic Reactions: Some people react to the medications with orthostatic hypotension, manifested in dizziness when they sit or stand up quickly. Patients often complain of anticholinergic effects, including blurred vision, dry mouth, urinary retention, and constipation.

If a patient complains of autonomic side effects, one might consider changing to Haldol, which has the lowest incidence of autonomic reactions. Table 8 shows some of the side effects and their frequency with various neuroleptics. In addition to the side effects mentioned in this table, all neuroleptics lower the seizure threshold and may also cause endocrinological side effects. Bassuk and Schoonover (1976) report that 10 percent of patients treated with phenothiazines have spontaneous clinical galactorrhea (lactation). This is due to elevated prolactin levels, which do not return to normal for two to three weeks after medication is discontinued. Amenorrhea and enlargement of the breasts may occur. Neuroleptics can also cause abnormal laboratory tests, including a false positive pregnancy test. Transient extrapyramidal effects (e.g., restlessness, rigidity, tremors, and dystonia) have been reported in newborns of mothers using phenothiazines in their last trimester.

TABLE 8: Nature and Frequency of Adverse Reactions to Various Types of Neuroleptic Drugs[1]

Adverse Reactions	Phenothiazines			Thioxanthenes	Butyrophenones
	Aliphatic Derivatives	Piperazine Derivatives	Piperidine Derivatives		
Behavioral					
Oversedation	+++	−	+++	+++	−
Extrapyramidal					
Parkinson's syndrome	++	+++	+	++	+++
Akathisia	++	+++	++	++	+++
Dystonic reactions	+	++	+	+	++
Autonomic					
Postural hypotension	+++	+	+++	++	++
Anticholinergic effects	+++	++	+++	++	+
Genitourinary					
Inhibition of ejaculation	++	++	+++	−	−
Cardiovascular					
EKG abnormalities	+	+	++	−	−
Hepatic					
Cholestatic jaundice	++	+	+	+	+
Hematological					
Blood dyscrasias	++	+	+	+	++
Ophthalmological					
Lenticular pigmentation	++	+	−	−	−
Pigmentary retinopathy	−	−	++	−	−
Dermatological					
Allergic skin reaction	++	+	+	+	+
Photosensitivity reaction	++	+	++	+	+
Skin pigmentation	++	−	−	−	−

Note: +++ = common; ++ = uncommon; + = rare.

1 Modified and expanded from *Medical Letter* (1970).

SOURCE: Table 2 from "Psychopharmacological Treatment of Schizophrenia," by H. E. Lehmann, in *Schizophrenia Bulletin,* No. 13, 1975.

Extrapyramidal Effects:

PARKINSONIAN SIDE EFFECTS: Generally the syndrome begins with tremors, but it may begin with rigidity, trouble in initiating movement, or weakness and muscle fatigue. Increased salivation, slurred speech, masklike face, and festinating gait often appear. These symptoms are continuous and appear two to three months after the initiation of treatment.

ACUTE DYSTONIC REACTIONS: These symptoms occur during the first five days of treatment. The symptoms are episodic, recurring, and dose-dependent. They consist of bizarre, involuntary contractions of the head muscles; less often they include contraction of the back and limbs.

TARDIVE DYSKINESIA: This is a long-term side effect of neuroleptics for which there is no known treatment. Its frequency, especially after the discontinuation of neuroleptic treatment, has been increasing. Medication seems to mask the symptoms of tardive dyskinesia, i.e., involuntary movements of the oral facial region and chorealike movements of other muscle groups. Unlike the extrapyramidal side effects, which appear early in neuroleptic treatment and respond to lowered dosage or antiparkinsonian medication, tardive dyskinesia occurs only after a year or more of drug treatment and is irreversible. Several recent malpractice suits have led doctors to advise patients of these side effects before or during treatment with neuroleptics. The increased use of drug holidays has also been a consequence of concern about this side effect.

Despite these side effects, neuroleptic drugs are the primary form of treatment in schizophrenia, and for good reason. Numerous studies have found that neuroleptics are superior to other medications, placebos, and psychotherapy in alleviating schizophrenic symptoms, e.g., hallucinations, delusions, projection, suspiciousness, confusion, ideas of reference, blunted affect, withdrawal, and agitation (Davis & Cole, 1975).

ELECTROCONVULSIVE THERAPY (ECT)

Before neuroleptics became available, insulin shock and electroconvulsive therapy (ECT) were widely used in the treatment of schizophrenia. Insulin shock is no longer in use, but ECT, which is frequently used for psychotic depression, is sometimes still used in the treatment of schizophrenia. There have been few controlled studies of its effectiveness with schizophrenia., and existing data are controversial. ECT sometimes gives more rapid results than neuroleptics, and it may be the treatment of choice for those experiencing extreme catatonic stupor or persistent paranoid delusions. However, ECT results are more temporary and maintenance is more difficult than is the case with antipsychotic medication (Lehmann, 1975). In many hospitals it is the treatment of last resort for schizophrenia, while other hospitals use it routinely.

CONCLUSION

The mounting concern about the cost and effectiveness of treatment has led to a search for the most efficient way of treating schizophrenia. Opposing camps have formed, with various sides favoring: medication, psychotherapy, behavior modification, family therapy, group therapy, milieu therapy, outpatient care, inpatient care, and even community organizing. Each side is armed with statistics and theories in support of its approach.

Obviously, there is no simple solution or cure; if there were, the problem would not be so serious and there would be no debate. In most cases, each therapy offers only a partial solution. A great deal depends on what is meant by "cure." Mosher (1973; Mosher & Menn, 1978) is fond of pointing out that, although phenothiazines permitted schizophrenics to leave state hospitals, they did not enable the majority of released patients to become integrated members of their communities. In other words, if we define "cure" as "being able to leave the hospital," then phenothiazines are the most efficient means of treating schizophrenics. But if we define "cure" as "the ability to interact with others in meaningful ways, to form intimate relationships, to take care of oneself and one's family, and to hold down a job," then phenothiazines alone are insufficient (Gunderson & Mosher, 1973; Klerman, 1977).

Antipsychotic medication certainly has its place. It intervenes in the schizophrenic's defective hardware by blocking dopamine transmission, thus inhibiting the excessive flow of information and decreasing arousal. In the process, it often eliminates or diminishes the secondary signs of schizophrenia, i.e., hallucinations, delusions, and agitation. Often these medications can also make the schizophrenic more approachable for other forms of therapy. Clearly, this is a valuable function, but it does not go far enough. In my view, the acute schizophrenic has "broken" under the strain of anxiety caused by information overload—too much novelty for the person's system (biochemical, cognitive, and emotional). It is not enough to modify the patient's biochemistry; the situation that became unbearable must be clarified, and the patient's capacity to adapt to this and future situations must be increased. To this end, individual psychotherapy and group psychotherapy are useful. One value of interpretations in psychotherapy is that they provide new constructs for understanding, and thus adapting to, the world. Shared interpretations or systems of meaning also diminish the schizophrenic's real and imagined isolation. In short-term therapy, ego interpretations and reality testing are enormously useful in reorienting schizophrenics to the real conflicts and dilemmas they must face—making it possible for them to say what must be said in *this* world. In addition to this cognitive impact of therapy, there is the therapeutic relationship itself. Certainly in intensive psychoanalytic treatment, and to a lesser extent in many briefer forms of therapy, the therapist's interest in and respect for the patient as a separate human being constitute a unique experience for some patients. It is this unique relationship that, in the most dramatic cases, permits a new beginning, a resolution of the basic fault, however deep it lies. Psychoanalytic treatment has as its goal an alteration and strengthening of the person's underlying character structure—a much more basic "cure" than that attempted by other treatment modalities, which strive to stabilize the patient outside the hospital and to inhibit maladaptive, inappropriate behavior.

No matter which treatment is chosen, the schizophrenic must remain alive and well while awaiting the benefits of medication or therapy. At times patients require a "holding environment" that can protect them from themselves and others by taking over some ego functions and thereby simplifying the environment. Structured milieus provide clear routines that serve to diminish the amount of individual thought and behavior necessary for survival. A clear implication of current knowledge about acute schizophrenia is that treatment wards should be minimally distracting. One can hardly expect improvement on a ward where the noise level and rates of assault and rape are higher than on the streets outside. Yet this is often the case in overcrowded, understaffed state facilities.

When schizophrenics are treated as outpatients, it is often necessary to enlist others in the family or community in the care and protection of the patient—they become the "holding environment." Frequently, hospitalized schizophrenics are still living with families that as cause, consequence, or coincidence, are extremely chaotic and confusing. Whatever the reason for this chaos, something must be done to alter the chaotic family pattern of communication and its pathological impact on the patient. Even if this pattern did not make the patient crazy, it certainly won't let him or her become sane. It is, therefore, often useful to use family therapy with schizophrenics who either live with their families or remain actively involved with them.

According to the model of normal development presented above, adaptation proceeds best when the rate of novelty is quite slow and the individual is "held" by a wall of constancies; this view has important implications for treatment. Consistent with this view is the proposal put forth by Wechsler (1960) for a program of graduated, sheltered workshops and environments in which the schizophrenic could progress from relatively simple tasks to more complex ones, and from the exceedingly structured, protective environment of the hospital to the halfway house and eventually to communal apartments. Common sense suggests that the usual course is a foolhardy one:

sending the patient from the mental institution, with all its restrictions, to the streets, where there are no limits, with only a weekly appointment at an outpatient clinic and some medication. This change itself is enough to cause immediate rehospitalization for some.

In general, extreme changes can act as precipitating factors in cognitive, as well as emotional, terms. Frequently, these changes necessitate new skills. Social services—education, rehabilitational, and financial—are not merely adjuncts to treatment but are necessary to enable schnizophrenics to make a gradual transition into full responsibility for their lives. They need to adapt to the changing demands of an increasingly complex world, a world that won't stand still while they "get it together."

In this book I have stressed the interconnectedness of the physical, emotional, and cognitive worlds of the individual with the external environment in all its aspects (family, school, job, community). Extreme deviations in any one of these areas will have consequences for the others—they cannot be addressed independently. Social planning and social conditions affect families. Family structure and well-being affect the emotional, physical, and cognitive well-being of the individual. The state of the individual in turn affects the family, the demand for social services, and the very fabric of society as a whole.

Description of and Diagnostic Criteria for Schizophrenia, American Psychiatric Association, 1978 (DSM-III)	Appendix One

SCHIZOPHRENIC DISORDERS

The essential features of this group of disorders* are: disorganization of a previous level of functioning; characteristic symptoms involving multiple psychological processes; the presence of certain psychotic features during the active phase of the illness; the absence of a full affective syndrome concurrent with or developing prior to the active phase of the illness; a tendency towards chronicity; and the disturbance is not explainable by any of the Organic Mental Disorders.

As defined here, at some time during the illness a Schizophrenic Disorder always involves at least one of the following: delusions, hallucinations, or certain characteristic types of thought disorder. No single clinical feature is unique to this condition or evident in every case or at every phase of the illness, except that by definition, the diagnosis is not made unless the period of illness has persisted for at least six months.

The limits of the concept of Schizophrenia are still unclear. Some approaches to defining the concept have emphasized the tendency towards a deteriorating course (Kraepelin), the presence of specific underlying disturbances in psychological processes (Bleuler), or pathognomonic symptoms or symptom complexes (Schneider). The approach taken here does not limit the concept to illnesses with a deteriorating course, although a minimal duration of illness is required because of the accumulated evidence that suggests that illnesses of briefer duration (here called Schizophreniform) are likely to have different correlates. The approach taken here also

---

*Although this classification acknowledges that Schizophrenia is a group of disorders, common usage refers to Schizophrenia. Therefore, throughout this manual whenever the term Schizophrenia appears it should be understood that conceptually the more accurate terminology would be Schizophrenic Disorders.

244

excludes illnesses without overt psychotic features, that have been referred to as latent, borderline, or simple schizophrenia. Such cases are likely to be diagnosed in this manual as having a Personality Disorder. Furthermore, individuals who develop either a depressive or manic syndrome before, or concurrent with psychotic symptoms, are not classified as having a Schizophrenic Disorder, but rather as having either an Affective or a Schizoaffective Disorder. Thus, this manual utilizes clinical criteria that include both a minimal degree of chronicity and a characteristic symptom picture, in an effort to identify a group of conditions that has validity in terms of differential response to somatic therapy, presence of a familial pattern, a tendency towards onset in early adult life, recurrence, and severe functional impairment.

Disorganization of a previous level of functioning. Schizophrenia always involves a disorganization of a previous level of functioning. Significant impairment always occurs in areas of routine daily functioning, such as work, social relations, and self-care. Family and friends often observe that the person is "no longer himself."

Characteristic symptoms involving multiple psychological processes. Invariably there are characteristic disturbances in several of the following areas: language and communication, content of thought, perception, affect, sense of self, volition, relationship to the external world, and motor behavior. It should be noted that no one of these features is invariably present or seen only in Schizophrenia.

A disturbance in *language and communication* is often present. This has been referred to as "formal thought disorder," or a disorder in form of thought, as distinguished from content of thought. As defined here, a language disorder involves the failure to follow semantic and syntactic rules, and is not attributable to lack of education, low intelligence or cultural background. The most common example of this is incoherence, in which statements are incomprehensible. A rare form of language disorder in Schizophrenia is neologism. Communication disorders are here defined as disturbances of speech or writing such that there is an obstacle to the understanding of the message by a listener or reader. This is due to deviations in rate, content, or form, and is not explainable by a language disorder, intellectual defect, or cultural background. The common communication disorders in Schizophrenia are derailment, poverty of content of speech, and illogicality. In derailment (loosening of associations), ideas slip off one track onto another one that is clearly but obliquely related, or onto one that is completely unrelated. Things may be said in juxtaposition which lack a meaningful relationship, or the individual may shift idiosyncratically from one frame of reference to another. In poverty of content of speech, the speech is adequate in amount but conveys little information because it is vague, overabstract or overconcrete, repetitive, or stereotyped. The listener may recognize this disturbance by noting that little if any information has been conveyed although the individual has spoken at some length. In illogicality, apart from delusional thinking that may be present, facts are obscured, distorted or excluded, and conclusions are arrived at on the basis of inadequate or faulty evidence. Less common communication disorders in Schizophrenia include perseveration and blocking.

Content of thought. The major disturbance in the content of thought involves delusions which often are multiple, fragmented and bizarre. However, simple persecutory delusions involving the belief that others are spying or surveilling on, spreading false rumors about, or planning harm to the individual, are common. Delusions of reference, in which unrelated events are given personal significance, are also common. For example, a newspaper article or television program may be interpreted as giving a special personal message, usually of a negative or pejorative nature. Certain delusions appear to be very characteristic of this disorder. These include, for instance, the belief or experience that an individual's thoughts, as they occur, are broadcast from his head into the external world so that others can hear them (thought broadcasting); that thoughts, which are not his own, are inserted into his mind (thought insertion); that thoughts have been removed from his head (thought withdrawal); or that his feelings, impulses, thoughts, or actions are not his own and are imposed upon him by some external force (delusions of being controlled or delusions of passivity). Less commonly, somatic, grandiose, religious, and nihilistic delusions are seen. Overvalued ideas may occur, such as preoccupation with the special significance of particular dietary habits.

Perception. The major disturbances in perception are various forms of hallucinations. Although they may occur in all modalities, by far the most common are auditory hallucinations, frequently involving voices heard from outside of the head. The voices may be familiar, may be responded to, and commonly make insulting statements. The voices may be solitary or multiple. Voices speaking directly to the individual or commenting on his ongoing behavior are particularly characteristic. Occasionally the auditory hallucinations are of sounds rather than voices. Tactile (haptic) hallucinations may be present and typically involve electrical, tingling, or burning sensations. Somatic hallucinations, such as the sensation of snakes crawling inside the abdomen, are occasionally seen. Visual, gustatory and olfactory hallucinations also occur, but with less frequency, and should always raise the question of the possible presence of an Organic Mental Disorder.

Affect. The disturbance in affective expression often involves blunting or flattening or inappropriateness of affect. In blunted affect there is a severe reduction in the intensity of affective expression. In flat affect there are virtually no signs of affective expression. In such instances, the voice may be monotonous and the face immobile. The individual may complain that he no longer responds emotionally with his normal intensity or, in extreme cases, that he no longer has any feelings at all. Affect is inappropriate when it is clearly discordant with the content of the individual's speech or ideation. For example, while discussing how he is being tortured by electrical shocks administered by his persecutors, an individual with Paranoid Schizophrenia may laugh or smile. Sudden and unpredictable changes in affect, which may involve inexplicable outbursts of anger, may occur.

Unfortunately, despite the importance of affective disturbance in Schizophrenia, its usefulness in making the diagnosis is limited because the judgment of it is often unreliable except when it is present in an extreme form. Furthermore, the antipsychotic drugs can produce a state that is nearly identical to the affective flattening seen in Schizophrenia.

Sense of self. The sense of self that gives the normal person his feeling of individuality, uniqueness, and self-direction is frequently disturbed. This is sometimes referred to as a loss of ego boundaries and may manifest itself in morbid perplexity about one's own identity and the meaning of existence, or in some of the specific delusions described above, particularly those involving control by some outside forces.

Volition. Nearly always there is some disturbance in self-initiated goal-directed activity, which may grossly impair work or other role functioning. It may take the form of inadequate interest or drive, or inability to complete successfully a course of action. Pronounced ambivalence regarding two opposite courses of action may lead to near cessation of goal-directed activity. Antipsychotic medication may produce akinesia, which often appears nearly identical to a disturbance in volition. Antipsychotic medication may also produce sedation, which does cause a disturbance in volition.

Relationship to the external world. Frequently there is a tendency to withdraw from involvement with the external world and to become preoccupied with ideas and fantasies that are egocentric and illogical, and in which objective facts then tend to be obscured, distorted, or excluded. Severe forms of this are referred to as autism. Family members or friends may comment that the individual seems preoccupied, in his own world, and emotionally detached from others.

Motor behavior. Various disturbances in motor behavior may be seen, particularly in the severe and chronic or more acutely florid forms of Schizophrenia. There may be a marked decrease in reactivity to the environment, with a reduction of spontaneous movements and activity, and the individual may appear to be unaware of the nature of his surroundings (as in catatonic stupor). The individual may maintain a rigid posture against any efforts to move him (as in catatonic rigidity). There may be apparently purposeless and stereotyped excited motor activity not influenced by external stimuli (as in catatonic excitement). The individual may voluntarily assume inappropriate or bizarre postures (as in catatonic posturing). The individual may resist and actively counteract instructions or attempts to move him (catatonic negativism). In addition, there may be mannerisms, grimacing, or waxy flexibility.

Associated features. Almost any psychiatric symptom can occur as an associated feature. The individual may appear perplexed, disheveled or eccentrically groomed or dressed. Abnormalities of psychomotor activity are common with either pacing, rocking, or apathetic immobility. Ritualistic or stereotyped behavior which may be associated with magical thinking may occur. Dysphoric mood is common; it may take the form of depression, anxiety, anger, or a mixture of these. Depersonalization, derealization, simple ideas of reference and illusions are commonly present, as are hypochondriacal concerns that may or may not be delusional. Typically there is no disturbance in sensorium, although during a period of exacerbation, the individual may be confused, perplexed and even disoriented, or show impairment in memory.

Age at onset. Onset is usually during adolescence or early adult life. Rarely, it may be in childhood or middle or late adult life.

Course. As noted previously, the diagnosis of Schizophrenia requires that continuous signs of the illness have lasted for at least six months during the person's life. The six month period must include an active phase of psychotic symptoms, with or without a prodromal or residual phase.

A *prodromal phase* occurs frequently. That is, prior to the development of the active phase of the illness there is a clear deterioration in functioning with such symptoms as social isolation or withdrawal, impairment in role functioning, eccentric, odd or peculiar behavior, impairment in personal hygiene and grooming, blunted or inappropriate affect, disturbances in communication, odd or bizarre ideation, and unusual perceptual experiences. A change in personality may be noted by friends or relatives. The length of this prodromal phase is extremely variable and its onset may be difficult to date accurately. In those cases in which the prodromal phase is characterized by an insidious downhill course over many years, the prognosis is especially poor.

During the *active phase* there are prominent psychotic symptoms, such as delusions, hallucinations, derailment (loosening of associations), incoherence, poverty of content of speech, illogicality and behavior that is grossly disorganized or catatonic. The specific psychotic symptoms, at least one of which is necessary to make the diagnosis, are noted in criterion A of the diagnostic criteria (p. 240). The onset of the active phase, either initially or as an exacerbation, is frequently associated with the occurrence of a psychosocial stressor . . . .

Usually there is a *residual phase* which follows the active phase of the illness. The clinical picture of this phase is similar to that seen in the prodromal phase, although affective blunting or flattening and impairment in role functioning tend to be more common. During the residual phase some of the psychotic symptoms, such as delusions or hallucinations, may persist but have lost their affective coloring.

A complete return to premorbid functioning is unusual. In fact, some clinicians would question the diagnosis under such circumstances. However, the concept of Schizophrenia used here does not exclude the possibility of full remission or recovery, but the frequency of this course is unknown. There is a strong tendency for acute exacerbations requiring therapeutic intervention, usually with increasing residual impairment between episodes.

Numerous studies have indicated a group of factors that are associated with a good prognosis: good premorbid personality with adequate social functioning, the presence of precipitating events, abrupt onset, onset late in life, a clinical picture that involves confusion or perplexity, and a family history of Affective Disorder.

Because a knowledge of course is of such importance for planning treatment, and because differences in course may reflect fundamental differences in subgroups of the Schizophrenic Disorders, course . . . [should be noted].

Since a six-month duration of illness is required for a diagnosis of Schizophrenia, there is no acute subtype. The diagnosis of Schizophreniform Disorder is the nearest equivalent to the [Diagnostic and Statistical Manual of Mental Disorders, 2nd ed.] concept of Acute Schizophrenic Episode. Frequently, an episode of Schizophreniform Disorder will persist for more than six months, requiring a change of diagnosis to Schizophrenia.

Impairment. During the active phase of the illness, the psychotic symptoms are associated with significant impairment in several areas of routine daily functioning, such as work, social relations, or self-care. The person may require supervision to insure that his biological needs are met and that he is protected from the consequences of his poor judgment, cognitive impairment, or acting on the basis of his delusional beliefs. Following an initial episode, and between subsequent exacerbations, the degree of disability can vary widely. Some individuals have virtually none, whereas others are severely impaired and may require prolonged institutional care.

Complications. The illness is so pervasive that it is difficult to separate the complications from the manifestations of the impairment. Complications include failure of educational achievement, work performance below that appropriate to education, social isolation, and inability to develop or maintain close interpersonal relationships. Although violent acts performed by individuals with this disorder may achieve notoriety, it is not known whether the incidence of violent acts is higher than in the nonschizophrenic population. The life expectancy is shorter than that of the general population due to an increased suicide rate and death from a variety of other causes, some of which have, at least previously, been associated with institutional care. Others are probably associated with the economically deprived environments in which many individuals with these disorders live.

Premorbid personality. The personalities of individuals who later develop Schizophrenia are often described as suspicious, introverted, withdrawn or eccentric. Such individuals may meet the criteria for Paranoid, Introverted, Schizotypal or Borderline Personality Disorder. In such cases, the premorbid Personality Disorder should be noted . . . since it may have prognostic significance.

Predisposing factors. The diagnosis is made more commonly amongst the lower socioeconomic groups. The reasons for this are still under investigation, but downward social drift and increased stress are likely contributors.

Various specific patterns of family interaction have been posited as being of etiological significance in the development of the illness. None of the various hypotheses has as yet been confirmed.

Prevalence. Many studies done in Europe and Asia have reported that a sizable proportion of members of a population alive at any given moment in time have had at some time in their lives an episode of a disorder which research workers in these areas have called Schizophrenia, using a relatively narrow concept of the disorder. The proportion has ranged from approximately .2% to almost 1%. In every location where these studies have been done, the cases designated as Schizophrenia constitute a sizable proportion of all psychoses. Some studies done in the United States, which have used broader criteria and surveyed urban populations, have reported higher rates.

Sex ratio. The disorder is apparently equally common in males and females.

Familial pattern. All investigators have found a higher prevalence of the disorder among biologically related family members. This includes studies in which the adopted offspring of individuals with Schizophrenia have been raised by normal parents. Twin studies consistently show a higher concordance rate for monozygotic twins than dizygotic twins, while dizygotic twins have the same concordance rate as nontwin siblings. However, being a monozygotic twin does not in itself predispose to the development of a Schizophrenic Disorder. Although genetic factors have been proven to be involved in the development of the illness, the relatively low concordance rate even in monozygotic twins indicates the importance of nongenetic factors.

Differential diagnosis. Organic Mental Disorders often present with symptoms that suggest Schizophrenia, such as delusions, hallucinations, incoherence, and blunted or inappropriate affect. In particular, Organic Delusional Syndromes, such as associated with amphetamines or phencyclidine, may cross-sectionally be identical in phenomenology to Schizophrenia. Even though an exacerbation of Schizophrenia may be associated with confusion, the presence of disorientation or memory impairment strongly suggests an Organic Mental Disorder. The diagnosis of Schizophrenia should not be made until the evidence indicates that the episode of illness is not due to any of the Organic Mental Disorders. This does not mean that Organic Mental Disorders and Schizophrenia as two separate disorders may not coexist in the same individual.

Paranoid Disorders are distinguished from Schizophrenia by the absence of prominent hallucinations, incoherence, derailment (loosening of associations), or those delusions listed in criterion A of the diagnostic criteria for Schizophrenia (see p. 240), such as delusions of being controlled or thought broadcasting.

In Schizoaffective and Affective Disorders, there is always a full affective syndrome and it either precedes or develops concurrently with any psychotic symptoms that may be present. In Schizophrenia, by definition, if an affective syndrome develops at all, it occurs *after* the development of the psychotic symptoms. The differential diagnosis from psychotic forms of the Affective Disorders, particularly mania, is of special importance because of the different treatment implications.

Atypical Depressive Disorder or Adjustment Disorder with Depressed Mood may be superimposed on Residual Schizophrenia, providing that there is no exacerbation of the psychotic Schizophrenic symptoms. In such instances, both diagnoses should be made.

In Schizophreniform Disorder, by definition, the duration of the illness is less than six months. The cross-sectional symptom picture may be indistinguishable from Schizophrenia although emotional turmoil and confusion are more likely in Schizophreniform Disorder. It should be noted that the six-month duration of illness required for Schizophrenia refers to a continuous period of illness. Thus, an individual with several episodes of Schizophreniform Disorder from which there was always a full recovery, would not be diagnosed as having Schizophrenia merely because the total period of illness exceeded six months. Often it is difficult to determine the duration of illness required to make the differential between Schizophreniform Disorder and Schizophrenia.

Atypical Psychosis should be diagnosed in those unusual instances in which some of the characteristic Schizophrenic psychotic symptoms are present but without any impairment in routine daily functioning. An example is an encapsulated delusion of bodily change.

In Obsessive Compulsive Disorder, and more rarely, Phobic Disorder, the individual occasionally develops explanatory ideas to account for his symptoms and that are difficult to distinguish from delusions. However, the individual with Obsessive Compulsive or a Phobic Disorder recognizes that his symptoms and thinking are irrational, even when dominated by them.

In Factitious Illness with Psychological Symptoms, any seemingly psychotic symptoms are under the individual's voluntary control and are likely to be present only when the individual thinks he is being observed.

In Atypical Somatoform Disorder the individual may have chronic hypochondriacal concerns which may be difficult to distinguish from somatic delusions.

In severe Personality Disorders, transient psychotic symptoms may occur. However, a quick return to the usual level of functioning distinguishes this exacerbation from Schizophrenia. The more difficult differential is to distinguish severe forms of Paranoid and Schizotypal Personality Disorders from Schizophrenia because of the difficulty in determining whether the paranoid ideation is of delusional intensity and whether the oddities of communication and perception are severe enough to meet the criteria for Schizophrenia. Furthermore, it is often difficult to differentiate the prodromal phase of Schizophrenia from the manifestations of some of the Personality Disorders, since both Personality Disorders and Schizophrenia usually develop during adolescence or early adult life.

Individuals who are members of religious or other subcultural groups may have beliefs or experiences that are difficult to distinguish from pathological delusions or hallucinations. When such experiences are explainable by identification with such subcultural groups or values, they should not be considered evidence of Schizophrenia. Useful clues that such experiences should not be considered pathological include the occurrence of the experiences during religious ceremonies or in other religious contexts, and the acceptance by the subgroup and the individual himself of the behavior as normal or desirable.

In Mental Retardation, the low level of social functioning, the oddities of behavior, and the impoverished affect and cognition all may suggest a chronic form of Schizophrenia. Both diagnoses in the same individual should be made only when there is certainty that the symptoms suggesting Schizophrenia, such as delusions or hallucinations, are definitely present and not the result of difficulties in communication. . . .

Diagnostic criteria for a Schizophrenic Disorder.

A. *Characteristic schizophrenic symptoms.* At least one symptom from any of the following 10 symptoms was present during an active phase of the illness (because a single symptom is given such diagnostic significance, its presence should be clearly established):

Characteristic delusions

(1) Delusions of being controlled: Experiences his thoughts, actions, or feelings as imposed on him by some external force.
(2) Thought broadcasting: Experiences his thoughts, as they occur, as being broadcast from his head into the external world so that others can hear them.
(3) Thought insertion: Experiences thoughts, which are not his own, being inserted into his mind (other than by God).
(4) Thought withdrawal: Belief that thoughts have been removed from his head, resulting in a diminished number of thoughts remaining.
(5) Other bizarre delusions (patently absurd, fantastic or implausible).
(6) Somatic, grandiose, religious, nihilistic or other delusions without persecutory or jealous content.
(7) Delusions of any type if accompanied by hallucinations of any type.

Characteristic hallucinations

(8) Auditory hallucinations in which either a voice keeps up a running commentary on the individual's behaviors or thoughts as they occur, or two or more voices converse with each other.

(9) Auditory hallucinations on several occasions with content having no apparent relation to depression or elation, and not limited to one or two words.

Other characteristic symptoms

(10) Either incoherence, derailment (loosening of associations), marked illogicality, or marked poverty of content of speech—if accompanied by either blunted, flat or inappropriate affect, delusions or hallucinations, or behavior that is grossly disorganized or catatonic.

B. During the active phase of the illness, the symptoms in A have been associated with significant impairment in two or more areas of routine daily functioning, e.g., work, social relations, self-care.

C. *Chronicity:* Signs of the illness have lasted continuously for at least six months at some time during the person's life and the individual now has some signs of the illness. The six month period must include an active phase during which there were symptoms from A with or without a prodromal or residual phase, as defined below.

Prodromal phase: A clear deterioration in functioning not due to a primary disturbance in mood or to substance abuse, and involving at least *two* of the symptoms noted below.

Residual phase: Following the active phase of the illness, at least *two* of the symptoms noted below, not due to a primary disturbance in mood or to substance abuse.

Prodromal or Residual Symptoms

(a) social isolation or withdrawal
(b) marked impairment in role functioning as wage-earner, student, home-maker
(c) markedly eccentric, odd, or peculiar behavior (e.g., collecting garbage, talking to self in corn field or subway, hoarding food)
(d) impairment in personal hygiene and grooming
(e) blunted, flat, or inappropriate affect
(f) (speech that is tangential, digressive, vague, overelaborate, circumstantial, or metaphorical
(g) odd or bizarre ideation, or magical thinking, e.g., superstitiousness, clairvoyance, telepathy, "sixth sense," "others can feel my feelings," overvalued ideas, ideas of reference, or suspected delusions
(h) unusual perceptual experiences, e.g., recurrent illusions, sensing the presence of a force or person not actually present, suspected hallucinations

Examples: Six months of prodromal symptoms with 1 week of symptoms from A: no prodromal symptoms with six months of symptoms from A; no prodromal symptoms with two weeks of symptoms from A and six months of residual symptoms; six months of symptoms from A, apparently followed by several years of complete remission, with 1 week of symptoms in A in current episode.

D. The full depressive or manic syndrome (criteria A and B of Depressive or Manic Episode) is either not present, or if present, developed after any psychotic symptoms.
E. Not due to any Organic Mental Disorder [American Psychiatric Association, 1978, pp. C:1–C:12].

Suggested Readings	*Appendix Two*

At the time of writing, the best way to keep up with the literature and research on schizophrenia is through *Schizophrenia Bulletin* (Loren R. Mosher, Editor in Chief; published quarterly by the National Institute of Mental Health).

Chapter 1

Cancro, R. (Ed.). *The schizophrenic reactions: A critique of the concept, hospital treatment, and current research* (Part I). New York: Brunner/Mazel, 1971.

Feinstein, A. R. A critical overview of diagnosis in psychiatry. In V. M. Rakoff, A. C. Stancer, & H. B. Kedward (Eds.), *Psychiatric diagnosis*. New York: Brunner/Mazel, 1977.

Grinker, R. R. The inadequacies of contemporary psychiatric diagnosis. In V. M. Rakoff, A. C. Stancer, & H. B. Kedward (Eds.), *Psychiatric diagnosis*. New York: Brunner/Mazel, 1977.

Meehl, P. E. Why I do not attend case conferences. In *Psychodiagnosis: Selected papers of Paul E. Meehl*. New York: Norton, 1973.

Schizophrenia Bulletin, 1975, No. 11.

Spitzer, R. L. & Klein, D. F. *Critical issues in psychiatric diagnosis*. New York: Raven Press, 1978.

Chapter 2

Alexander, F., & Selesnick, S. *The history of psychiatry*. New York: Harper & Row, 1966.

Foucault, M. *Madness and civilization*. New York: Vintage Books, 1973.

Zilboorg, G. *A history of medical psychology*. New York: Norton, 1941.

General References for Chapters 3–10 Covering Research in Schizophrenia

Bellak, L. (Ed.). *Disorders of the schizophrenic syndrome.* New York: Basic Books, 1980.
Bellak, L., & Loeb, L. (Eds.). *The schizophrenic syndrome.* New York: Grune & Stratton, 1969.
Cancro, R. *Annual review of the schizophrenic syndrome* (4 vols.). New York: Brunner/Mazel, 1971–1976. [A selection of critical articles that appeared in the years 1970–1975.]
Rosenthal, D., & Kety, S. (Eds.). *The transmission of schizophrenia.* Oxford: Pergamon, 1968.
Schizophrenia Bulletin. Published quarterly.
Wynne, L., Cromwell, R., & Matthysse, S. (Eds.). *The nature of schizophrenia.* New York: Wiley, 1978.

Chapter 3

Rosenthal, D. *Genetics of psychopathology.* New York: McGraw-Hill, 1971.
Rosenthal, D. The genetics of schizophrenia. In S. Arieti & E. Brody (Eds.), *American handbook of psychiatry* (Vol. 3) (2nd ed.). New York: Basic Books, 1974.
Schizophrenia Bulletin, 1976, *2*(3).
Shields, J. Summary of genetic evidence. In D. Rosenthal & S. Kety (Eds.), *The transmission of schizophrenia.* Oxford: Pergamon, 1968.

Chapter 4

Frohman, C. E., & Gottlieb, J. S. The biochemistry of schizophrenia. In S. Arieti & E. Brody (Eds.), *American handbook of psychiatry* (Vol. 3) (2nd ed.). New York: Basic Books, 1974.
Schizophrenia Bulletin, 1976, *2*(1).

Chapter 5

Schizophrenia Bulletin, 1977, *3*(1).

Chapter 6

Chapman, L. J., & Chapman, J. P. *Disordered thought in schizophrenia.* Englewood Cliffs, N. J.: Prentice-Hall, 1973.
Schizophrenia Bulletin, 1977, *3*(3).

Chapter 7

Arieti, S. *The interpretation of schizophrenia* (2nd ed.). New York: Basic Books, 1974.
Boyer, L. B., & Giovacchini, P. L. *Psychoanalytic treatment of schizophrenic and character disorders.* New York: Science House, 1967, Chapters 2 and 3.

Chapter 8

Bateson, G. Toward a theory of schizophrenia. *Behavioral Science,* 1956, *4*, 251–265.
Lidz, T. *The origin and treatment of schizophrenic disorders.* New York: Basic Books, 1973.

Mishler, E. G., & Waxler, N. (Eds.). *Family process and schizophrenia.* New York: Jason Aronson, 1975.

Chapter 10

Schizophrenia Bulletin, 1974, Nos. 8, 9.

Chapter 13

Arieti, S. *The interpretation of schizophrenia* (2nd ed.). New York: Basic Books, 1974, Part 7.

Gunderson, J. G., & Mosher, L. *Psychotherapy of schizophrenia.* New York: Jason Aronson, 1975.

Schizophrenia Bulletin, 1975, No. 13 [special issue on treatment].

References

Adler, G., & Buie, D. H. *The process of change in the psychotherapy of borderline patients.* Paper presented at 11th Annual Symposium on Psychotherapy, Tufts University, April 9, 1976.

Alanen, Y. O. From the mothers of schizophrenic patients to interactional family dynamics. In D. Rosenthal & S. Kety (Eds.), *The transmission of schizophrenia.* Oxford: Pergamon, 1968.

Alanen, Y. O. The families of schizophrenic patients. In R. Cancro (Ed.), *Annual review of the schizophrenic syndrome 1971.* New York: Brunner/Mazel, 1972.

Alexander, F. C., & Selesnick, S. T. *The history of psychiatry: An evaluation of psychiatric thought from prehistoric times to the present.* New York: Mentor, 1966.

Allan, L. G. The attention switching model: Implications for research in schizophrenia. In L. C. Wynne, R. L. Cromwell, & S. Matthysse (Eds.), *The nature of schizophrenia.* New York: Wiley, 1978.

Almond, R. Issues in milieu treatment. *Schizophrenia Bulletin,* 1975, No. 13, 12–26.

Altschule, M. D. Disease entity, syndrome, state of mind or figment? In R. Cancro (Ed.), *The schizophrenic reactions: A critique of the concept, hospital treatment, and current research.* New York: Brunner/Mazel, 1970.

American Psychiatric Association. *DSM-II: Diagnostic and statistical manual* (2nd ed.). Washington, D.C.: American Psychiatric Association, 1968.

American Psychiatric Association. *DSM-III: Diagnostic and statistical manual* (Draft of 3rd ed.). Washington, D.C.: American Psychiatric Association, 1978.

Anthony, E. J. The developmental precursors of adult schizophrenia. In D. Rosenthal & S. Kety (Eds.), *The transmission of schizophrenia.* Oxford: Pergamon, 1968.

Anthony, E. J. The impact of mental and physical illness on family life. *American Journal of Psychiatry,* 1970, *127,* 56–64.

Anthony, E. J. A clinical and experimental study of high risk children and their schizophrenic parents. In A. R. Kaplan (Ed.), *Genetic factors in schizophrenia.* Springfield, Ill.: Charles C Thomas, 1971a.

257

Anthony, E. J. A clinical evaluation of children with psychotic parents. In R. Cancro (Ed.), *The schizophrenic syndrome.* New York: Brunner/Mazel, 1971b.

Anthony, E. J. The contagious subculture of psychosis. In C. J. Sager & H. S. Kaplan (Eds.), *Progress in group and family therapy.* New York: Brunner/Mazel, 1972.

Anthony, E. J. A risk-vulnerability intervention model for children of psychotic parents. In E. J. Anthony & C. Koupernik (Eds.), *The child in his family: Children at psychiatric risk* (Vol. 3). New York: Wiley, 1974a.

Anthony, E. J. The syndrome of the psychologically invulnerable child. In E. J. Anthony & C. Koupernik (Eds.), *The child in his family: Children at psychiatric risk* (Vol. 3). New York: Wiley, 1974b.

Anthony, E. J. Preventive measures of children and adolescents at high risk for psychosis. In G. W. Albee & J. M. Joffe (Eds.), *Primary prevention of psychopathology: The issues* (Vol. 1). Hanover, N. H.: University Press of New England, 1977.

Ariès, P. *Centuries of childhood.* New York: Vintage Books, 1962.

Arieti, S. *The interpretation of schizophrenia.* New York: Robert Brunner, 1955.

Arieti, S. *The interpretation of schizophrenia* (2nd ed.). New York: Basic Books, 1974a.

Arieti, S., & Brody, E. (Eds.). *American handbook of psychiatry* (2nd ed.). New York: Basic Books, 1974.

Arlow, J. A., & Brenner, C. The psychopathology of the psychoses: A proposed revision. *International Journal of Psycho-Analysis,* 1969, *50,* 5–14.

Ashby, W. R. *Design for a human brain.* London: Chapman & Hall, 1965.

Auerbach, C. *Some general characteristics of human development, with particular reference to adaptation, regulation, and models.* Unpublished paper, 1977.

Bagshaw, M. H., & Benzies, S. Multiple weakness of the orienting reaction and their dissociation after amygdalectomy in monkeys. *Experimental Neurology,* 1968, *20,* 175–187.

Bagshaw, M. H., Kimble, D. P., & Pribram, K. H. The GSR of monkeys during orienting and habituation and after ablation of the amygdala, hippocampus, and inferotemporal cortex. *Neuropsychologia,* 1965, *3,* 111–119.

Bannister, D. B. The genesis of schizophrenic thought disorder: A retest of the serial invalidation hypothesis. *British Journal of Psychiatry,* 1965, *113,* 377–382.

Bannister, D. B., & Fransella, F. *Inquiring man.* Baltimore: Penguin Books, 1971.

Bassuk, E. L., & Schoonover, S. C. *The practitioner's guide to psychoactive drugs.* New York: Plenum, 1976.

Bateson, G. Minimal requirements for a theory of schizophrenia. *Archives of General Psychiatry,* 1960, *2,* 477–491.

Bateson, G., Jackson, D. D., Haley, J., & Weakland, J. Toward a theory of schizophrenia. *Behavioral Science,* 1956, *1,* 251–264.

Bateson, G., Jackson, D. D., Haley, J., & Weakland, J. A note on the double bind family process. *Family Process,* 1963, *2,* 154–161.

Beck, H. Minimal requirements for a biobehavioral paradigm, *Behavioral Science,* 1971, *16,* 442–455.

Beels, C. C. Family and social management of schizophrenia. *Schizophrenia Bulletin,* 1975, No. 13, 97–118.

Bellak, L. *Dementia praecox. The past decade's work and present status: A review and evaluation.* New York: Grune & Stratton, 1948.

Bellak, L. The validity and usefulness of the concept of the schizophrenic syndrome. In R. Cancro (Ed.), *The schizophrenic reactions.* New York: Brunner/Mazel, 1970.

Bellak, L. A "mini-max": A research strategy for establishing subgroups of the schizophrenic syndrome. *Schizophrenia Bulletin,* 1979, *5,* 443–446.

Bellak, L., & Charles E. Schizophrenic syndrome related to minimal brain dysfunction: A possible neurological subgroup. *Schizophrenia Bulletin,* 1979, *5,* 480–489.

Bellak, L., Hurvich, M., & Gediman, H. K. *Ego functions in schizophrenics, neurotics and normals.* New York: Wiley, 1973.

Bellak, L., & Loeb, L. (Eds.). *The schizophrenic syndrome.* New York: Grune & Stratton, 1969.

Bemporad, J. R., & Pinsker, H. Schizophrenia: The manifest symptomatology. In S. Arieti & E. Brody (Eds.), *American handbook of psychiatry* (2nd ed.) (Vol. 3). New York: Basic Books, 1974.

Bergen, J. R., Koella, W. P., Freeman, H., & Hoagland, H. A human plasma factor inducing behavior and electrophysical changes in animals. II. Changes in animals. *Annals of the New York Academy of Science,* 1962, *96,* 469.

Bergman, P., & Escalona, S. Unusual sensitivities in very young children. *Psychoanalytic Study of the Child,* 1949, *3/4,* 333–352.

Bernstein, A. S., & Taylor, K. W. *The interaction of stimulus information with potential stimulus significance in eliciting the skin conductance orienting response.* Presented at the NATO Conference on Orienting, Amsterdam, 1978.

Bleuler, E. *Dementia praecox, or the group of schizophrenias.* New York: International Universities Press, 1950. (Originally published, 1911.)

Bleuler, M. *Krankheitsverlauf, Persönlichkeit and verwandtschaft Schizophrener & ihre gegenseitigen Beziehungen.* Leipzig: Thieme, 1941.

Bleuler, M. The offspring of schizophrenics. *Schizophrenia Bulletin,* 1974, No. 8, 93–109.

Blumenthal, R. The effects of level of mental health, premorbid history and interpersonal stress upon the speech disruption of chronic schizophrenics. *Journal of Nervous and Mental Disease,* 1964, *139,* 313–323.

Boch, E., Weeke, B., & Rafaelson, O. J. Serum proteins in acutely psychotic patients. *Journal of Psychiatric Research,* 1971, *9,* 1–9.

Böök, J. A. A genetic and neuropsychiatric investigation of a North-Swedish population with special regard to schizophrenia and mental deficiency. *Acta Genetica,* 1953, *4,* 1–139.

Bowen, M. A family concept of schizophrenia. In D. D. Jackson (Ed.), *The etiology of schizophrenia.* New York: Basic Books, 1960.

Bowers, M. B., Jr. Central dopamine turnover in schizophrenic syndromes. *Archives of General Psychiatry,* 1974, *31,* 50–54.

Boyer, B. L., & Giovacchini, P. C. *Psychoanalytic treatment of characterological and schizophrenic disorders.* New York: Science House, 1967.

Broadbent, D. E. *Perception and communication.* New York: Pergamon, 1958.

Brody, E. B., & Redlich, F. C. (Eds.). *Psychotherapy with schizophrenics.* New York: International Universities Press, 1952.

Broen, W. E., Jr. *Schizophrenia: Research and theory.* New York: Academic, 1968.

Broen, W. J., Jr., & Storms, L. H. Lawful disorganization: The process underlying a schizophrenic syndrome. *Psychological Review,* 1966, *73,* 265–277.

Buchsbaum, M. S. *Neurophysiology of schizophrenia.* Paper delivered at Downstate Medical Center Grand Rounds, November 24, 1976.

Buchsbaum, M. S. The middle evoked response components and schizophrenia. *Schizophrenia Bulletin,* 1977a, *3,* 93–104.

Buchsbaum, M. S. Psychophysiology and schizophrenia. *Schizophrenia Bulletin,* 1977b, *3,* 7–14.

Buchsbaum, M. S. Neurophysiological aspects of the schizophrenic syndrome. In L. Bellak (Ed.), *Disorders of the schizophrenic syndrome.* New York: Basic Books, 1980.

Buchsbaum, M. S., Murphy, D. L., Coursey, R. D., Lake, C. R., & Zeigler, M. G. Platelet monoamine oxidase, plasma dopamine-beta-hydroxylase, and attention in a "biochemical high-risk" sample. In L. C. Wynne, R. L. Cromwell, & S. Matthysse (Eds.), *The nature of schizophrenia.* New York: Wiley, 1978.

Burnham, D., Gladstone, A., & Gibson, R. *Schizophrenia and the need-fear dilemma.* New York: International Universities Press, 1969.

Burton, D. (Ed.). *Psychotherapy of the psychoses.* New York: Basic Books, 1961.

Buss, A. H., & Lang, P. J. Psychological deficit in schizophrenia: 1. Affect, reinforcement and concept attainment. *Journal of Abnormal Psychology,* 1965, *70,* 2–24.

Bychowski, G. Physiology of schizophrenic thinking. *Journal of Nervous and Mental Disease,* 1943, *98,* 368–386.

Bychowski, G. *Psychotherapy of psychosis.* New York: Grune & Stratton, 1952.

Callaway, E., III. Schizophrenia and interference. In R. Cancro (Ed.), *Annual review of the schizophrenic syndrome 1971.* New York: Brunner/Mazel, 1972.

Cameron, N. Experimental analysis of schizophrenic thinking. In J. S. Kasanin (Ed.), *Language and thought in schizophrenia.* New York: Norton, 1964. (Originally published, 1944.)

Cancro, R. (Ed.). *The schizophrenic reactions: A critique of the concept, hospital treatment, and current research.* New York: Brunner/Mazel, 1970.

Cancro, R. (Ed.). *Annual review of the schizophrenic syndrome 1971* (Vol. 1). New York: Brunner/Mazel, 1972.

Cancro, R. (Ed.). *Annual review of the schizophrenic syndrome 1972* (Vol. 2). New York: Brunner/Mazel, 1973.

Cancro, R. (Ed.). *Annual Review of the schizophrenic syndrome 1973* (Vol. 3). New York: Brunner/Mazel, 1974.

Cancro, R. (Ed.). *Annual review of the schizophrenic syndrome 1974/1975* (Vol. 4). New York: Brunner/Mazel 1976a.

Cancro, R. *Visual attention in schizophrenia.* Paper presented at the Scottish Rite Schizophrenia Research Program Conference on Attention and Information Processing in Schizophrenia. Rochester, N.Y., 1976b.

Cancro, R., & Pruyser, P. A historical review of the development of the concept of schizophrenia. In R. Cancro (Ed.), *The schizophrenic reactions.* New York: Brunner/Mazel, 1970.

Cancro, R., Sutton, S., Kerr, J., & Sugarman, A. A. Reaction time and prognosis in acute schizophrenia. *Journal of Nervous and Mental Disease,* 1971, *153,* 351–359.

Caputo, D. U. The parents of the schizophrenic. *Family Process,* 1963, *2,* 339–356.

Carlsson, A., & Lindquist, M. Effect of chlorpromazine and haloperidol on the formation of 3-methoxytyramine and normetanephrine in mouse brain. *Acta Pharmac.* (KBH), 1963, *20,* 140.

Carpenter, W. T., Jr., Strauss, J. S., & Bartko, J. J. An approach to the diagnosis and understanding of schizophrenia. *Schizophrenia Bulletin,* 1976, *2,* 35–79.

Chapman, L. J., & Chapman, J. P. *Disordered thought in schizophrenia.* Englewood Cliffs, N.J.: Prentice-Hall, 1973.

Chapman, J. P., & McGhie, A. A comparative study of disordered attention in schizophrenia. *Journal of Mental Science,* 1962, *108,* 487–500.

Cheek, F. E. The fathers of the schizophrenic: The function of a peripheral role. *Archives of General Psychiatry,* 1965, *13,* 336–345.

Clark, R. E. The relationship of schizophrenia to occupational income and occupational prestige. *American Sociology Review,* 1948, *13,* 26–31.

Clark, R. E. Psychoses, income and occupational prestige. *American Journal of Sociology,* 1949, *54,* 433–440.

Conant, R. C., & Ashby, W. R. Every good regulator of a system must be a model of that system. *International Journal of Systems Science,* 1970, *1,* 89–97.

Corbett, L. Perceptual dyscontrol: A possible organizing principle for schizophrenia research. *Schizophrenia Bulletin,* 1976, *2,* 249–265.

Crandell, D. L., & Dohrenwend, B. P. Some relations among psychiatric symptoms, organic illness, and social class. *American Journal of Psychiatry,* 1967, *123,* 1527–1538.

Crocetti, G. M., et al. Selected aspects of the epidemiology of schizophrenia in Croatia (Yugoslavia). *Milbank Memorial Fund Quarterly,* 1964, *42,* 9–37.

Cromwell, R. L. Attention and information processing: A foundation for understanding schizophrenia? In L. C. Wynne, R. L. Cromwell, & S. Matthysse (Eds.), *The nature of schizophrenia.* New York: Wiley, 1978.

Dasberg, H., & Robinson, S. Correlation between electroencephalographic deviations following antipsychotic drug treatment and the course of mental illness. *Israeli Annals of Psychiatry,* 1969, *7,* 185–200.

Davis, J. M. Critique of single amine theories: Evidence for a cholinergic influence in the major illnesses. In D. X. Freedman (Ed.), *Biology of the main psychoses.* New York: Raven Press, 1975.

Davis, J. M. Dopamine theory of schizophrenia: A two-factor theory. In L. C. Wynne, R. L. Cromwell, & S. Matthysse (Eds.), *The nature of schizophrenia.* New York: Wiley, 1978.

Davis, J. M., & Cole, J. O. Antipsychotic drugs, In A. M. Freedman, H. I. Kaplan, & B. J. Sadock (Eds.), *Comprehensive textbook of psychiatry* (2nd ed.) (2 vols.). Baltimore: Williams & Wilkins, 1975.

Day, J. F., & Kwiatkowska, H. The psychiatric patient and his "well" sibling. *Bulletin of Art Therapy,* 1962, *2,* 51–66.

Diefendorf, A. R., & Dodge, R. An experimental study of the ocular reactions of the insane from photographic records. *Brain,* 1908, *31,* 451.

Dohrenwend, B. P., & Dohrenwend, B. S. *Social status and psychological disorder: A causal inquiry.* New York: Wiley, 1969.

Durell, J., & Archer, E. G. Plasma proteins in schizophrenia: A review. *Schizophrenia Bulletin,* 1976, *2,* 147–161.

Erikson, E. H. *Childhood and society* (rev. ed.). New York: Norton, 1963.

Erlenmeyer-Kimling, L. Studies on the offspring of two schizophrenic parents. In D. Rosenthal & S. Kety (Eds.), *The transmission of schizophrenia.* Oxford: Pergamon, 1968.

Erlenmeyer-Kimling, L. A prospective study of children at risk for schizophrenia: Methodological considerations and some preliminary findings. In R. D. Wirt, G. Winokur, & M. Roff (Eds.), *Life history research on psychopathology* (Vol. 4). Minneapolis: University of Minnesota Press, 1975.

Erlenmeyer-Kimling, L., & Cornblatt, B. Attentional measures in a study of children at high risk for schizophrenia. In L. C. Wynne, R. L. Cromwell, & S. Matthysse (Eds.), *The nature of schizophrenia.* New York: Wiley, 1978.

Erlenmeyer-Kimling, L., Cornblatt, B., & Fleiss, J. High risk research. *Psychiatric Annals,* 1979, *9,* 79–102.

Fairbairn, W. R. D. *Psychoanalytic studies of the personality.* London: Routledge, 1952a.

Fairbairn, W. R. D. A revised psychopathology of the psychoses and psychoneuroses. In *Psychoanalytic studies of the personality.* London: Routledge, 1972b. (Originally published, 1941.)

Fairbairn, W. R. D. Schizoid factors in the personality. In *Psychoanalytic studies of the personality.* London: Routledge, 1952c. (Originally published, 1941.)

Falconer, D. S. The inheritance of liability to certain diseases. *Annals of Human Genetics,* 1965, *29,* 51–76.

Faris, R. E. L., & Dunham, H. W. *Mental disorders in urban areas: An ecological study of schizophrenia and other psychoses.* Chicago: University of Chicago Press, 1939.

Federn, P. The analysis of psychotics. *International Journal of Psycho-Analysis,* 1934, *15,* 209–214.

Federn, P. Psychoanalysis of psychoses. 1. Errors and how to avoid them. 2. Transference. *Psychiatric Quarterly*, 1943, *17*, 3, 246.

Federn, P. *Ego psychology and the psychoses.* New York: Basic Books, 1952.

Fenichel, O. *The psychoanalytic theory of neurosis.* New York: Norton, 1945.

Ferenczi, S. Some clinical observations on paranoia and paraphrenia. In *Sex and psychoanalysis,* New York: Robert Brunner, 1950a. (Originally published, 1914.)

Ferenczi, S. Stages in the development of the sense of reality. In *Sex in psychoanalysis.* New York: Robert Brunner, 1950b. (Originally published, 1913.)

Ferenczi, S. Paranoia. In *Final contributions to the problems and methods of psychoanalysis.* New York: Basic Books, 1955. (Originally published, 1922.)

Fink, M. EEG response strategies in psychiatric diagnosis. In R. L. Spitzer & D. F. Klein (Eds.), *Critical issues in psychiatric diagnosis.* New York: Raven Press, 1978.

Fish, B. The detection of schizophrenia in infancy: A preliminary report. *Journal of Nervous and Mental Disease,* 1957, *125,* 1–24.

Fish, B. Longitudinal observation of biological deviation in a schizophrenic infant. *American Journal of Psychiatry,* 1959, *116,* 25–31.

Fish, B. Discussion: Genetic or traumatic developmental deviation? *Social Biology,* 1971, *18,* 3117–3119.

Fish, B. An approach to prevention in infants at risk for schizophrenia: Developmental deviations from birth to 10 years. *Journal of the American Academy of Child Psychiatry,* 1976, *15,* 62–82.

Fish, B. Neurobiological antecedents of schizophrenia in children: Evidence for an inherited congenital neurointegrative defect. *Archives of General Psychiatry,* 1977, *34,* 1297–1313.

Foster, B. The recapitulation of development during regression: A case report. In J. G. Gunderson & L. R. Mosher (Eds.), *Psychotherapy of schizophrenia.* New York: Jason Aronson, 1975.

Foucault, M. *Madness and civilization* (R. Howard, trans.). New York: Pantheon, 1965.

Franzen, G., & Ingvar, D. H. Abnormal distribution of cerebral activity in chronic schizophrenia. *Journal of Psychiatric Research,* 1975a, *12,* 199–214.

Franzen, G., & Ingvar, D. H. Absence of activation in frontal structures during psychological testing of chronic schizophrenics. *Journal of Neurology, Neurosurgery and Psychiatry.* 1975b, *38,* 1027–1032.

Freedman, A. M., Kaplan, H. I., & Sadock, B. J. *Modern synopsis of comprehensive textbook of psychiatry.* Baltimore: William & Wilkins, 1972.

Freedman, A. M., Kaplan, H. I., & Sadock, B. J. (Eds.). *Comprehensive textbook of psychiatry* (2nd ed.) (2 vols.). Baltimore: Williams & Wilkins, 1975.

Freedman, B. The subjective experience of perceptual and cognitive disturbances in schizophrenia. In R. Cancro (Ed.), *Annual review of the schizophrenic syndrome 1974/1975.* New York: Brunner/Mazel, 1976.

Freud, A. The mutual influences in the development of ego and id. *Psychoanalytic Study of the Child,* 1952, *7,* 42–50.

Freud, A. *The ego and the mechanisms of defense.* New York: International Universities Press, 1966. (Originally published, 1936.)

Freud, S. The unconscious. *Standard edition* (Vol. 14). London: Hogarth, 1957. (Originally published, 1915.)

Freud, S. Formulations on the two principles of mental functioning. *Standard edition* (Vol. 12). London: Hogarth, 1958a. (Originally published, 1911.)

Freud, S. Psycho-analytic notes on an autobiographical account of a case of paranoia (dementia paranoides). *Standard edition* (Vol. 12). London: Hogarth, 1958b. (Originally published, 1911.)

Freud, S. The ego and the id. *Standard edition* (Vol. 19). London: Hogarth, 1961a. (Originally published, 1923.)

Freud, S. Neurosis and psychosis. *Standard edition* (Vol. 19). London: Hogarth, 1961b. (Originally published, 1924).

Freud, S. The loss of reality in neurosis and psychosis. *Standard edition* (Vol. 19). London: Hogarth, 1961c. (Originally published, 1924.)

Freud, S. Fetishism. *Standard edition* (Vol. 21). London: Hogarth, 1961d. (Originally published, 1927.)

Freud, S. The neuro-psychoses of defence. *Standard edition* (Vol. 3). London: Hogarth, 1962a. (Originally published, 1894.)

Freud, S. Further remarks on the neuro-psychoses of defence. *Standard edition* (Vol. 3). London: Hogarth, 1962b. (Originally published, 1896.)

Friedhoff, A. J., & Alpert, M. Receptor sensitivity modification as a potential treatment. In M. A. Lipson, A. DiMascio, & K. F. Killam (Eds.), *Psychopharmacology: A generation of progress*. New York: Raven Press, 1978.

Friedhoff, A. J., Park, S., Schweitzer, J. W., Burdock, E. I., & Armour, M. Excretion of 3, 4-dimethoxyphenethylamine (DMPEA) by acute schizophrenics and controls. *Biological Psychiatry*, 1977, *12*, 643–654.

Friedhoff, A. J., & Van Winkle, E. The characteristics of an amine found in the urine of schizophrenic patients. *Journal of Nervous and Mental Disease*, 1962, *135*, 550.

Friedrich, O. *Going crazy*. New York: Avon, 1977.

Frohman, C. E., & Gottlieb, J. S. The biochemistry of schizophrenia. In S. Arieti & E. Brody (Eds.), *American handbook of psychiatry* (2nd ed.) (Vol. 3). New York: Basic Books, 1974.

Frohman, C., Harmison, C. R., Arthur, R. E., & Gottlieb, J. S. Conformation of a unique plasma protein in schizophrenia. *Biological Psychiatry*, 1971, *3*, 113–121.

Fromm-Reichmann, F. Notes on the development of treatment of schizophrenics by psychoanalytic psychotherapy. In *Psychoanalysis and psychotherapy: Selected papers*. Chicago: University of Chicago Press, 1959a. (Originally published, 1948.)

Fromm-Reichmann, F. A preliminary note on the emotional significance of stereotypes in schizophrenics. In *Psychoanalysis and psychotherapy: Selected papers*. Chicago: University of Chicago Press, 1959b. (Originally published, 1942.)

Fromm-Reichmann, F. *Psychoanalysis and psychotherapy: Selected papers* (D. M. Bullard, Ed.). Chicago: University of Chicago Press, 1959c.

Fromm-Reichmann, F. Transference problems in schizophrenia. In *Psychoanalysis and psychotherapy: Selected papers*. Chicago: University of Chicago Press, 1959d. (Originally published, 1939.)

Garmezy, N. (with the collaboration of Streitman, S.). Children at risk: The search for the antecedents of schizophrenia. Part I: Conceptual models and research methods. *Schizophrenia Bulletin*, 1974a, No. 8, 14–90.

Garmezy, N. Children at risk: The search for the antecedents of schizophrenia. Part II: Ongoing research programs, issues, and intervention. *Schizophrenia Bulletin*, 1974b, No. 9, 55–125.

Garmezy, N. The study of competence in children at risk for severe psychopathology. In E. J. Anthony & C. Koupernik (Eds.), *The child in his family: Children at psychiatric risk* (Vol. 3). New York: Wiley, 1974c.

Garmezy, N. The experimental study of children vulnerable to psychopathology. In A. Davids (Ed.), *Child personality and psychopathology: Current topics*. New York: Wiley, 1975.

Garmezy, N. Psychology of attention. *Schizophrenia Bulletin*, 1977, *3*, 360–369.

Garmezy, N. Current status of a sample of other high-risk research programs. In L. C. Wynne,

R. L. Cromwell, & S. Matthysse (Eds.), *The nature of schizophrenia.* New York: Wiley, 1978a.

Garmezy, N. Observations on high-risk research and premorbid development in schizophrenia. In L. C. Wynne, R. L. Cromwell, & S. Matthysse (Eds.), *The nature of schizophrenia.* New York: Wiley, 1978b.

Gerard, D., & Siegel, J. The family background of schizophrenics. *Psychiatric Quarterly,* 1950, *24,* 47–73.

Gittelman, M., & Birch, H. Childhood schizophrenia: Intellect, neurologic status, perinatal risk, prognosis and family pathology. *Archives of General Psychiatry,* 1967, *17,* 16–25.

Goffman, E. *Asylums.* Garden City, N.Y.: Doubleday, 1961.

Goldberg, E. M., & Morrison, S. L. Schizophrenia and social class. *British Journal of Psychiatry,* 1963, *109,* 785–802.

Goldstein, K. Methodological approach to the study of schizophrenic thought disorder. In J. S. Kasanin (Ed.), *Language and thought in schizophrenia.* New York: Norton, 1964. (Originally published, 1944.)

Goldstein, L., & Sugarman, A. A. EEG correlates of psychopathology. In J. Zubin (Ed.), *Neurobiological aspects of psychopathology.* New York: Grune & Stratton, 1969.

Goldstein, M. J., Rodnick, E. H., Jones, J. E., McPherson, S. R., & West, K. C. Familial precursors of schizophrenic spectrum disorders. In L. C. Wynne, R. L. Cromwell, & S. Matthysse (Eds.), *The nature of schizophrenia.* New York: Wiley, 1978.

Gottesman, I. I., Schizophrenia and genetics: Where are we? Are you sure? In L. C. Wynne, R. L. Cromwell, & S. Matthysse (Eds.), *The nature of schizophrenia.* New York: Wiley, 1978.

Gottesman, I. I. Toward understanding uncertainty. *Psychiatric Annals,* 1979, *9,* 54–78.

Gottesman, I. I., & Shields, J. A polygenic theory of schizophrenia. *Proceedings of the National Academy of Sciences, USA,* 1967, *58,* 199–205.

Gottesman, I. I., & Shields, J. Genetic theorizing and schizophrenia. *British Journal of Psychiatry,* 1973, *22,* 15–30.

Gottesman, I. I., & Shields, J. A critical review of recent adoption, twin and family studies of schizophrenia: Behavioral genetics perspectives. *Schizophrenia Bulletin,* 1976, *2,* 360.

Green, H. *I never promised you a rose garden.* New York: Holt, Rinehart & Winston, 1964.

Grice, G. R., & Hunter, J. J. Stimulus intensity effects depend upon the type of experimental design. *Psychological Review,* 1964, *71,* 247–256.

Grotstein, J. S. A theoretical rationale for psychoanalytic therapy of schizophrenia. In J. G. Gunderson & L. R. Mosher (Eds.), *Psychotherapy of schizophrenia.* New York: Jason Aronson, 1975.

Gruzelier, J. H. Bilateral asymmetry of skin conductance orienting activity and levels in schizophrenics. *Biological Psychology,* 1973, *1,* 21–42.

Gruzelier, J. H. The cardiac responses of schizophrenics to orienting, signal and non-signal tones. *Biological Psychology,* 1975, *3,* 143–155.

Gruzelier, J. H. Bimodal states of arousal and lateralized dysfunction in schizophrenia: Effects of chlorpromazine. In L. C. Wynne, R. L. Cromwell, & S. Matthysse (Eds.), *The nature of schizophrenia.* New York: Wiley, 1978.

Gruzelier, J. H., & Venables, P. H. Skin conductance orienting activity in a heterogeneous sample of schizophrenics. *Journal of Nervous and Mental Disease,* 1972, *155,* 277–287.

Gunderson, J. G. The current metapsychology of schizophrenia. In J. G. Gunderson & L. R. Mosher (Eds.), *Psychotherapy of schizophrenia.* New York: Jason Aronson, 1975.

Gunderson, J. G., Autry, J. H., Mosher, L. R., & Buchsbaum, S. Special report: Schizophrenia, 1973. *Schizophrenia Bulletin,* 1974, No. 9, 15–55.

Gunderson, J. G., & Mosher, L. R. *The cost of schizophrenia.* Paper delivered at Conference on the Personal, Social, and Economic Cost of Schizophrenia. Minneapolis, 1973.

Gunderson, J. G., & Mosher, L. R. *Psychotherapy of schizophrenia.* New York: Jason Aronson, 1975.

Guntrip, H. *Schizoid phenomena, object relations and the self.* New York: International Universities Press, 1969.

Hagen, R. L. Behavioral therapies and the treatment of schizophrenics. *Schizophrenia Bulletin,* 1975, No. 13, 70–96.

Haier, R. J., Buchsbaum, M. S., Murphy, D. L., Gottesman, I. I., & Coursey, R. D. Psychiatric vulnerability, monoamine oxidase, and the average evoked potential. *Archives of General Psychiatry,* 1980, *37,* 340–345.

Halasz, P., & Nagy, T. A. The mitten pattern—an EEG abnormality in sleep. *Acta Med. Acad. Sci.* (Hungary), 1965, *21,* 311–318.

Hanfmann, E., & Kasanin, J. S. A method for the study of concept formation. *Journal of Psychology, 1936, 3,* 521–540.

Harris, J. G. Size estimation of pictures as a function of thematic content for schizophrenic and normal subjects. *Journal of Personality,* 1957, *25,* 651–671.

Hartmann, H. Ego psychology and the problem of adaptation. In D. Rapaport (Ed.), *Organization and pathology of thought.* New York: Columbia University Press, 1951. (Originally published, 1939.)

Hartmann, H. Contribution to the metapsychology of schizophrenia. *Psychoanalytic Study of the Child,* 1953, *8,* 177–197.

Heath, R. G. (and the Tulane University Department of Psychiatry and Neurology). *Studies in schizophrenia.* Cambridge: Harvard University Press, 1959.

Heath, R. G., Martens, S., Leach, B. E., Cohen, M., & Angel, C. Effect on behavior in humans with the administration of taraxein. *American Journal of Psychiatry,* 1957, *114,* 14.

Hertzig, M. E., & Birch, H. Neurological organization in psychiatrically disturbed adolescent girls. *Archives of General Psychiatry,* 1966, *15,* 590–598.

Heston, L. L. Psychiatric disorders in foster home reared children of schizophrenic mothers. *British Journal of Psychiatry,* 1966, *112,* 819–825.

Hoffer, A., Osmond, H., & Smythies, J. Schizophrenia: New approach; result of year's research. *Journal of Mental Science,* 1954, *100,* 29.

Hollingshead, A. B., & Redlich, F. C. *Social class and mental illness.* New York: Wiley, 1958.

Holzman, P. S., Kringlen, E., Levy, D. L., Proctor, L. R., & Haberman, S. Smooth pursuit eye movements in twins discordant for schizophrenia. In L. C. Wynne, R. L. Cromwell, & S. Matthysse (Eds.), *The nature of schizophrenia.* New York: Wiley, 1978.

Holzman, P. S., & Levy, D. L. Smooth pursuit eye movements and functional psychoses: A review. *Schizophrenia Bulletin,* 1977, *3,* 15–27.

Holzman, P., Proctor, L., Levy, D., Yasillo, N., Meltzer, H., & Hurt, S. Eye-tracking dysfunctions in schizophrenic patients and their relatives. *Archives of General Psychiatry,* 1974, *31,* 143–151.

Hoover, C. F. The embroiled family: A blueprint for schizophrenia. *Family Process,* 1965, *4,* 291–310.

Hoover, C. F., & Franz, J. D. Siblings in the families of schizophrenics. *Archives of General Psychiatry,* 1972, *26,* 334–342.

Inderbitzin, L. B., Buchsbaum, M., & Silverman, J. EEG averaged evoked response and perceptual variability in schizophrenics. In R. Cancro (Ed.), *Annual review of the schizophrenic syndrome 1972.* New York: Brunner/Mazel, 1973.

Ingvar, D. H., Sjolound, B., & Arno, A. Correlation between dominant EEG frequency, cerebral oxygen uptake and blood flow. *Electroencephalography and Clinical Neurophysiology,* 1976, *41,* 268–276.

Itil, T. M. Electroencephalography in psychiatry. In H. Dember (Ed.), *Psychopharmacologic treatment: Theory and practice.* New York: Marcel Dekker, 1975.

Itil, T. M., Marasa, J., Saletu, B., Davis, S., & Mucciardi, A. Computerized EEG: Predictor of outcome in schizophrenia. *Journal of Nervous and Mental Disease,* 1975, *160,* 188–203.

Itil, T. M., Saletu, B., & Davis, S. EEG findings in chronic schizophrenics based on digital computer period analysis and analog power spectra. *Biological Psychiatry,* 1972, *5,* 1–13.

Jackson, D. D. (Ed.). *The etiology of schizophrenia.* New York: Basic Books, 1960.

Jackson, D. D. Family therapy in the family of the schizophrenic. In M. Stein (Ed.), *Contemporary psychotherapies.* Glencoe, Ill.: Free Press, 1961.

Jackson, D. D. (Ed.). *Human communication: Communication, family and marriage* (Vol. 1). Palo Alto: Science and Behavior Books, 1968a.

Jackson, D. D. (Ed.). *Human communication: Therapy, communication and change* (Vol. 2). Palo Alto: Science and Behavior Books, 1968b.

Jackson, D. D., Block, J., & Peterson, U. Psychiatrists' conceptions of the schizophrenic parent. *Archives of Neurology and Psychiatry,* 1958, *79,* 448–459.

Jackson, D. D., & Weakland, J. Schizophrenic symptoms and family interaction. *Archives of General Psychiatry,* 1959, *1,* 618–621.

Jacobson, E. Contribution to the metapsychology of psychotic identifications. *Journal of the American Psychoanalytic Association,* 1954a, *2,* 239–261.

Jacobson, E. On psychotic identifications. *International Journal of Psycho-Analysis,* 1954b, *35,* 102–108.

Jones, J. *The therapeutic community: A new treatment method in psychiatry.* New York: Basic Books, 1953.

Jung, C. G. On the psychogenesis of schizophrenia. *Journal of Mental Science,* 1939, *85,* 999–1011.

Jung, C. G. *The psychology of dementia praecox.* New York: Nervous and Mental Disease Monograph Series, 1944. (Originally published, 1907.)

Jung, C. G. The psychogenesis of mental disease. *The collected works of C. G. Jung* (Vol. 3), Bollingen Series XX. Princeton, N.J.: Princeton University Press, 1960.

Kadri, Z. N. Schizophrenia in the university students. *Singapore Medical Journal,* 1963, *4,* 113–118.

Kahn, A. J., & Kammerman, S. *Not for the poor alone.* New York: Harper & Row, 1977.

Kallmann, F. J. *The genetics of schizophrenia.* Locust Valley, N.Y.: J. J. Augustin, 1938.

Kallmann, F. J. The genetic theory of schizophrenia. *American Journal of Psychiatry,* 1946, *103,* 309-322.

Kaplan, A. R. (Ed.). *Genetic factors in schizophrenia.* Springfield, Ill.: Charles C Thomas, 1972.

Kaplan, B. (Ed.). *The inner world of mental illness.* New York: Harper & Row, 1964.

Karlsson, J. L. *The biological basis of schizophrenia.* Springfield, Ill.: Charles C Thomas, 1966.

Karlsson, J. L. Genealogic studies of schizophrenia. In D. Rosenthal & S. Kety (Eds.), *The transmission of schizophrenia.* Oxford: Pergamon, 1968.

Karlsson, J. L. A 2-locus hypothesis for inheritance of schizophrenia. In A. R. Kaplan (Ed.), *Genetic factors in schizophrenia.* Springfield, Ill.: Charles C Thomas, 1972.

Kasanin, J. S. (Ed.). *Language and thought in schizophrenia.* New York: Norton, 1964. (Originally published, 1944.)

Katz, M. M., Sanborn, K. O., with Lowery, H. A., & Ching, J. Ethnic studies in Hawaii: On psychopathology and social deviance. In L. C. Wynne, R. L. Cromwell, & S. Matthysse (Eds.), *The nature of schizophrenia.* New York: Wiley, 1978.

Keith, S. J., Gunderson, J. G., Reifman, A., Buchsbaum, S., & Mosher, L. Special report: Schizophrenia 1976. *Schizophrenia Bulletin,* 1976, *2,* 510–565.

Kelly, G. *The psychology of personal constructs* (Vol. 1). New York: Norton, 1955.

Kempler, R. I., & Brissen, A. The adult schizophrenic and his siblings. *Family Process,* 1962, *1,* 224–235.

Kety, S. S. Biochemical hypotheses and studies. In L. Bellak & L. Loeb (Eds.), *The schizophrenic syndrome.* New York: Grune & Stratton, 1969.

Kety, S. S. Psychiatric concepts and treatment in the People's Republic of China. In R. Cancro (Ed.), *Annual review of the schizophrenic syndrome 1974/75.* New York: Brunner/Mazel, 1976.

Kety, S. S., Rosenthal, D., Wender, P. H., & Schulsinger, F. The types and prevalence of mental illness in the biological and adoptive families of adopted schizophrenics. In D. Rosenthal & S. Kety (Eds.), *The transmission of schizophrenia.* London: Pergamon, 1968.

Kety, S. S., Woodford, R. B., Harmel, M. H., Freyhan, F. A., Appel, K. E., & Schmidt, C. F. Cerebral blood flow and metabolism in schizophrenia. *American Journal of Psychiatry,* 1948, *104,* 765–770.

Kilborg, R. R., & Siegel, A. W. Formal operations in reactive and process schizophrenics. In R. Cancro (Ed.), *Annual review of the schizophrenic syndrome 1974/1975.* Brunner/Mazel, 1976.

Kirkegaard-Sorenson, L., & Mednick, S. A. Registered criminality in families with children at high risk for schizophrenia. *Journal of Abnormal Psychology,* 1975, *84,* 197–204.

Klein, M. The development of a child. *International Journal of Psycho-Analysis,* 1921, *4.*

Klein, M. The psychotherapy of the psychoses. *British Journal of Medical Psychology,* 1930, *10.*

Klein, M. *The psychoanalysis of children.* London: Hogarth, 1932.

Klein, M. Notes on some schizoid mechanisms. *International Journal of Psycho-Analysis,* 1945, *26.*

Klein, M. A contribution to the theory of anxiety and guilt. *International Journal of Psycho-Analysis,* 1948, *29.*

Klein, M. Some theoretical conclusions regarding the emotional life of the infant. In J. Riviere (Ed.), *Developments in psycho-analysis.* London: Hogarth, 1952.

Klein, M. *Envy and gratitude.* New York: Basic Books, 1957.

Kleist, H. *The Marquise of O . . . and other stories* (M. Greenberg, trans.). New York: Criterion Books, 1960.

Klerman, G. L. Social and ethical issues in the de-institutionalization of the mentally ill. *Schizophrenia Bulletin,* 1977, *3,* 617–631.

Kohn, M. L. Social class and schizophrenia: A critical review. In D. Rosenthal & S. Kety (Eds.), *The transmission of schizophrenia.* Oxford: Pergamon, 1968.

Kohn, M. L. Social class and schizophrenia: A critical review and a reformulation. *Schizophrenia Bulletin,* 1973, No. 7, 60–79.

Kornetsky, C., & Orzack, M. H. Physiologic and behavioral correlates of attention dysfunction in schizophrenic patients. In L. C. Wynne, R. L. Cromwell, & S. Matthysse (Eds.), *The nature of schizophrenia.* New York: Wiley, 1978.

Kraepelin, E. *Psychiatrie: Ein Lehrbuch für Studierende und Aertze* (5th ed.). Leipzig: Barth, 1896.

Kraepelin, E. *Dementia praecox and paraphrenia* (G. M. Robertson, Ed.; R. M. Barclay, trans.), New York: Robert E. Krieger, 1971. (Originally published as 8th edition, 1919.)

Kringlen, E. An epidemiological-clinical twin study of schizophrenia. In D. Rosenthal & S. Kety (Eds.), *The transmission of schizophrenia.* Oxford: Pergamon, 1968.

Lacey, J. I. Somatic response patterning and stress: Some revisions of activation theory. In M. H. Appley & E. Trumbull (Eds.), *Psychological stress.* New York: Appleton-Century Crofts, 1967.

Lacey, J. I., & Lacey, B. L. Some autonomic nervous system interrelationships. In P. Block (Ed.), *Psychological correlates of emotion.* New York: Academic, 1970.

Laing, R. D. *The divided self.* England: Penguin, 1965a. (Originally published, 1960.)

Laing, R. D. Mystification, confusion and conflict. In I. Boszormenyi-Nagy & J. L. Framo (Eds.), *Intensive family therapy.* New York: Harper & Row, 1965b.

Laing, R. D., & Esterson, A. *Sanity, madness, and the family.* Middlesex, England: Penguin, 1970. (Originally published, 1964.)

Lane, E. A., & Albee, G. W. Childhood intellectual differences between schizophrenic adults and their siblings. *American Journal of Orthopsychiatry,* 1965, *35,* 747–753.

Lang, P. J., & Buss, A. H. Psychological deficit in schizophrenia: II. Interference and activation. *Journal of Abnormal and Social Psychology,* 1965, *70,* 77–106.

Langner, T. S., & Michael, S. T. *Life stress and mental health.* New York: Free Press of Glencoe, 1963.

Lehmann, H. E. Psychopharmacological treatment of schizophrenia. *Schizophrenia Bulletin,* 1975, No. 13, 27–45.

Levit, R. A., Sutton, S., & Zubin, J. Evoked potential correlates of information processing in psychiatric patients. *Psychological Medicine,* 1973, *3,* 487–494.

Lidsky, A., Hakerem, G., & Sutton, S. Pupillary reactions to single light pulses in psychiatric patients and normals. *Journal of Nervous and Mental Disease,* 1971, *153,* 286–291.

Lidz, R. W., & Lidz, T. The family environment of schizophrenic patients. *American Journal of Psychiatry,* 1949, 106, 332–345.

Lidz, T. *The origin and treatment of schizophrenic disorders.* New York: Basic Books, 1973.

Lidz, T., Cornelison, A., Terry, D., et al. The transmission of irrationality. In T. Lidz, S. Fleck, & A. Cornelison (Eds.), *Schizophrenia and the family.* New York: International Universities Press, 1965. (Originally published, 1958.)

Lidz, T., & Fleck, S. Schizophrenia, human integration, and the role of the family. In D. D. Jackson (Ed.), *The etiology of schizophrenia.* New York: Basic Books, 1960.

Lidz, T., Fleck, S., & Cornelison, A. R. *Schizophrenia and the family.* New York: International Universities Press, 1965.

Lu, Y. C. Mother-child role relations in schizophrenia. *Psychiatry,* 1961, *24,* 133–142.

Luria, A. R. *The role of speech in the regulation of normal and abnormal behavior.* New York: Pergamon, 1961.

McDonald, R. L. The role of emotional factors in obstetric complications: A review. *Psychosomatic Review,* 1968, *30,* 222–237.

McGhie, A. *Pathology of attention.* Middlesex, England: Penguin, 1969.

McGhie, A., & Chapman, J. Disorders of attention and perception in early schizophrenia. *British Journal of Medical Psychology,* 1961, *34,* 103–117.

McGhie, A., & Chapman, J. Attention and perception in schizophrenia. In R. Cancro (Ed.), *Annual review of the schizophrenic syndrome 1972.* New York: Brunner/Mazel, 1973.

McGhie, A., Chapman, J., & Lawson, J. S. The effect of distraction on schizophrenic performance: 1. Perception and immediate memory. *British Journal of Psychology,* 1965a, *111,* 383–390.

McGhie, A., Chapman, J., & Lawson, J. S. The effect of distraction on schizophrenic performance: 2. Psychomotor ability. *British Journal of Psychiatry,* 1965b, *111,* 391–398.

McKinnon, T., & Singer, G. Schizophrenia and the scanning cognitive control: A re-evaluation. *Journal of Abnormal Psychology,* 1969, *74,* 242–248.

McNeil, E. B. *The psychoses.* Englewood Cliffs, N.J.: Prentice-Hall, 1970.

McNeil, T. F., & Kaij, L. Obstetric factors in the development of schizophrenia: Complications in the births of preschizophrenics and in reproduction by schizophrenic parents. In L. C. Wynne, R. L. Cromwell, & S. Matthysse (Eds.), *The nature of schizophrenia.* New York: Wiley, 1978.

McReynolds, P. Anxiety, perception and schizophrenia. In D. D. Jackson (Ed.), *The etiology of schizophrenia.* New York: Basic Books, 1960.

Maher, B. A. *Principles of psychopathology.* New York: McGraw-Hill, 1966.

Maher, B. A. The language of schizophrenia: A review and interpretation. *British Journal of Psychiatry,* 1972, *17,* 3–17.

Mahler, M. S. On child psychosis and schizophrenia: Autistic symbiotic infantile psychoses. *Psychoanalytic Study of the Child,* 1952, *7,* 286–305.

Mahler, M. S. *On human symbiosis and the vicissitudes of individuation: Infantile psychosis* (Vol. 1). New York: International Universities Press, 1968.

Mahler, M. S., Pine, F., & Bergman, A. *The psychological birth of the human infant: Symbiosis and individuation.* New York: Basic Books, 1975.

Main, T. F. The hospital as a therapeutic institution. *Bulletin of the Menninger Clinic,* 1946, *19,* 66–70.

Malmo, R. B., & Shagass, C. Physiologic studies of reaction to stress in anxiety and early schizophrenia. *Psychosomatic Medicine,* 1949, *11,* 9–24.

Malmo, R. B., Shagass, C., & David, F. H. Electromyographic studies of muscular tension in psychiatric patients under stress. *Journal of Clinical Experimental Psychopathology,* 1951, *12,* 45–66.

Malzberg, B. *Social and biological aspects of mental disease.* Utica, 1940.

Matthews, S. M., Roper, N. T., Mosher, L. R., & Menn, A. Z. A non-neuroleptic treatment for schizophrenia. *Schizophrenia Bulletin,* 1979, *5,* 322–333.

Matthysse, S. Overview: Biological research on schizophrenia. In R. Cancro (Ed.), *Annual review of the schizophrenic syndrome 1974/1975.* New York: Brunner/Mazel, 1976a.

Matthysse, S. Schizophrenia: Relationship to dopamine transmission, motor control and feature extraction. In R. Cancro (Ed.), *Annual review of the schizophrenic syndrome 1974/1975.* New York: Brunner/Mazel, 1976b.

Matthysse, S. A theory of the relation between dopamine and attention. In L. C. Wynne, R. L. Cromwell, & S. Matthysse (Eds.), *The nature of schizophrenia.* New York: Wiley, 1978.

May, P. R. A. Schizophrenia: Evaluation of treatment methods. In A. M. Freedman, H. I. Kaplan, & B. J. Sadock (Eds.), *Comprehensive Textbook of Psychiatry* (2nd ed.) (Vol. 1). Baltimore: Williams & Wilkins, 1975a.

May, P. R. A. Schizophrenia: Overview of treatment methods. In A. M. Freedman, H. I. Kaplan, & B. J. Sadock (Eds.), *Comprehensive Textbook of Psychiatry* (2nd ed.) (Vol. 1). Baltimore: Williams & Wilkins, 1975b.

Mednick, S. A. A learning theory approach to research in schizophrenia. *Psychological Bulletin,* 1958, *55,* 316–327.

Mednick, S. A. Breakdown in individuals at high risk for schizophrenia: Possible predispositional perinatal factors. *Mental Hygiene,* 1970, *54,* 50–61.

Mednick, S. A. Berkson's fallacy and high-risk research. In L. C. Wynne, R. L. Cromwell, & S. Matthysse (Eds.), *The nature of schizophrenia.* New York, Wiley, 1978.

Mednick, S. A., & Schulsinger, F. A longitudinal study of children with a high risk for schizophrenia: A preliminary report. In S. Vandenberg (Ed.), *Methods and goals in human behavior genetics.* New York: Academic, 1965.

Mednick, S. A. & Schulsinger, F. Some premorbid characteristics related to breakdown in children with schizophrenic mothers. In D. Rosenthal & S. Kety (Eds.), *The transmission of schizophrenia.* Oxford: Pergamon, 1968.

Mednick, S. A., Schulsinger, H., & Schulsinger, F. Schizophrenia in children of schizophrenic mothers. In A. Davids (Ed.), *Childhood personality and psychopathology: Current topics* (Vol. 2). New York: Wiley, 1975.

Mednick, S. A., Schulsinger, F., Teasdale, T. W., Venables, P., & Rock, R. Schizophrenia in high risk children: Sex differences in predisposing factors. In G. Serban (Ed.), *Cognitive defects in the development of mental illness.* New York: Brunner/Mazel, 1978.

Mednick, S. A., & Witkin-Lamoil, G. H. Intervention in children at high risk for schizophrenia.

In G. W. Albee & J. M. Joffe (Eds.), *Primary prevention of psychopathology: The issues* (Vol. 1). Hanover, N.H.: University Press of New England, 1977.

Meehl, P. E. Schizotaxia, schizotypy, schizophrenia. *American Psychologist,* 1962, *17,* 827–838.

Meehl, P. E. Hedonic capacity: Some conjectures. *Bulletin of the Menninger Clinic,* 1975, *35,* 255–307.

Meissner, W. W. Sibling relations in the schizophrenic family. *Family Process,* 1970, *9,* 1–25.

Meltzer, H. Y. Biochemical studies in schizophrenia. *Schizophrenia Bulletin,* 1976, *2,* 10–19.

Meltzer, H. Y. Biology of schizophrenia subtypes: A review and proposal for method of study. *Schizophrenia Bulletin,* 1979, *5,* 460–479.

Meltzer, H. Y., & Stahl, S. M. The dopamine hypothesis of schizophrenia: A review. *Schizophrenia Bulletin,* 1976, *2,* 19–77.

Meshover, P. *Communication processes in early development: With special reference to the deaf.* Unpublished doctoral dissertation, Yeshiva University, 1980.

Miller, G. A., Galanter, E., & Pribram, K. *Plans and the structure of human behavior.* New York: Holt, 1960.

Mishler, E. G., & Waxler, H. (Eds.). *Family processes and schizophrenia.* New York: Jason Aronson, 1975.

Money, J., & Ehrhardt, A. *Man and woman, boy and girl.* Baltimore: Johns Hopkins University Press, 1972.

Mosher, L. R. Etiological implications of studies of identical twins discordant for schizophrenia. *Orthomolecular Psychiatry,* 1972, *42,* 60–67.

Mosher, L. R. Psychiatric heretics and the extra-medical treatment of schizophrenia. In R. Cancro, N. Fox, & L. E. Shapiro (Eds.), *Strategic intervention in schizophrenia.* New York: Behavioral Publications, 1973.

Mosher, L. R., & Menn, A. Community residential treatment for schizophrenia: Two-year follow-up data. *Hospital and Community Psychiatry,* 1978, *29,* 715–723.

Mosher, L. R., Pollin, W., & Stabenau, J. R. Families with identical twins discordant for schizophrenia: Some relationships between identification, thinking styles, psychopathology and dominance-submission. *British Journal of Psychiatry,* 1971a, *118,* 29–42.

Mosher, L. R., Pollin, W., & Stabenau, J. R. Identical twins discordant for schizophrenia: Neurological findings. *Archives of General Psychiatry,* 1971b, *24,* 423–430.

Mowrer, O. H. Preparatory set (expectancy)—Further evidence of its "central" locus. *Journal of Experimental Psychology,* 1941, *28,* 116–133.

Mullahy, P. *Psychoanalysis and interpersonal psychiatry.* New York: Science House, 1970.

Murphy, H. B. M. Cultural factors in the mental health of Malayan students. In P. H. Funkenstein (Ed.), *The student and mental health: An international view.* World Federation for Mental Health, 1959.

Murphy, H. B. M. Cultural factors in the genesis of schizophrenia. In D. Rosenthal and S. Kety (Eds.), *The transmission of schizophrenia.* Oxford: Pergamon, 1968.

Murphy, H. B. M. Cultural influences on incidence, course, and treatment response. In L. C. Wynne, R. L. Cromwell, & S. Matthysse (Eds.), *The nature of schizophrenia.* New York: Wiley, 1978.

Myers, J. K., & Roberts, B. H. *Family and class dynamics in mental illness.* New York: Wiley, 1959.

Neale, J. M., & Cromwell, R. L. Attention and schizophrenia. In R. Cancro (Ed.), *Annual review of the schizophrenic syndrome 1972.* New York: Brunner/Mazel, 1973.

Nuechterlein, K. H. Reaction time and attention. *Schizophrenia Bulletin,* 1977, *3,* 373–428.

O'Brien, C. P. Group therapy for schizophrenia: A practical approach. *Schizophrenia Bulletin,* 1975, No. 13, 119–130.

Ødegaard, Ø. The incidence of psychoses in varying occupations. *International Journal of Social Psychiatry,* 1956, *2,* 85–104.

O'Doherty, E. F. The high proportion of mental hospital beds in the Republic (abstract). *Transcultural Psychiatric Research,* 1965, *2,* 134–136.

Ornitz, E. R. Disorders of perception common to early infantile autism and schizophrenia. In R. Cancro (Ed.), *The schizophrenic syndrome.* New York: Brunner/Mazel, 1971.

Pao, P.-N. Notes on Freud's theory of schizophrenia. *International Journal of Psycho-Analysis,* 1973, *54,* 469–476.

Pasamanick, B., & Knobloch, H. Epidemiological studies on the complications of pregnancy and the birth process. In G. Caplan (Ed.), *Prevention of mental disorders in children.* New York: Basic Books, 1961.

Patterson, T. Skin conductance recovery and pupillometics in chronic schizophrenics. *Psychophysiology,* 1976a, *13,* 189–195.

Patterson, T. Skin conductance responding/nonresponding and pupillometics in chronic schizophrenia: A confirmation of Gruzelier and Venables. *Journal of Nervous and Mental Disease,* 1976b, *163,* 200–209.

Payne, R. W. The measurement and significance of overinclusive thinking and retardation in schiziophrenic patients. In P. Hoch & J. Zubin (Eds.), *Psychopathology of schizophrenia.* New York: Grune & Stratton, 1966.

Piaget, J. *The language and thought of the child* (3rd ed.). Atlantic Highland, N.J.: Humanities, 1962. (Originally published, 1923.)

Pollack, M., Woerner, M., Goodman, W., & Greenberg, I. Childhood development patterns of hospitalized adult schizophrenics and non-schizophrenic patients and their siblings. *American Journal of Orthopsychiatry,* 1966, *36,* 510–517.

Pollack, M., Woerner, M., Goldberg, P., & Klein, D. Siblings of schizophrenic and non-schizophrenic psychiatric patients. *Archives of General Psychiatry,* 1969, *20,* 652–658.

Pollock, H. M. A statistical study of the foreign born insane in New York state hospitals. *State Hospitals Bulletin,* 1913, special issue, 10–27.

Pollock, H. M. Frequency of schizophrenia in relation to sex, age, environment, nativity and race. *Schizophrenia.* New York: Assn. Res. Nerv. Ment. Dis., 1928.

Pollin, W. The pathogenesis of schizophrenia. In R. Cancro (Ed.), *Annual review of the schizophrenic syndrome 1973.* New York: Brunner/Mazel, 1974.

Pollin, W., & Stabenau, J. Biological, psychological, and historical differences in a series of monozygotic twins discordant for schizophrenia. In D. Rosenthal & S. Kety (Eds.), *The transmission of schizophrenia.* Oxford: Pergamon, 1968.

Pollin, W., Stabenau, J., Mosher, L., & Tupin, J. Life history differences in identical twins discordant for schizophrenia. *American Journal of Orthopsychiatry,* 1966, *36,* 492–509.

Pollin, W., Stabenau, J., & Tupin, J. Family studies with identical twins discordant for schizophrenia. *Psychiatry,* 1965, *28,* 60–78.

Prout, C. T., & White, M. A. The schizophrenic's sibling. *Journal of Nervous and Mental Disease,* 1956, *123,* 162–170.

Rapaport, D. (Ed.). *Organization and pathology of thought.* New York: Columbia University Press, 1951.

Rattan, R. B., & Chapman, L. J. Associative intrusions in schizophrenic verbal behavior. *Journal of Abnormal Psychology,* 1973, *82,* 169–173.

Read, P. P. *Alive: The story of the Andes survivors.* Philadelphia: Lippincott, 1974.

Redlich, F. C. The concept of schizophrenia and its implications for therapy. In E. B. Brody & F. C. Redlich (Eds.), *Psychotherapy with schizophrenics.* New York: International Universities Press, 1952.

Rieder, R. B. Children at risk. In L. Bellak (Ed.), *Disorders of the schizophrenic syndrome.* New York: Basic Books, 1980.

Robbins, L. N. *Deviant children grown up.* Baltimore, Md.: Williams & Wilkins, 1966.

Rogler, L. H., & Hollingshead, A. B. *Trapped: Families and schizophrenia.* New York: Wiley, 1965.

Rosen, J. N. The treatment of schizophrenic psychosis by direct analytic therapy. *Psychiatric Quarterly,* 1947, *21,* 3–37.

Rosen, J. N. *Direct analysis: Selected papers.* New York: Grune & Stratton, 1953.

Rosenfeld, H. A. Analysis of a schizophrenic state with depersonalization. *International Journal of Psycho-Analysis,* 1947, *28,* 130–139.

Rosenfeld, H. A. *Psychotic states.* New York: International Universities Press, 1965.

Rosengarten, H., & Friedhoff, A. J. A review of recent studies of the biosynthesis and excretion of hallucinogens formed by methylation of neurotransmitters or related substances. *Schizophrenia Bulletin,* 1976, *2,* 90–106.

Rosenthal, D. The heredity-environment issue in schizophrenia: Summary of the conference and present status of our knowledge. *Journal of Psychiatric Research,* 1968, *6,* (Suppl. 1), 413.

Rosenthal, D. *Genetics of psychopathology.* New York: McGraw-Hill, 1971.

Rosenthal, D. The genetics of schizophrenia. In S. Arieti & E. Brody (Eds.), *American handbook of psychiatry* (2nd ed.) (Vol. 3). New York: Basic Books, 1974.

Rosenthal, D. Searches for the mode of genetic transmission in schizophrenia: Reflections and loose ends. *Schizophrenia Bulletin,* 1977, *3,* 268–276.

Rosenthal, D., & Kety, S. (Eds.). *The transmission of schizophrenia.* Oxford: Pergamon, 1968.

Rüdin, E. *Zur Vererbung und Neuentstehung der Dementia Praecox.* Berlin: Springer, 1916.

Ryckoff, I., Day, J., & Wynne, L. C. Maintenance of stereotyped roles in the families of schizophrenics. *Archives of General Psychiatry,* 1959, *1,* 109–114.

Sachar, E. J., Gruen, P. H., Altman, N., Langer, G., & Halpern, F. S. Neuroendocrine studies of brain dopamine blockade in humans. In L. C. Wynne, R. L. Cromwell, & S. Matthysse (Eds.), *The nature of schizophrenia.* New York: Wiley, 1978.

Sachar, E. J., Kanter, S., Buie, D., Engle, R., & Mehlman, R. Psychoendocrinology of ego disintegration. In R. Cancro (Ed.), *Annual review of the schizophrenic syndrome 1971.* New York: Brunner/Mazel, 1972.

Sagan, C. *The dragons of Eden.* New York: Random House, 1977.

Sameroff, A. J., & Zax, M. Perinatal characteristics of the offspring of schizophrenic women. *Journal of Nervous and Mental Disease,* 1973, *157,* 191–199.

Sameroff, A. J., & Zax, M. In search of schizophrenia: Young offspring of schizophrenic women. In L. C. Wynne, R. L. Cromwell, & S. Matthysse (Eds.), *The nature of schizophrenia.* New York: Wiley, 1978.

Sandler, J. The concept of the representational world. *Psychoanalytic Study of the Child,* 1962, *17,* 128–145.

Sanua, V. Sociocultural aspects. In L. Bellak & L. Loeb (Eds.), *The schizophrenic syndrome.* New York: Grune & Stratton, 1969.

Sartorius, N., Jablensky, A., & Shapiro, R. Cross-cultural differences in prognosis of schizophrenic psychosis. *Schizophrenia Bulletin,* 1978, *4,* 102–113.

Schilder, P. *Brain and personality.* New York: Nervous and Mental Disease Monograph Series No. 53, 1931.

Searles, H. *Collected papers on schizophrenia and related subjects.* New York: International Universities Press, 1965a.

Searles, H. The effort to drive the other person crazy—An element in the aetiology and psychotherapy of schizophrenia. In *Collected papers on schizophrenia and related subjects.* New York: International Universities Press, 1965b. (Originally published, 1959.)

Sechehaye, M. A. *Autobiography of a schizophrenic girl.* New York: Grune & Stratton, 1951a.

Sechehaye, M. A. *Symbolic realization.* New York: International Universities Press, 1951b.

Segal, H. *Introduction to the work of Melanie Klein.* New York: Basic Books, 1973.

Shagass, C. Neurophysiological studies. In L. Bellak & L. Loeb (Eds.), *The schizophrenic syndrome*. New York: Grune & Stratton, 1969.

Shagass, C., Amadeo, M., & Overton, P. A. Eye tracking performance in psychiatric patients. *Biological Psychiatry*, 1974, *9*, 245–260.

Shagass, C., Roemer, R. A., & Amadeo, M. Eye tracking performance and engagement of attention. *Archives of General Psychiatry*, 1976, *33*, 121–125.

Shakow, D. Segmental set. *Archives of General Psychiatry*, 1962, *6*, 1–17.

Shakow, D. Psychological deficit in schizophrenia. *Behavioral Science*, 1963, *8*, 275–305.

Shakow, D. Some observations on the psychology (and some fewer, on the biology) of schizophrenia. In R. Cancro (Ed.), *Annual review of the schizophrenic syndrome 1973*. New York: Brunner/Mazel, 1974.

Shapiro, S. A. *A cybernetic organizing principle for schizophrenia research*. Unpublished doctoral dissertation, Yeshiva University, 1978.

Shields, J. Summary of genetic evidence. In D. Rosenthal & S. Kety (Eds.), *The transmission of schizophrenia*. Oxford: Pergamon, 1968.

Silverman, J. The problem of attention in research and theory in schizophrenia. *Psychological Review*, 1964a, *71*, 352–379.

Silverman, J. Perceptual control of stimulus intensity in paranoid and non-paranoid schizophrenia. *Journal of Nervous and Mental Disease*, 1964b, *139*, 544–548.

Simmel, E. Psychoanalytic treatment in a sanitorium. *International Journal of Psycho-Analysis*, 1929, *10*, 70.

Singer, M. T., & Wynne, L. Thought disorder and family relations of schizophrenics: III. Methodology using projective techniques. IV. Results and interpretations. *Archives of General Psychiatry*, 1965, *12*, 187–212.

Slater, E. The nongenetic theory of schizophrenia. *Acta Genetica*, 1958, *8*, 50–56.

Slater, E. A review of earlier evidence on genetic factors in schizophrenia. In D. Rosenthal & S. Kety (Eds.), *The transmission of schizophrenia*. Oxford: Pergamon, 1968.

Snyder, S. H. Dopamine and schizophrenia. In L. C. Wynne, R. L. Cromwell, & S. Matthysse (Eds.), *The nature of schizophrenia*. New York, Wiley, 1978.

Solod, R., & Lapidus, L. B. Concrete operational thinking, diagnosis, and psychopathology in hospitalized schizophrenics. *Journal of Abnormal Psychology*, 1977, *86*, 199–202.

Spitz, R. A. Hospitalism: An inquiry into the genesis of psychiatric conditions in childhood. *Psychoanalytic Study of the Child*, 1945, *1*, 53–74.

Spitzer, R. L., & Klein, D. F. (Eds.). *Critical issues in psychiatric diagnosis*. New York: Raven Press, 1978.

Spitzka, E. C. Race and insanity. *Journal of Nervous and Mental Disease*, 1880, *7*, 342–348.

Spohn, H. E., Cancro, R., & Thetford, P. E. Visual scanning and size estimation in acute schizophrenics. In R. Cancro (Ed.), *Annual review of the schizophrenic syndrome 1974/1975*. New York: Brunner/Mazel, 1976.

Spohn, H. E., Lacoursie, R., Thompson, K., & Coyne, L. The effect of phenothiazines on psychological and psychophysiological dysfunction in chronic schizophrenics. *Archives of General Psychiatry*, 1977, *34*, 633–644.

Spohn, H. E., & Patterson, T. Recent studies of psychophysiology in schizophrenia. *Schizophrenia Bulletin*, 1959, *5*, 581–611.

Spohn, H. E., Thetford, P. E., & Cancro, R. The effects of phenothiazine medication on skin conductance and heart rate in schizophrenic patients. *Journal of Nervous and Mental Disease*, 1971, *152*, 129–139.

Spring, B. *Vulnerability to schizophrenic episodes in adults*. Unpublished grant proposal, 1975.

Spring, B., Nuechterlein, K. H., Sugarman, J., & Matthysse, S. The "new look" in studies of schizophrenic attention and information processing. *Schizophrenia Bulletin*, 1977, *3*, 470–482.

Spring, B., & Zubin, J. Vulnerability to schizophrenic episodes and their prevention in adults. In G. W. Albee & J. M. Joffe (Eds.), *Primary prevention of psychopathology: The issues* (Vol. 1). Hanover, N.H.: University Press of New England, 1977.

Spring, B. J., & Zubin, J. Attention and information processing as indicators of vulnerability to schizophrenic episodes. In L. C. Wynne, R. L. Cromwell, & S. Matthysse (Eds.), *The nature of schizophrenia*. New York: Wiley, 1978.

Srole, L., Langner, T. S., Michael, S. T., Opeler, M. K., & Rennie, T. A. C. *Mental health in the metropolis: The midtown Manhattan study*. New York: McGraw-Hill, 1962.

Stanton, A., & Schwartz, M. *The mental hospital*. New York: Basic Books, 1954.

Stevens, J. R. An anatomy of schizophrenia? *Archives of General Psychiatry*, 1973, *29*, 177–189.

Struve, F., & Becka, D. R. The relative incidence of the B-mitten EEG pattern in process and reactive schizophrenia. *Electroencephalogr. Clin. Neurophysiol.*, 1968, *24*, 80–82.

Sullivan, H. S. *Conceptions of modern psychiatry*. New York: William Alanson White Psychiatric Foundation, 1940.

Sullivan, H. S. *The interpersonal theory of psychiatry*. New York: Norton, 1953.

Sullivan, H. S. *Clinical studies in psychiatry*. New York: Norton, 1956.

Sullivan, H. Environmental factors in etiology and course under treatment of schizophrenia. In *Schizophrenia as a human process*. New York: Norton, 1962a. (Originally published, 1931.)

Sullivan, H. Peculiarity of thought in schizophrenia. In *Schizophrenia as a human process*. New York: Norton, 1962b. (Originally published, 1925.)

Sullivan, H. S. Research in schizophrenia. In *Schizophrenia as a human process*. New York: Norton, 1962c. (Originally published, 1929.)

Sullivan, H. S. *Schizophrenia as a human process*. New York: Norton, 1962d.

Sullivan, H. S. Schizophrenia: Its conservative and malignant factures. In *Schizophrenia as a human process*. New York: Norton, 1962e. (Originally published, 1924.)

Sullivan, H. S. The language of schizophrenia. In J. S. Kasanin (Ed.), *Language and thought in schizophrenia*. New York: Norton, 1964. (Originally published, 1944.)

Sutton, S. A psychophysiological approach to psychopathology. *Annual Review of Psychology*, 1975, *26*, 648–656.

Sutton, S., Braren, M., Zubin, J., & John, E. R. Evoked potential correlates of stimulus uncertainty. *Science*, 1965, *150*, 1187–1188.

Sutton, S., & Tueting, P. Evoked potentials and diagnosis. In R. L. Spitzer & D. F. Klein (Eds.), *Critical issues in psychiatric diagnosis*. New York: Raven Press, 1978.

Sutton, S., Tueting, P., Zubin, J., & John, E. R. Information delivery and the sensory evoked potential. *Science*, 1967, *155*, 1436–1438.

Swift, H. M. Insanity and race. *American Journal of Insanity*, 1913, *70*, 143–154.

Szasz, T. *The myth of mental illness*. New York: Hoeber-Harper, 1961.

Tausk, V. On the origin of "the influencing machine" in schizophrenia. *Psychoanalytic Quarterly*, 1933, *2*, 519–556. (Originally published, 1919.)

Thomas, A., Chess, S., & Birch, H. *Temperament and behavior disorders in children*. New York: New York University Press, 1969.

Tienari, P. Schizophrenia in monozygotic male twins. In D. Rosenthal & S. Kety (Eds.), *The transmission of schizophrenia*. Oxford: Pergamon, 1968.

Toffler, A. *Future shock*. New York: Random House, 1970.

Torrey, E. F. Is schizophrenia universal: An open question. *Schizophrenia Bulletin*, 1973, No. 7, 53–60.

Torrey, E. F. Tracking the causes of madness. *Psychology Today*, 1979, *12*, 78–82.

Torrey, E. F., & Peterson, M. The viral hypothesis of schizophrenia. *Schizophrenia Bulletin*, 1976, *2*, 136–147.

Tueting, P., Sutton, S., & Zubin, J. Quantitative evoked potential correlates of the probability of events. *Psychophysiology,* 1971, *7,* 385–394.

Turner, R. J., & Wagenfeld, M. O. Occupational mobility and schizophrenia: An assessment of social causation and social selection hypotheses. *American Sociological Review,* 1967, *32,* 104–113.

United States–United Kingdom Cross-National Project. The diagnosis and psychopathology of schizophrenia in New York and London. *Schizophrenia Bulletin,* 1974, No. 11, 80–102.

Vartanyan, M. E., & Gindilis, V. M. The role of chromosomal aberrations in the clinical polymorphism of schizophrenia. In L. Erlenmeyer-Kimling (Ed.), Genetics and mental disorders. *International Journal of Mental Health,* 1971, *1,* 93–106.

Vaughan, H. G., Jr. Toward a neurophysiology of schizophrenia. In L. C. Wynne, R. L. Cromwell, & S. Matthysse (Eds.), *The nature of schizophrenia.* New York: Wiley, 1978.

Venables, P. H. Input dysfunction in schizophrenia. In B. A. Maher (Ed.), *Progress in experimental personality research* (Vol. 1). New York: Academic, 1964.

Venables, P. H. The recovery limb of the skin conductance response in high risk research. In S. A. Mednick, F. Schulsinger, J. Higgins, & B. Bell (Eds.), *Genetics, environment and psychopathology.* Amsterdam: North-Holland/American Elsevier, 1975.

Venables, P. H., & Wing, J. K. Level of arousal and the subclassification of schizophrenia. *Archives of General Psychiatry,* 1962, *7,* 114–119.

von Domarus, E. The specific laws of logic in schizophrenia. In J. S. Kasanin (Ed.), *Language and thought in schizophrenia.* New York: Norton, 1964. (Originally published, 1944.)

Vonnegut, M. *How to tell someone they're crazy in a way that makes sense.* Downstate Grand Rounds, January, 1977.

Vygotsky, L. S. *Thought and Language.* Cambridge: M.I.T. Press, 1962.

Wasz-Höckert, O., Lind, J., Vuorenkoski, V., Partanen, T., & Valanne, E. The infant cry: A spectrographic and auditory analysis. *Clinics in Developmental Medicine,* 1968, *29.*

Weakland, J. H. The "double-bind" hypothesis of schizophrenia and three-party interaction. In D. D. Jackson (Ed.), *The etiology of schizophrenia.* New York: Basic Books, 1960.

Wechsler, H. Half-way houses for former mental patients. *Journal of Social Issues,* 1960, *16,* 20–26.

Wender, P., Rosenthal, D., & Kety, S. A psychiatric assessment of the adoptive parents of schizophrenics. In D. Rosenthal & S. Kety (Eds.), *The transmission of schizophrenia.* Oxford: Pergamon, 1968.

Wender, P. H., Rosenthal, D., Kety, S. S., et al. Crossfostering: A research strategy for clarifying the role of genetic and experiential factors in the etiology of schizophrenia. *Archives of General Psychiatry,* 1974, *30,* 121.

Wexler, M. The evolution of a deficiency view of schizophrenia. In J. Gunderson & L. Mosher (Eds.), *Psychotherapy of schizophrenia.* New York: Jason Aronson, 1975.

Wiener, N. *Cybernetics.* Cambridge: M.I.T. Press, 1965.

Will, O. A. Process, psychotherapy, and schizophrenia. In A. Burton (Ed.), *Psychotherapy of the psychoses.* New York: Basic Books, 1961.

Wilson, L. *This stranger, my son.* New York: Putnam, 1968.

Winnicott, D. W. *Collected papers: Through pediatrics to psychoanalysis.* London: Tavistock, 1958.

Winnicott, D. W. *The family and individual development.* London: Tavistock, 1965a.

Winnicott, D. W. *The maturational processes and the facilitating environment.* New York: International Universities Press, 1965b.

Winnicott, D. W. From dependence towards independence in the development of the individual. In *The Maturational processes and the facilitating environment.* New York: International Universities Press, 1965c. (Originally published, 1963.)

Wolff, P. The causes, controls, and organization of behavior in the neonate. *Psychological Issues,* Monograph No. 17. New York: International Universities Press, 1966.

Wolstein, B. *Theory of psychoanalytic therapy.* New York: Grune & Stratton, 1967.

Woolf, L. I. Large scale screening for metabolic disease in the newborn, Great Britain. In J. A. Anderson & K. F. Swaiman (Eds.), *Phenylketonuria and allied metabolic diseases.* Washington D.C.: Superintendent of Documents, U.S. Government Printing Office, 1967.

Wyatt, R. J., Murphy, D. L., & Belmaker, R., et al. Reduced monoamine oxidase in platelets: A possible genetic marker for vulnerability to schizophrenia. *Science,* 1973, *179,* 916–918.

Wyatt, R. J., & Murphy, D. L. Low platelet monoamine oxidase activity and schizophrenia. *Schizophrenia Bulletin,* 1976, *2,* 77–90.

Wynne, L. C. Communication disorder and the quest for relatedness in families of schizophrenics. In C. Sager & H. Kaplan (Eds.), *Progress in group and family therapy.* New York: Brunner/Mazel, 1972a.

Wynne, L. C. Family research on the pathogenesis of schizophrenia: Intermediate variables in the study of families at high risk. In C. Sager & H. Kaplan (Eds.), *Progress in group and family therapy.* New York: Brunner/Mazel, 1972b.

Wynne, L. C., Cromwell, R. L., & Matthysse, S. (Eds.). *The nature of schizophrenia: New approaches to research and treatment.* New York: Wiley, 1978.

Wynne, L., Ryckoff, I. M., Day, J., & Hirsch, S. Pseudomutuality in the family relations of schizophrenics. *Psychiatry,* 1958, *21,* 205–220.

Wynne, L., & Singer, M. Thought disorder and family relations of schizophrenics: I. A research strategy. II. A classification of forms. *Archives of General Psychiatry,* 1963, *9,* 191–206.

Wynne, L., Singer, M., & Bartko, J. J. Schizophrenics and their families: Recent research on parental communication. In J. M. Tanner (Ed.), *Psychiatric research: The widening perspective.* New York: International Universities Press, 1975.

Zahn, T. P. Effects of reduction of uncertainty on reaction time in schizophrenic and normal subjects. *Journal of Experimental Research in Personality,* 1970, *4,* 135–143.

Zahn, T. P. On the bimodality of the distribution of electrodermal orienting responses in schizophrenic patients. *Journal of Nervous and Mental Disease,* 1976, *162,* 195–199.

Zubin, J. The biometric approach to psychopathology—Revisited. In J. Zubin & C. Shagass (Eds.), *Neurobiological aspects of psychopathology.* New York: Grune & Stratton, 1969.

Zubin, J. Problem of attention in schizophrenia. In M. C. Kietzman, S. Sutton, & J. Zubin (Eds.), *Experimental approaches to psychopathology.* New York: Academic, 1975.

Zubin, J., & Spring, B. Vulnerability—A new view of schizophrenia. *Journal of Abnormal Psychology,* 1977, *86,* 103–120.

Name Index

277

Subject Index

Abstract attitude, loss of, 64–65
Abstract thought (see Thought; Thought disorders)
Acetylcholine/dopamine balance, 80
ACTH (adrenocorticotropic hormone), 48
Active phase of schizophrenia, described, 248
Acute dystonic reactions, 240
Acute schizophrenia, 39, 57, 63, 101, 166
  arousal in, 77
    (See also Arousal)
  attention disorders in, 70, 71, 73
    (See also specific disorders)
  biochemical basis of, 39–40
  incidence of, 1
    (See also Incidence rates of schizophrenia)
  insomnia before episode of, 55
  sensory and perceptual alterations in, 58
    (See also Perceptual disorders; Sensory disorders)
  treatment of, 227, 230, 233, 235, 237, 242
  withdrawal of (see Withdrawal)
  (See also Reactive schizophrenia)
Adaptation:
  critical features of, 60
  ego's role in, 88
  learning and, 156–157
  risk and, 150
  (See also Development)
Adolescence:
  normal, 173
  schizophrenia and, 204–207, 223–224
  (See also Development)
Adoption studies, 31–32
Adrenocortical stress response studies, 45
Adrenocorticotropic hormone (ACTH), 48
Adulthood:
  normal, 173
  schizophrenia and, 208–211, 224–226
AEPs (see Average evoked potentials)
AERs (average evoked responses), 50–51

Affective disturbances, 10, 18
  biochemistry and, 45
  brain lesions as causes of, 15
  defined, 20, 246
  dopamine level and, 44
  stimuli and, 66
    (See also Stimuli)
  (See also Emotional development)
Age of onset of schizophrenia, 37, 247
  (See also specific developmental stages, for example: Adolescence)
Akathesias, 238
Alienation, social, 17, 63
  (See also Withdrawal)
Alpha methyl paratyrosine (AMPT), 43
Alpha-2-globulin, 38–39
Ambivalence, psychotic, 17, 20
Amphetamine psychoses, 12, 42
AMPT (alpha methyl paratyrosine), 43
ANS (see Autonomic nervous system)
Antipsychotic drugs (neuroleptics), 60, 77, 232, 233, 235–241
  effects of: on evoked potentials, 51–53
    on eye scanning, 58–59
  middle components of average evoked potentials and, 53
  treatment with, 235–241
    mechanism of action of, 241
    side effects of, 45, 235, 237–240
  (See also Butyrophenones; Phenothiazines)
Anti-S protein, 39
Anxiety:
  arousal and, 68, 77, 78
    (See also Arousal)
  biochemistry and, 145
  defined, 61
  excess stimuli as source of, 61
    (See also Stimuli)
  infant, 100, 101
  maternal, preschizophrenia and, 118

About the Author

SUE A. SHAPIRO received her B.A. from Brandeis University, and her M.A. and Ph.D. from Yeshiva University. While writing this book, she co-administered the inpatient unit at Kingsboro Psychiatric Center in New York, later concentrating on teaching, supervising staff, and conducting seminars on schizophrenia. Currently she is affiliated with the New York University postdoctoral program and in private practice.